IMAGES
of America

FLORENCE REVISITED

I0806365

ACKNOWLEDGMENTS

Thank you, to my daughters, Carol Borbi and Tina Grabowski, as well as my son-in-law, Louis Borbi—who are all very interested in preserving town history. Their encouragement and assistance in collecting memorabilia is greatly appreciated.

—Mary Tapper

Thanks also goes to Raymond Carugno, Richard Glass, and Stuart Foulks Sr. These three local historians were always ready to share their knowledge about our town and its people.

—Jack Ulmer

My dedication goes to all who have contributed and will contribute to the growth of the Florence Historical Society's Museum through pictures, artifacts, and reminisces—and also to one of our behind-the-scene workers, Paul Anderson.

—Margie Anderson

My thank-yous go to Judy King, who got me interested in this in the first place, and to my husband, Dave, who puts up with all my absences. I also thank my cats, who don't care if I am here or not as long as somebody feeds them.

—Lynda Borgstrom

A final thanks goes to the Florence Historical Society Book Committee, whose varied talents have coalesced to make this book possible, and to my husband, Dave Monti, for his willingness to accomplish any task needed for the Florence Historical Society.

—Judith King

INTRODUCTION

There have been some changes over the past 100 years in Florence. The most devastating was the closing of the foundry, or Griffin Pipe, which occurred several years ago. This foundry on West Front Street was the main industry in Florence since 1850, when Richard Jones started the enterprise. Several of the buildings have been demolished, but some still stand, with dates in the brick from the 1920s to the 1930s. As a mainstay of the community, the foundry employed many generations and many nationalities of Florence people as skilled labor.

Part of the airport is now a housing development. Several large farms across the highway are also housing developments. The cement plant, which stood on Railroad Avenue near ReadyPac, and the train station have been gone since the early 1960s. Part of the A&P warehouse on Cedar Lane, built in 1964, has been demolished to make way for new warehouses. Other large properties have given way to warehouses to provide township tax ratable. The foundry farm, which was vacant for many years, is now the Oak Mill housing development. Birch Hollow Condominiums on Columbus Road now stand on the Walnut Farm land, which included harness racing, stables, and pastures. The farms along Schuyler Ferry Road have been gone since the 1970s, as has Potts Lumber Yard. Part of that property is now a New Jersey Light Rail station. Recently, the Duffy School on West Second Street has been converted to senior citizen apartments. The restoration of this old building is exceptional, and many features, both inside and out, have been preserved. In a better light, the Clover Valley Farm on Columbus Road near Interstate 295 has been marked as farmland preservation, keeping the large acreage from development. Despite these changes, Florence is still considered a bedroom community. Some historic homes and public buildings have been lost to fire and neglect; however, others still stand to give the town its historical character and charm. With the help of local authorities and our historical society, Florence will still remain an excellent example of small-town America. The mayor and council, as well as Joy Weiler and Tom Sahol, have helped the society in many endeavors, chief among these the permission to use the old Third Street firehouse as its museum. As we approach our 20th year, we have every hope to continue our participation in community activities and make our extensive collection available to townspeople.

It is amusing to learn that many people in town had nicknames, both men and women. Some of these, which need explanation from the older generation, are Harry the Hummer, Toodles, Topsy, Scat, Icky, Scoots, Jingles, Mumbles, Ichabod, Shanks, Choo Choo, Bugs, Windy, Sweaty, Beans, Gas Tank, Clothesline, Beanpole, Shine, Pint, Cracker, Plunger, Boots, Flutter, Duder, Trip, Zip, Flash, Skip, Ace, Hawks, Chicken, Sacky, Pidge, Hambone, Buzz, and Zit. From the 1950s generation are Woody, Smokey, Beak, and, of course, Smitty.

Although the township is 9.68 square miles, the majority of stores, pizza shops, and restaurants are still in the middle of Florence. The corner candy stores are gone, but the auto repair shops, hardware store, news shop, and beauty parlors remain successful. Recreation includes many sports fields, boating and fishing along the Delaware River, and social organization activities. Churches abound, and Florence has been recognized as a Tree City USA community.

As our first book on Florence was well received, we hope this volume will also capture the interest of our readers and inspire them to share family histories, photographs, and other memorabilia with us and the community.

It is our great pleasure to share these wonderful pictures and stories about Florence and its people, and we hope to continue this in the future. This is all possible because of the Florence residents who gave us this opportunity to share their many generations of rich cultural history.

One

Across the Highway

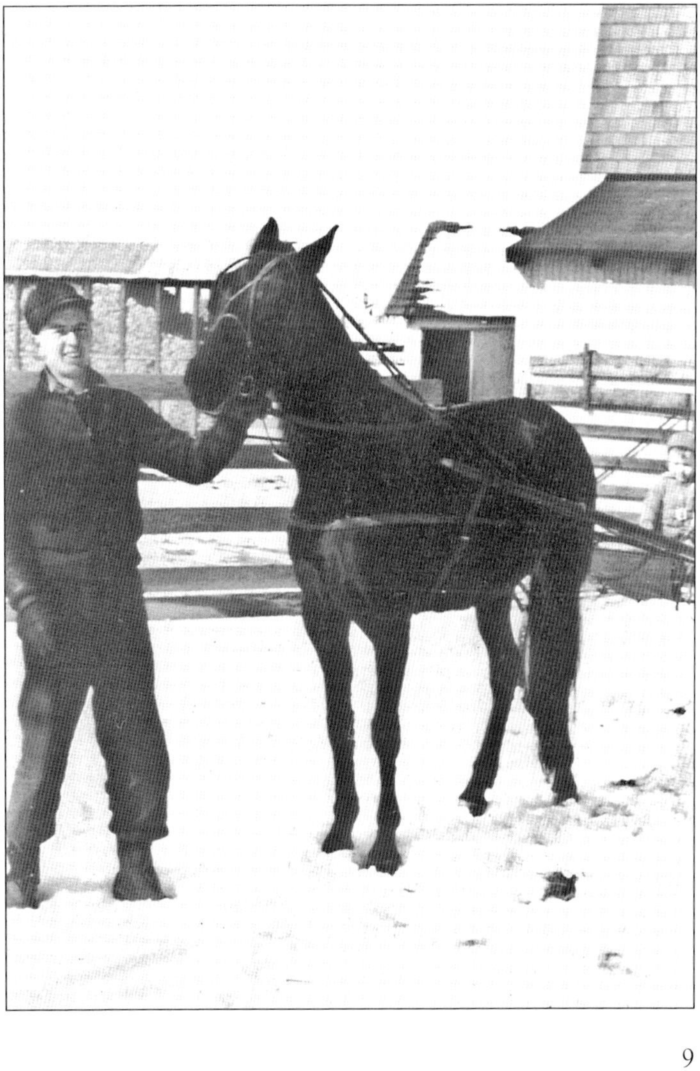

Walnut Farm. Jack Smith is shown with one of his harness racers at Walnut Farm around 1940. Jake Millerline is on the sulky. This property, once a slaughterhouse, was a horse farm for many years and ultimately became the Birch Hollow townhomes on Florence-Columbus Road. (Courtesy of the Florence Historical Society.)

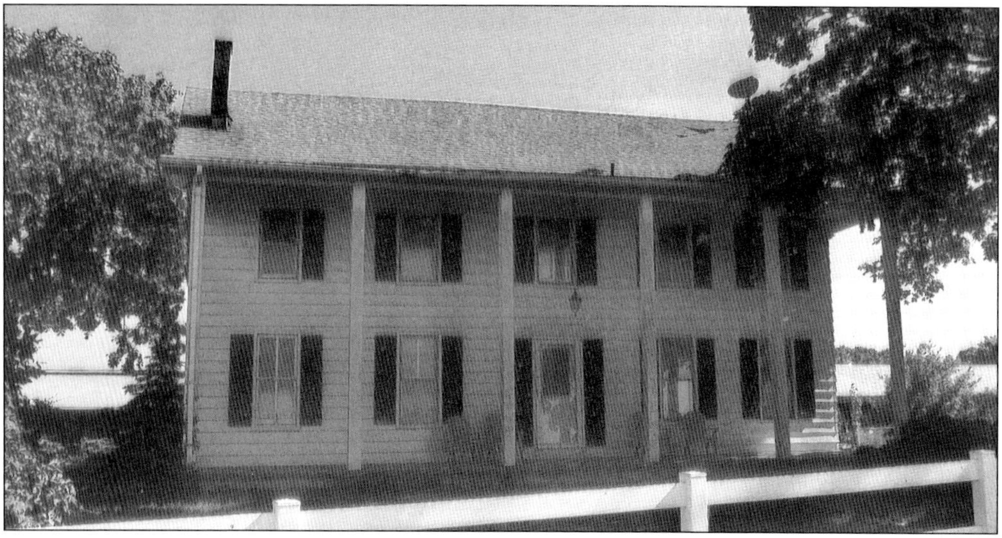

FRED WAINWRIGHT FARMHOUSE. Pictured is the front porch of the farmhouse, facing south toward Route 295. The house has several additions and many outbuildings. Known as Clover Valley Farm, this large dairy operation is located on Florence-Columbus Road, comprising 204 acres. The house has been used for many generations of the Wainwright family, who have been in the area since the 1800s. (Courtesy of the Florence Historical Society.)

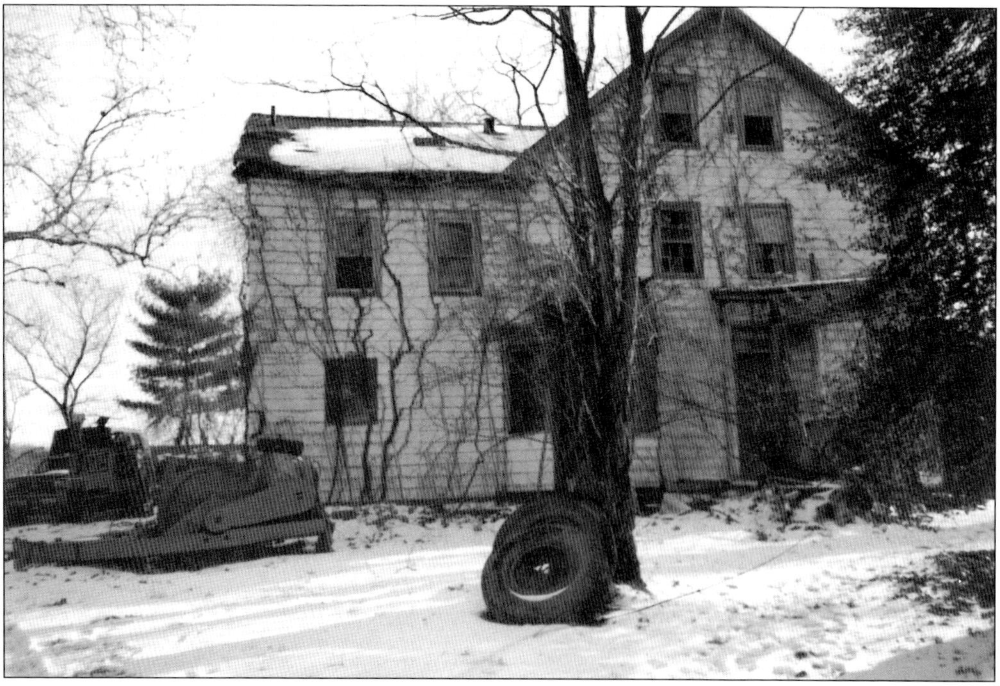

SIMPKINS FARMHOUSE. The northeast side of Simpkins's farmhouse offers an idea of the size of this large building. Originally in the Carty family, it belonged to Jim Christy during the 1930s as a speakeasy. It has fallen into disrepair and is currently vacant. Located on the east side of Cedar Lane after crossing Route 130, the property still retains most of the original farm buildings, including a silo marked "Stout." Charles Stout was a previous owner and a county freeholder. (Courtesy of the Florence Historical Society.)

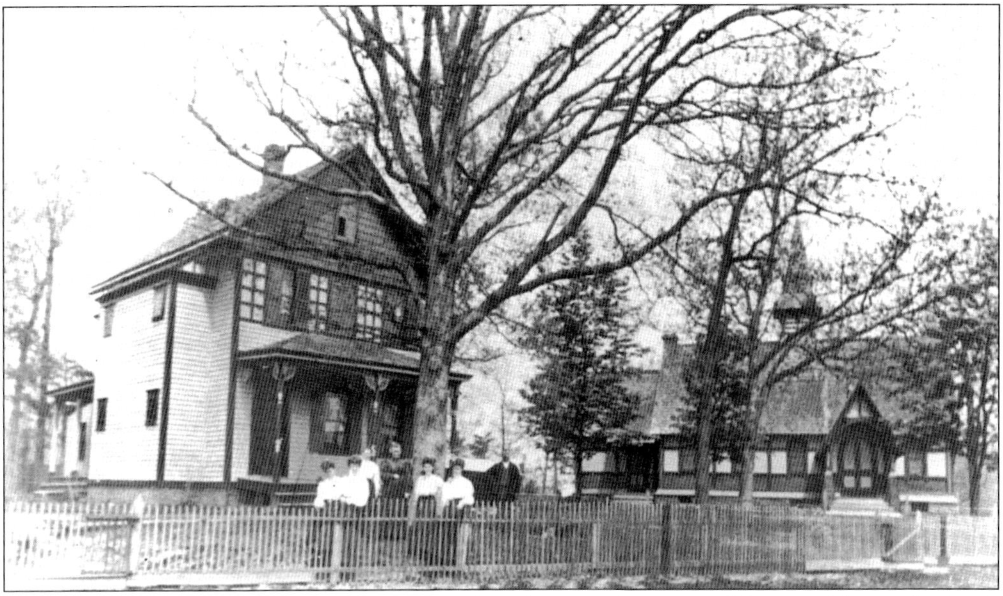

Providence Presbyterian Church. Named to the State Register of Historic Places, the Stick Style Providence Presbyterian Church in Bustleton (Florence Township) was erected in 1863 and is pictured on the right side of the photograph around the early 1900s. The building on the left is the parsonage, built in 1888. Located on the corner of Cedar Lane and Bustleton Road, the land was donated by Joseph Zelley. (Courtesy of the Florence Historical Society)

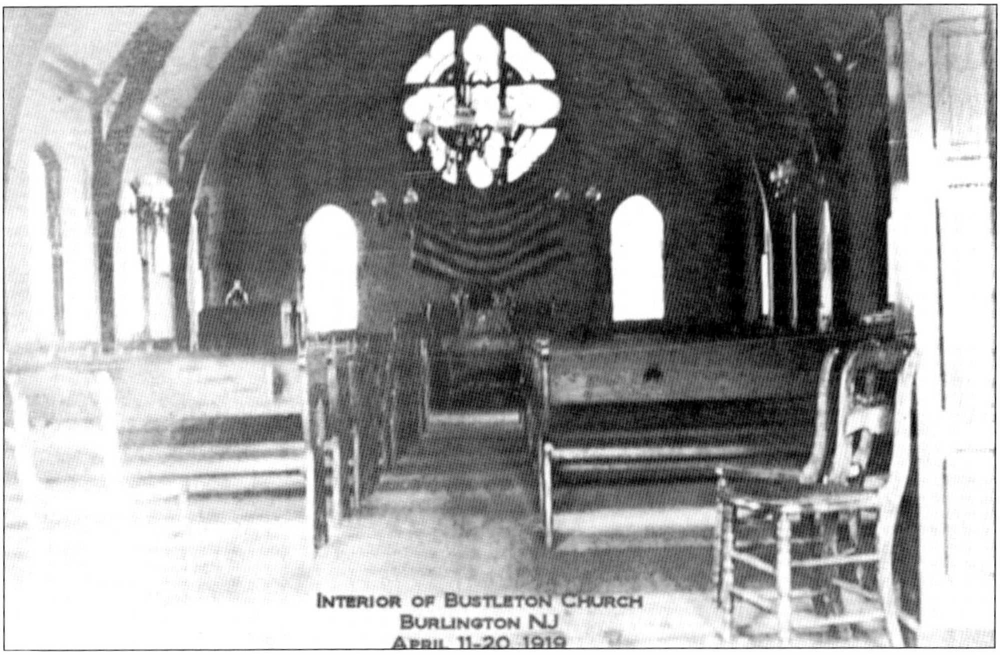

Providence Church Interior. In 1919, the interior of Providence Presbyterian Church in Bustleton contains 24 oak pews, ruby carpets, an arched ceiling with hanging translucent cylindrical lamps and a wooden lectern with a heavy black Bible. The oval stained-glass window is the focal point of the interior. The majority of parishioners were local farmers in Bustleton. (Courtesy of the Florence Historical Society.)

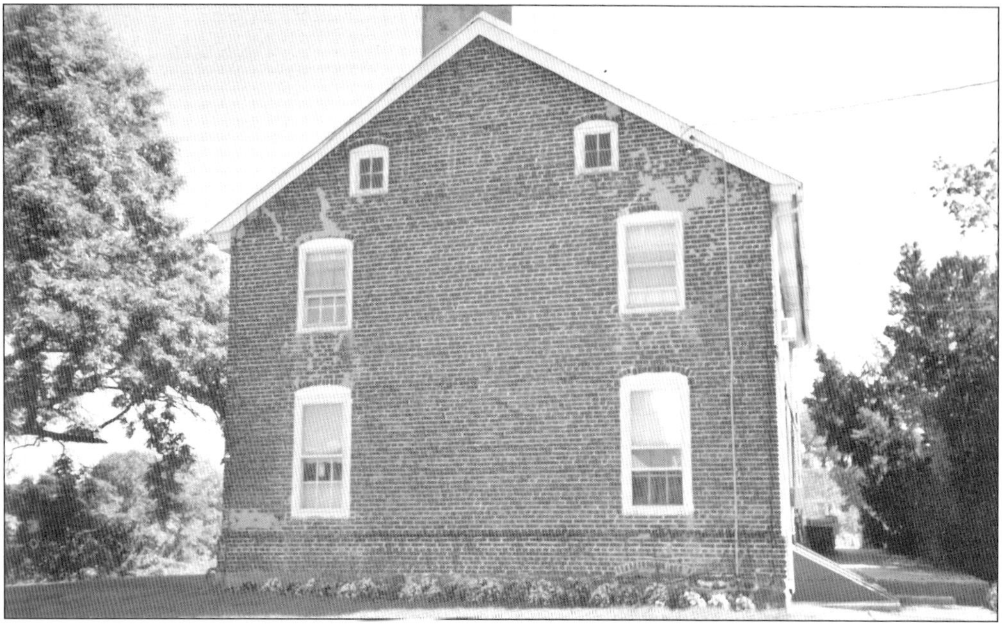

The Von Thaden House. The Von Thaden House is pictured on Old York Road in Florence Township. This home—built in 1762, as marked in the brick—was constructed of distinctive Flemish bond, a more expensive brickwork at that time. Marked on the 1876 map as being owned by J.W. Tallman, the property contained 208 acres. Part was lost to the turnpike in the 1950s, but this is still a working farm today. (Courtesy of the Florence Historical Society.)

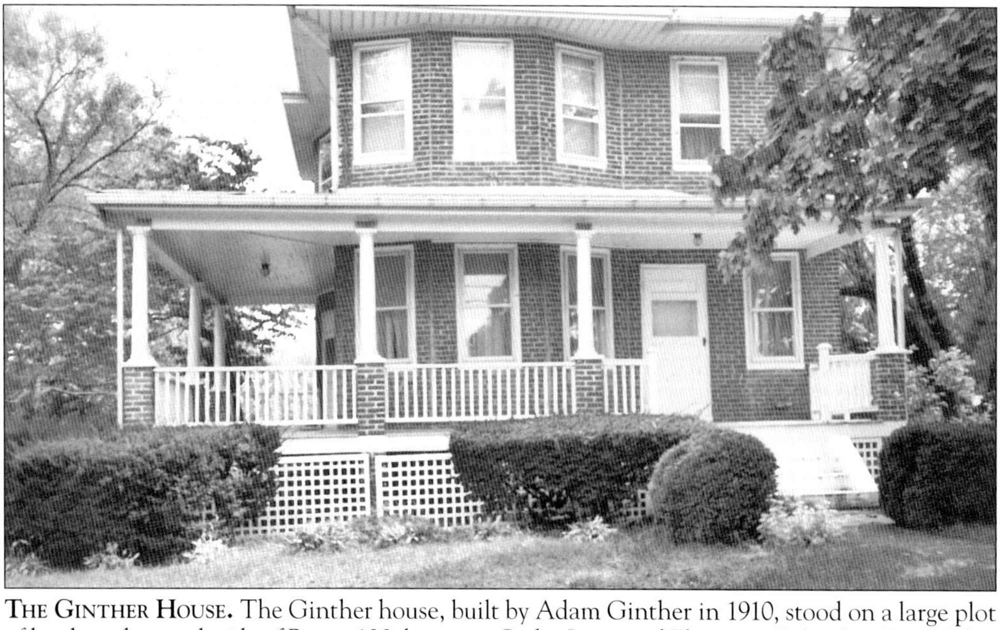

The Ginther House. The Ginther house, built by Adam Ginther in 1910, stood on a large plot of land on the north side of Route 130, between Cedar Lane and Florence-Columbus Road. This beautiful brick Queen Anne house with wraparound porch was demolished in 1998 to make way for the New Jersey Turnpike ramp. (Courtesy of the Florence Historical Society.)

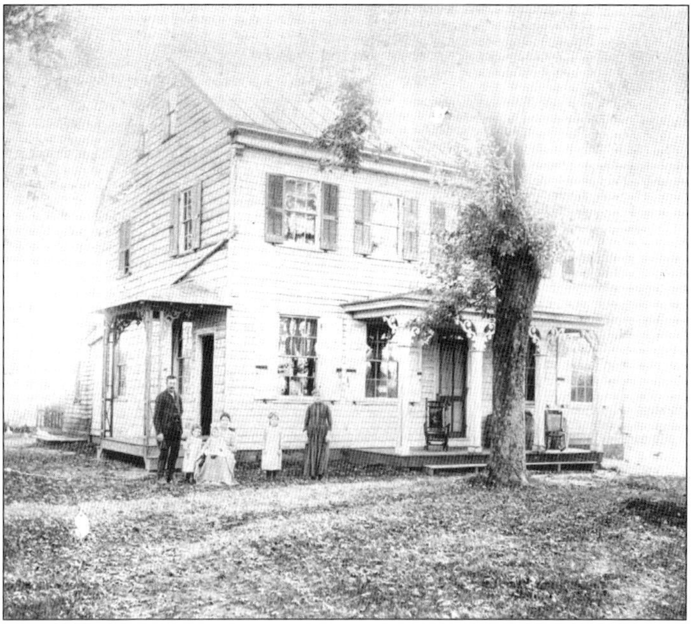

Wainwright Farmhouse. The Wainwright family stands in front of their farmhouse on Old York Road in the early 1900s. Known as Brooklet Farm, the house appears on an 1849 map and had pegged beams and hand-hewn lumber. The Wainwrights retained ownership of this large dairy farm for many generations until it was demolished in 2003 to make way for the Greenbriar Horizons adult community. (Courtesy of Fred Wainwright.)

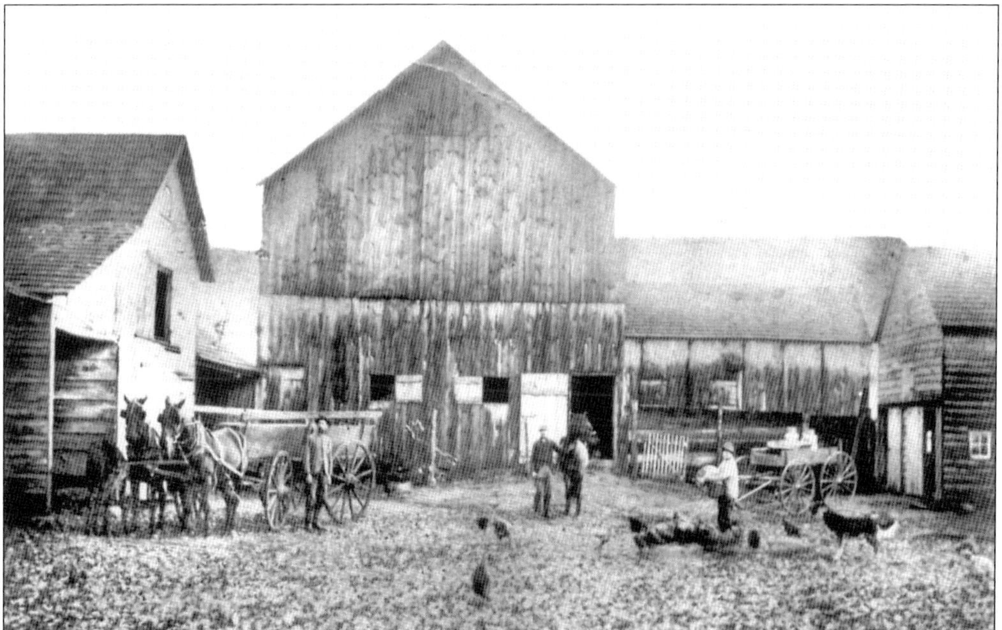

Wainwright Farm. The Wainwright farm on Old York Road and its original barn are pictured in the 1890s. Lost in a fire, the barn was rebuilt, and dairy farming continued. As shown here, both mules and horses were used by family members and outside help. From an old journal, it is also known that neighboring farmers helped each other at harvesttime and during barn raisings. (Courtesy of Fred Wainwright.)

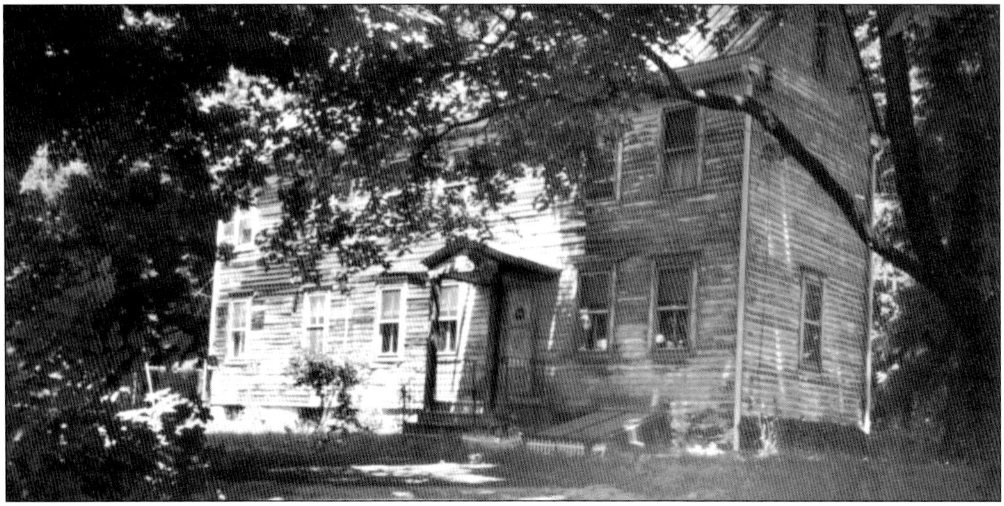

THOMAS SUTTON FARMHOUSE. Largely unchanged since being built, this large clapboard house on Old York Road has been occupied by the Suttons for many generations. With two and a half stories and seven bays wide, it was probably built in two sections in the 18th century. It is situated on the border of Florence and Burlington Townships. A record of the first T. Sutton in the area was documented in 1814. The farm consists of 65 acres, and it is still in use today. (Courtesy of the Florence Historical Society.)

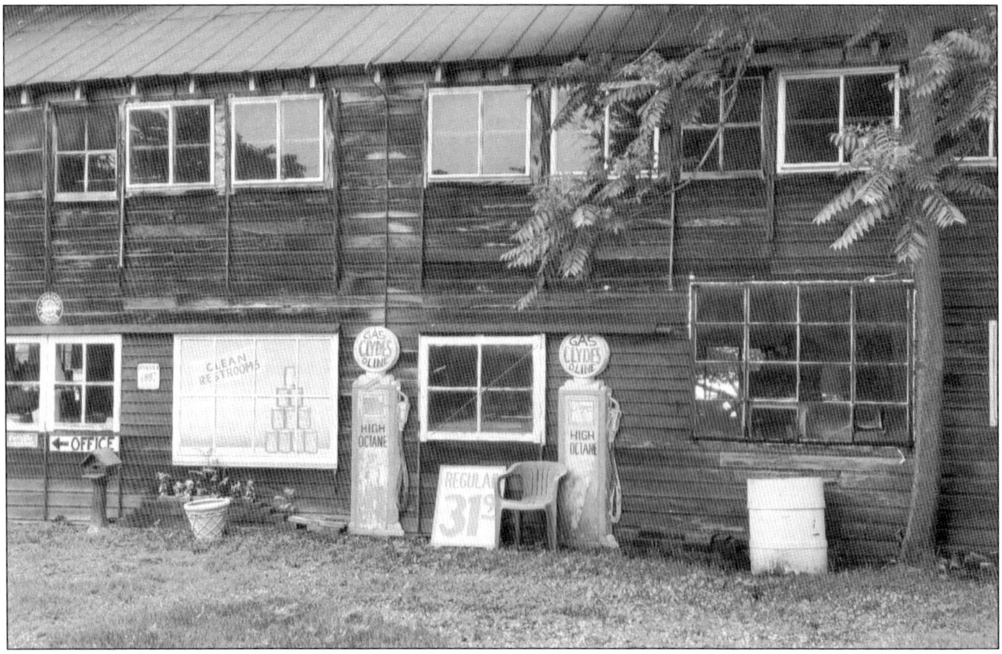

CARTY CHICKEN HOUSE. Byron Carty's farm was on the north side of Route 130 (Route 25 in those days) a short distance from Cedar Lane. The property consisted of the farmhouse and the large chicken house. The farmhouse burned down some years ago, but the chicken house, over 70 feet long, still stands. It is now occupied by Clyde Boiston Sheds and looks much the same, other than the attached signs. (Courtesy of the Florence Historical Society.)

Two

AROUND TOWN

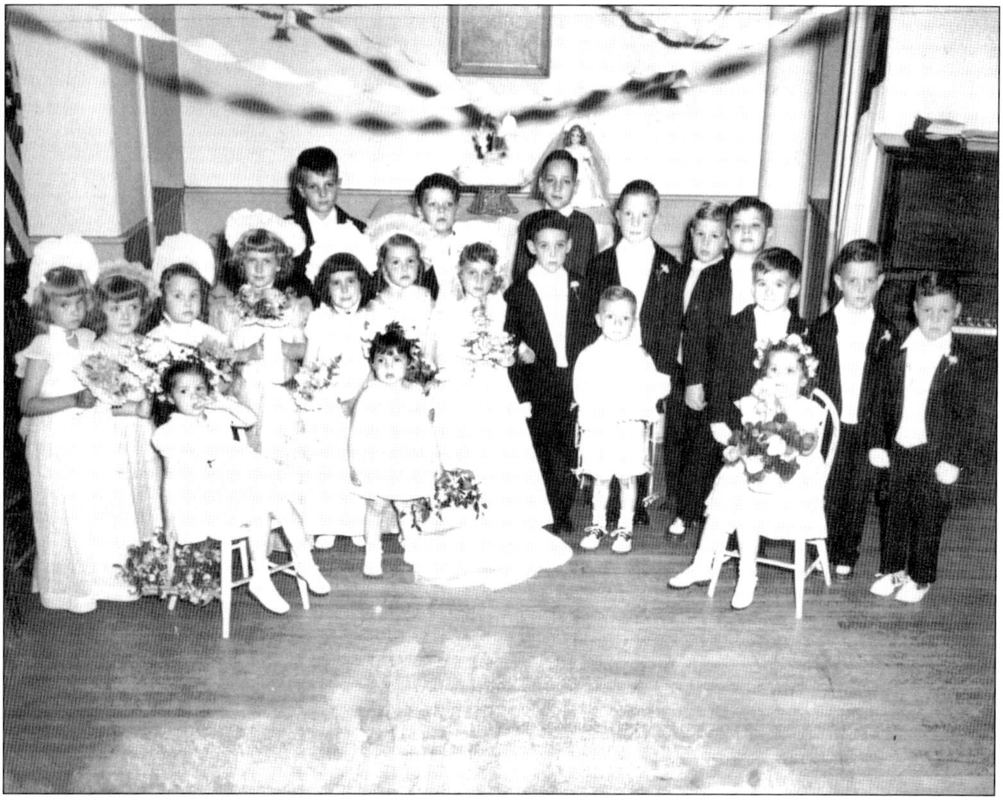

TOM THUMB WEDDING. A Tom Thumb wedding is held at the Florence United Methodist Church in May 1951. As far back as 1931, these weddings were held as fundraisers. Pictured are, from left to right, (first row) Arlene Jones, Cheryl Rainier, Jimmy Meadows, and Linda Sutphin; (second row) Nancy Adams, Sue Ellen Brown, Ann Jobes, Lois Hennessy, Jeanne Marshall, Kathy Fisher, Rosilyn Miller, Gerry Simpkins, Buddy Gilbert, Glenn Miller, Nelson Eckert, Richie Robinson, Terry Bodine, and Gregory VanArsdale; (third row) Wilmer Bauer Jr., Glendon Bryden (father of the bride), and minister Terry Hennessy. (Courtesy of Barbara Miller Harvey.)

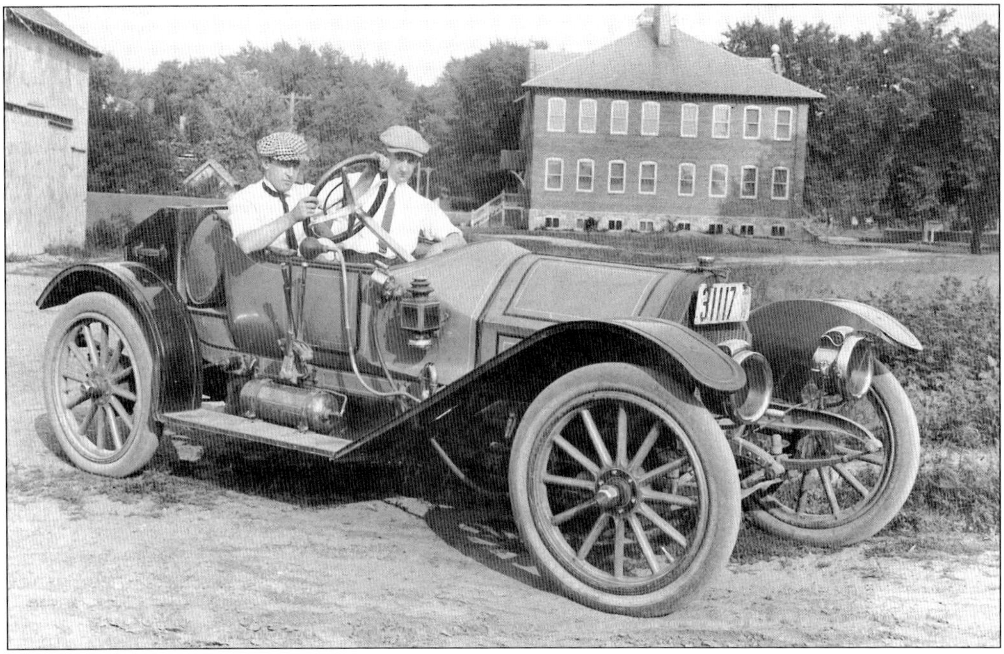

The Peacock Brothers. In 1903, driver Robert Peacock, 20 years old, and his brother Charles, age 18, prepare for an outing near the Florence School No. 1 on West Second Street. Robert later became a prominent attorney and a member of many well-known organizations. Charles was a first baseman for the Florence baseball team and made spectacular catches during part of his career from 1900 to 1924. (Courtesy of Thelma Peacock Tilghman.)

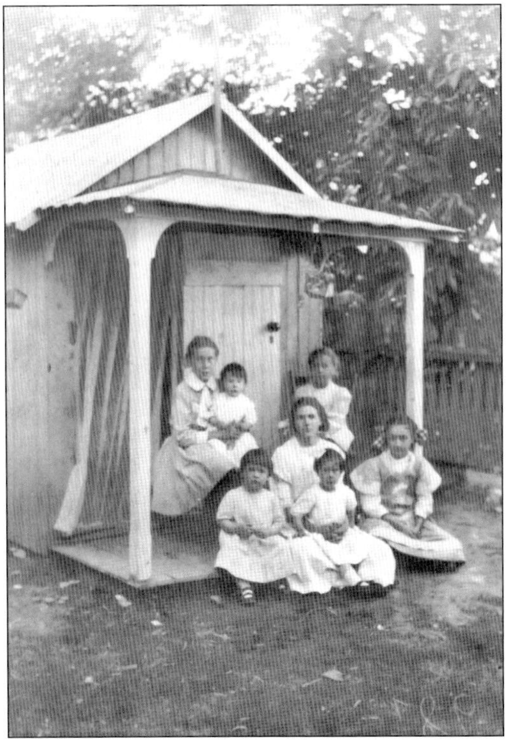

The Hoffner-Quig Family. The Hoffner-Quig family sits in front of their playhouse at Florence Station in the early 1900s. Jacob Hoffner owned a large farm in Florence Station, which was later sold into lots and known as the Hoffner tract. (Courtesy of Jack Quig.)

Florence Pipe Foundry and Machine Truck. The Florence Pipe Foundry and Machine Company added a new phase to its production during World War II, as advertised on the large truck used in a local parade. Shipyard equipment, castings for B-29 bombers, and 200-ton flanging presses were the company's specialty in helping the war effort. (Courtesy of the Florence Historical Society.)

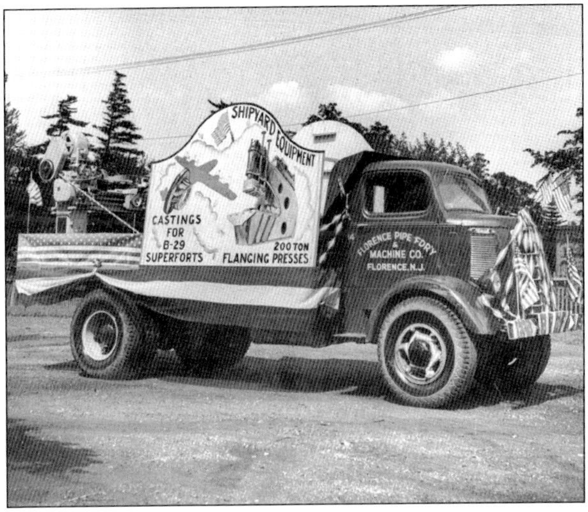

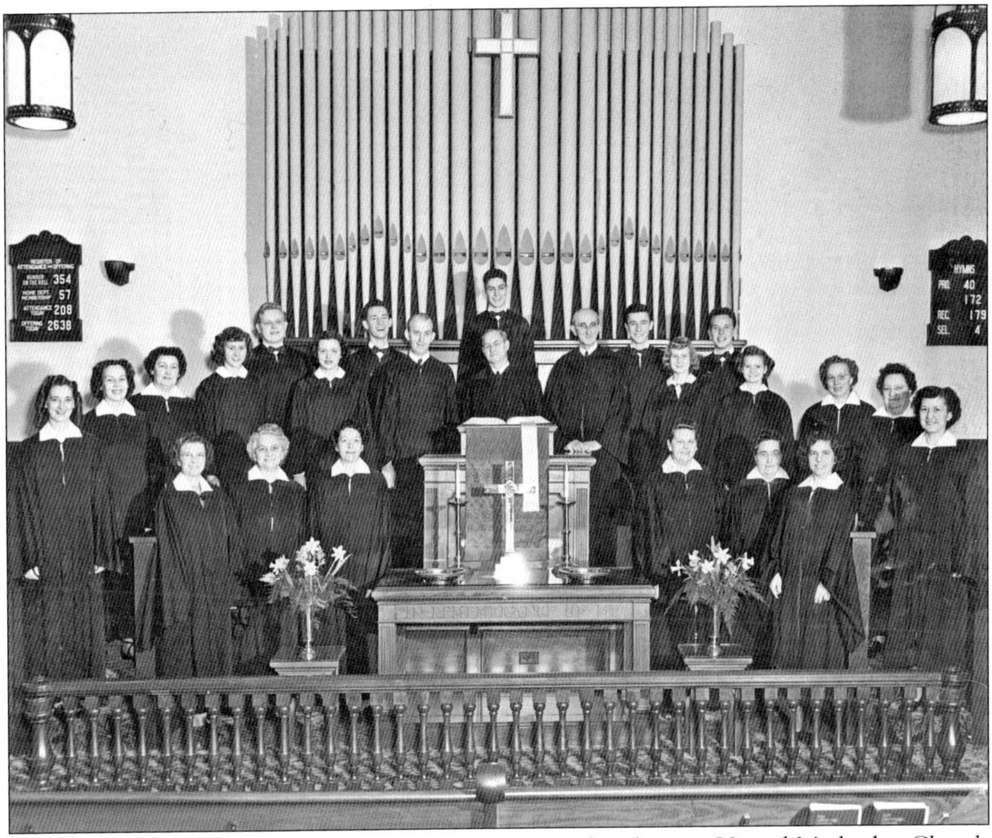

Methodist Church Choir. Between 1948 and 1950, the Florence United Methodist Church choir is quite impressive with its many members. From left to right are (first row) Mrs. Duvall, Bess Hamilton, Esther Denneler, Lilly Evans, Melvina Weber and Mary Dubell; (second row) Naomi Spotts, Iris Rainier, Gladys Cooper, Betty Gaskill, Bill Hamilton, Ruth Arden Speed, Ed Patterson, Presley Hamilton, Donald Cooper, George Brown, Karl Weber, Leroy Patterson, Donald Jones, Hazel Weeks, Phyllis Weeks, Mary Jones, Lillian Hughes, and Betty Book. (Courtesy of Roy Patterson.)

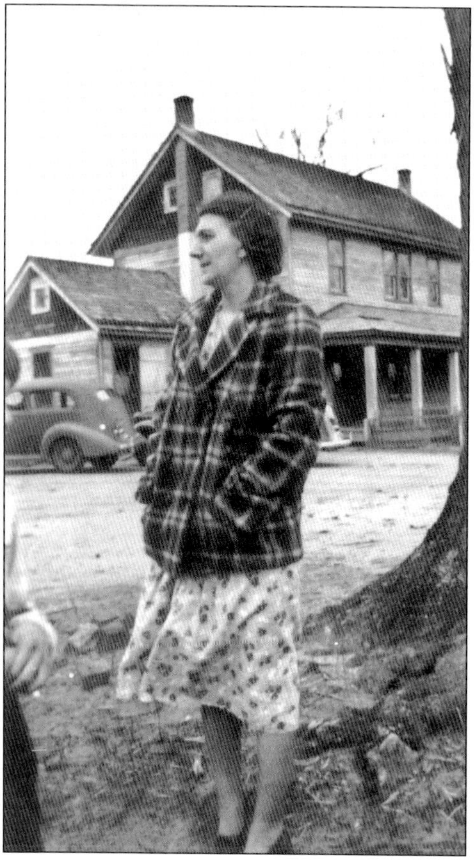

BESSIE IVINS. Bessie Ivins stands across the street from what is believed to be the Richardson farmhouse, although the property is marked on the 1859 map as being owned by W. Thompson. Standing on the northeast corner of Front and Summer Streets, this large farmhouse was demolished in the 1960s. The Richardson and Ivins families were two of the earliest families in the Florence/ Mansfield area. James Richardson kept the Florence Hotel from 1855 to 1857. (Courtesy of the Florence Historical Society.)

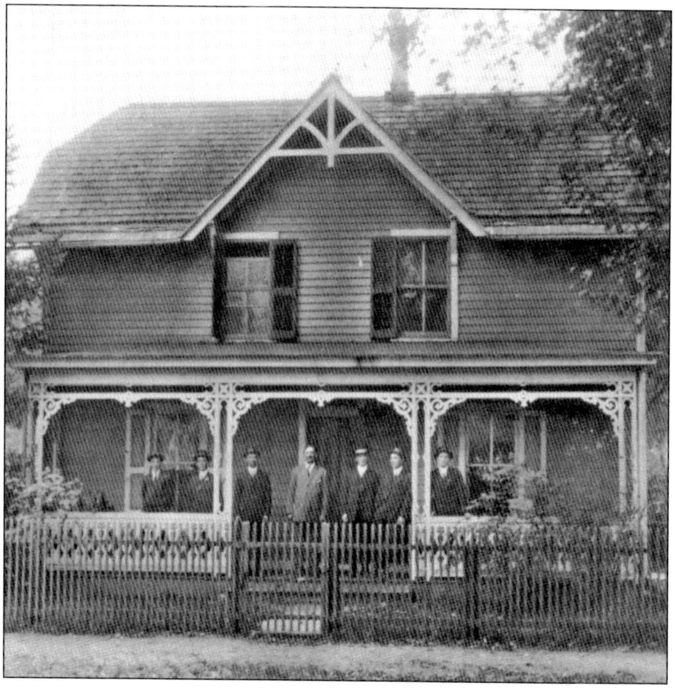

THE MCGRATH HOUSE. Some of the McGrath family stands on their porch around 1905. From left to right are sons Leo Carrol McGrath, William McGrath, Michael McGrath, Michael J. McGrath (father), Philip McGrath, Martin McGrath, and James McGrath. This lovely old home is virtually unchanged outside other than removal of the upstairs shutters, different gingerbread on the porch, and a similar fence. Located at the southeast corner of Second and Iron Streets, it also housed Mary McGrath and her daughters Sadie, Mary, and Nora. (Courtesy of John Williams.)

Cheerleaders, 1953. The Florence High School class of 1953 included the cheerleaders pictured here. From left to right are (first row) Jean Othmer, Julia Russ, and Janice Lundin; (second row) Shirley Brewer, Wilma Luyber, and Carol Hamilton. The uniforms were more modest in those days. (Courtesy of Julia Russ Foulks.)

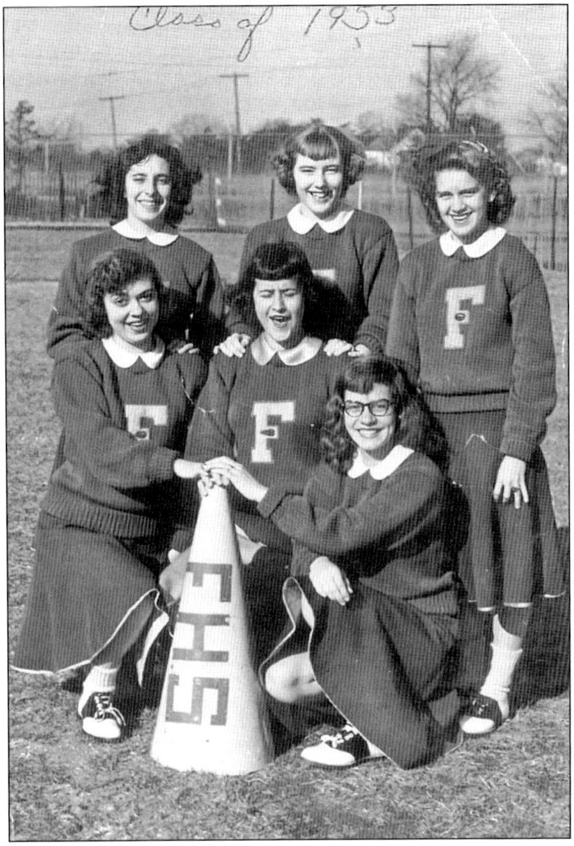

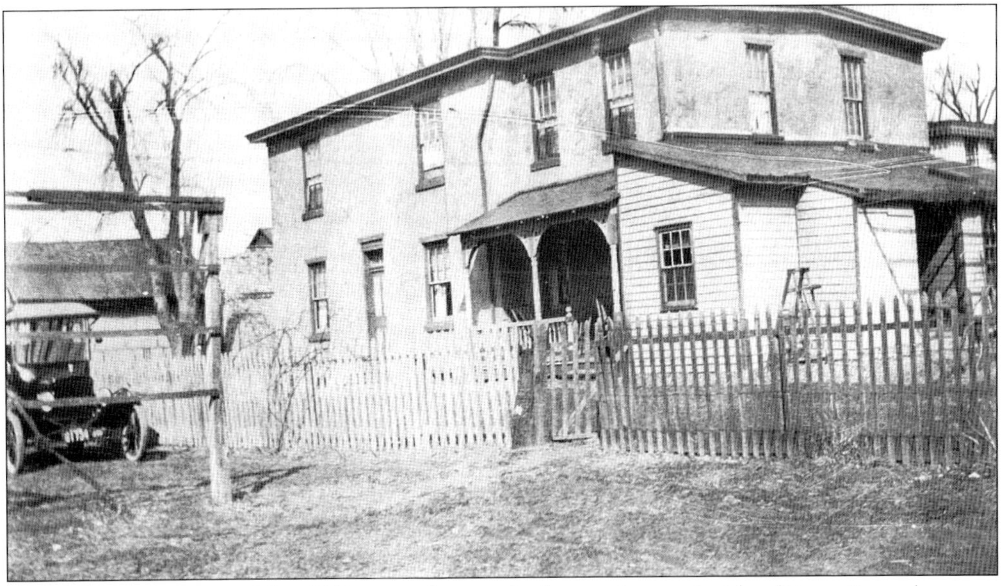

E.T. Baker Trucking. This 1914 scene shows a duplex on the south side of Front Street between Foundry and Iron Streets. On the right was the home and business of E.T. Baker; his company furnished building materials for Florence Supply Company in 1928. These homes were built by the R.D. Wood Company for its foundry employees. (Courtesy of the Florence Historical Society.)

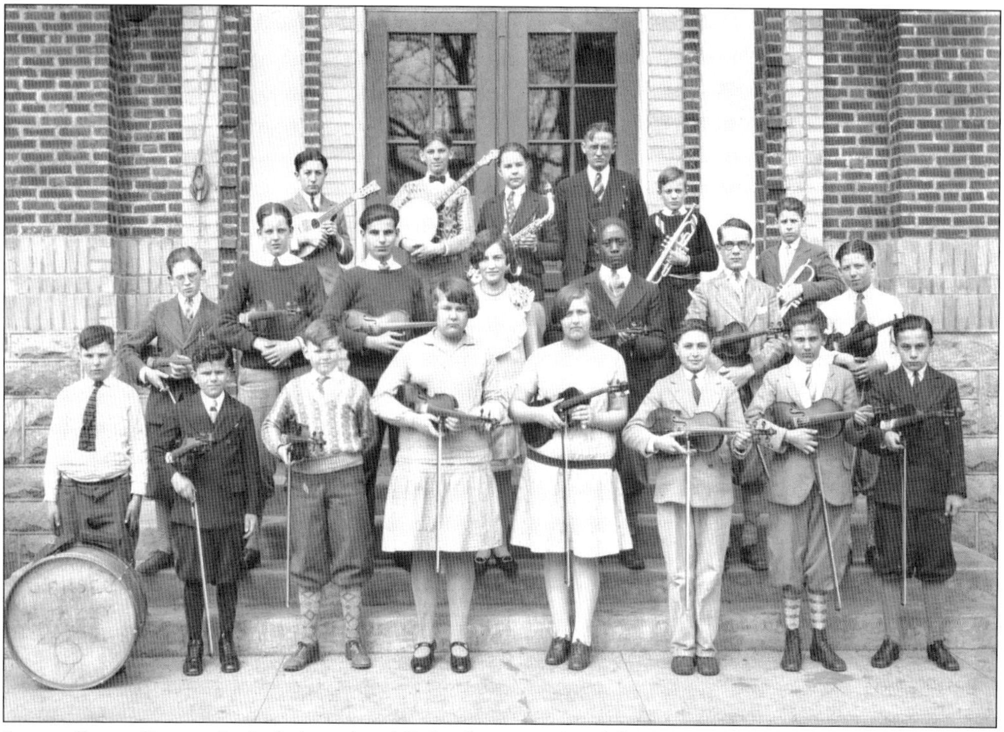

Jersey Jazzy Band. Included in this 1930s photograph of the Jersey Jazzy sixth-grade band are, from left to right, (first row) Olin Brining, Gilbert Halasz, William Roberts, Laura Horn, Florie Dubo, William "Mimi" Wallace, Michael Malmos, and Stephen Bogdani; (second row) John Goddard, Vincent O'Donnell, John Magyar, Grace Hoover, John Trask, Bert Naismith, and William Van Ness; (third row) Ralph Hamilton, "Bud" Reed, James Alvord, director H.E. Moore, James Gardner, and Warren Shepherd. (Courtesy of the Florence Historical Society.)

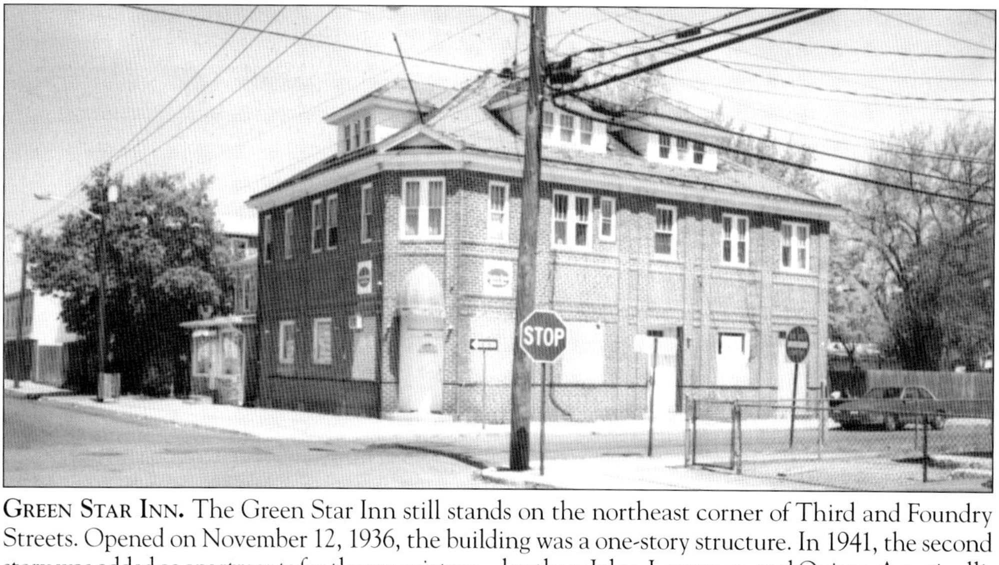

Green Star Inn. The Green Star Inn still stands on the northeast corner of Third and Foundry Streets. Opened on November 12, 1936, the building was a one-story structure. In 1941, the second story was added as apartments for the proprietors—brothers John, Lawrence, and Quinto Agostinelli. The inn had a beautiful bar and spacious dining room, with ample space for dancing. It has now been remodeled into roomy private apartments (Courtesy of the Florence Historical Society.)

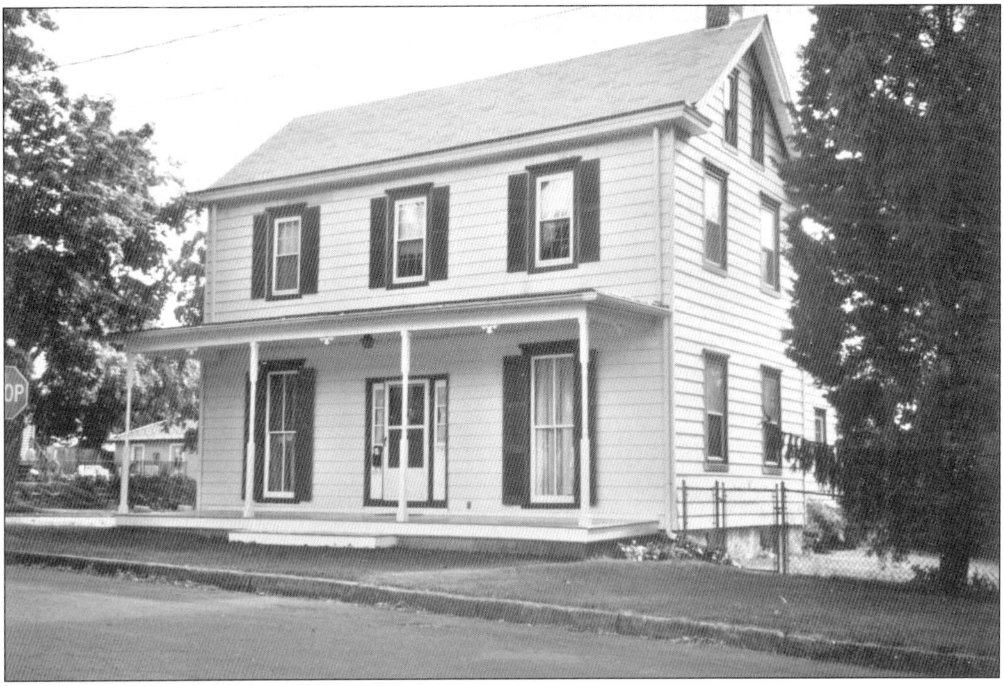

The Lanning House. Located on the southwest corner of East Second and Walnut Streets, this house was built by William A. Lanning on land that was purchased from Robert Pettit in 1872. William Lanning was a Civil War veteran. The house was later occupied by his descendant, Susie Lanning, who married William M.R. Brown. Brown formerly worked at Hanover Furnace and then at the Florence Iron Works. (Courtesy of the Florence Historical Society.)

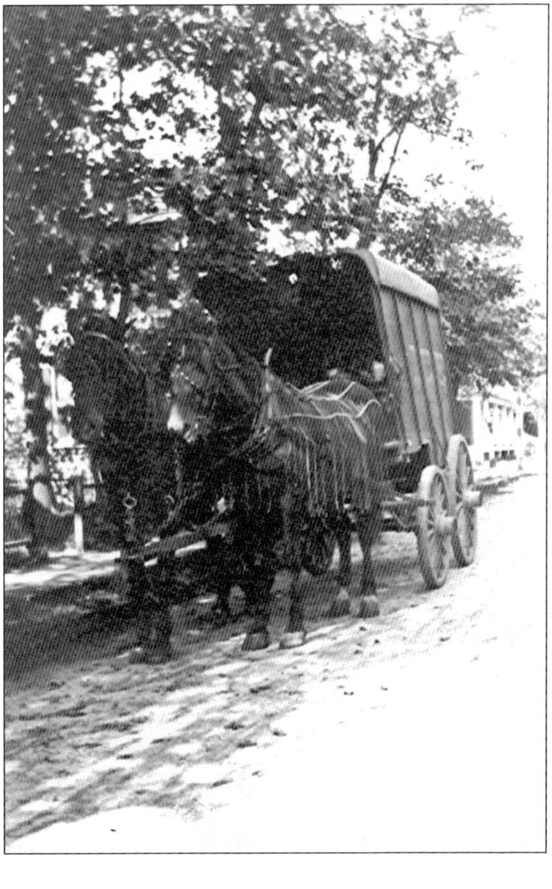

An Ice Wagon. This ice wagon is pictured on Front Street in the early 1900s. The street is unpaved, which is kinder on horses' hooves. The horses wear light blankets with long fringe to keep the flies away. At the right is the Florence Hotel, later the Municipal Building, which burned down in 1979. (Courtesy of Jack Quig.)

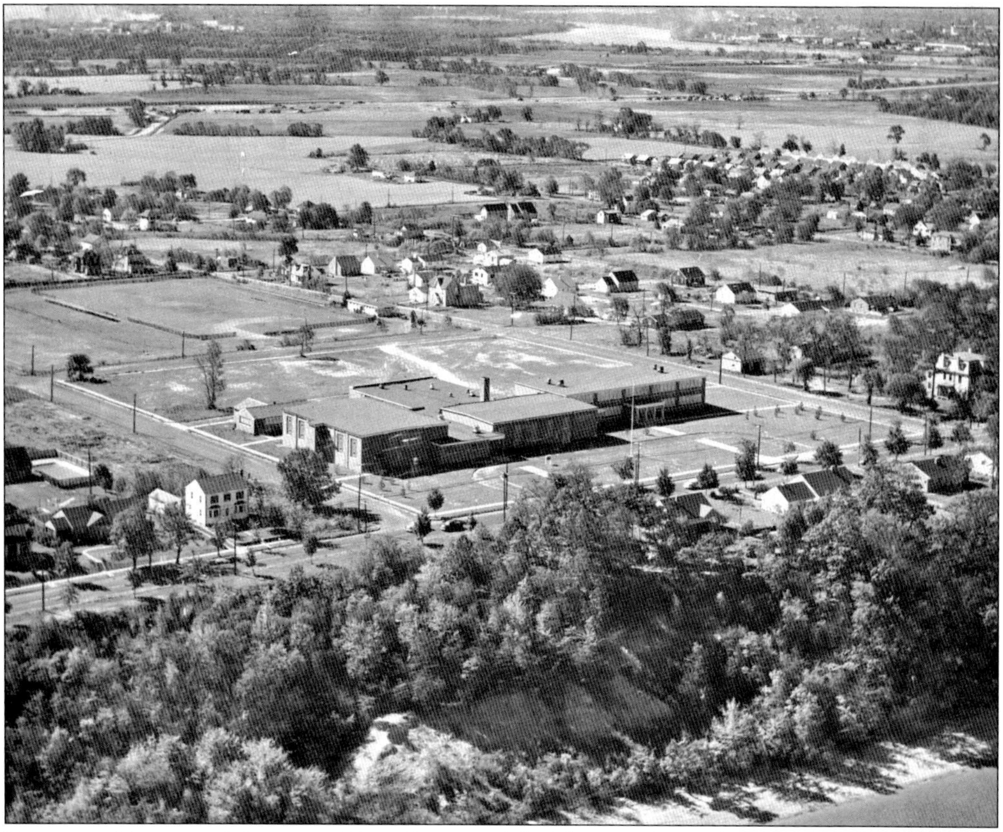

Florence Township Memorial High School. The Florence Township Memorial High School on Front Street was erected in 1952. Currently named the Riverfront School, it houses fourth to eighth grades and preschool programs. Behind the building, and also located between Third and Fifth Streets, was the football field, affectionately known as "the Pit." The bottom right corner shows the Delaware River, which makes a major bend and can be seen again at upper right. (Courtesy of the Florence Historical Society.)

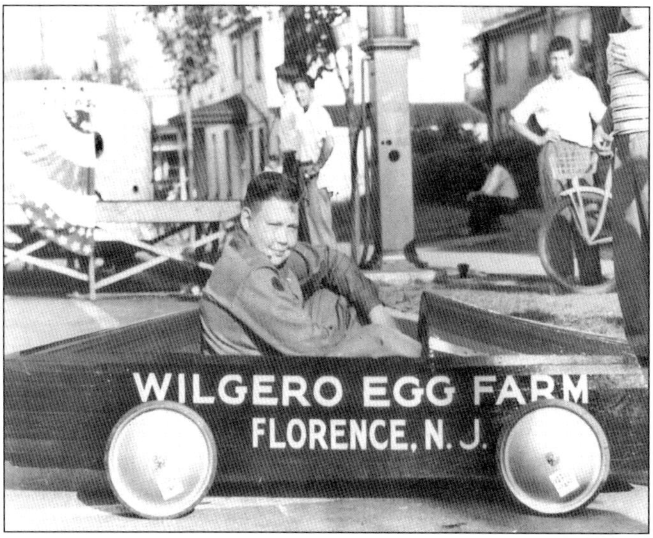

William Dempsey. William Dempsey, son of Raymond Dempsey, steers his soapbox racer about 1948 near the reviewing stand on Front Street in the annual soapbox derby. His father raised chickens as a hobby and won three first prizes at the New York Poultry Show. "Wilgero" on the car represents the three Dempsey children: William, Geraldine, and Rose. (Courtesy of William Dempsey.)

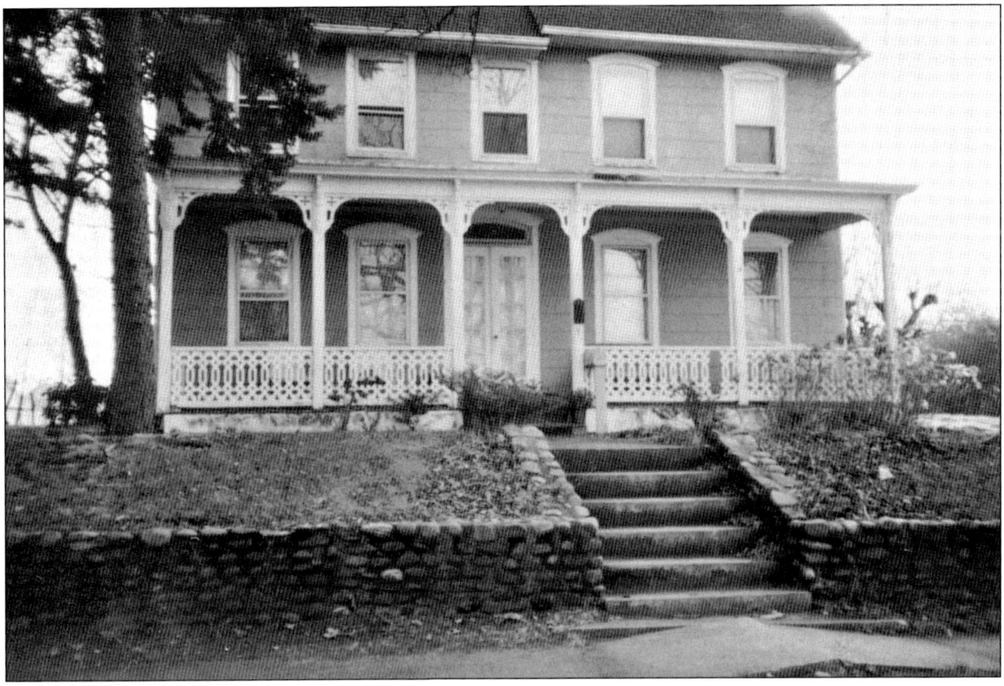

THE DURELL HOUSE. Early preaching services of the Methodist Church were held in the home of William Durell, located on the southwest corner of Front and Chestnut Streets. It was in the home that the first Methodist Episcopal Sunday school was started by Alfred Carty and Julia Durell. This house still stands today. (Courtesy of the Florence Historical Society.)

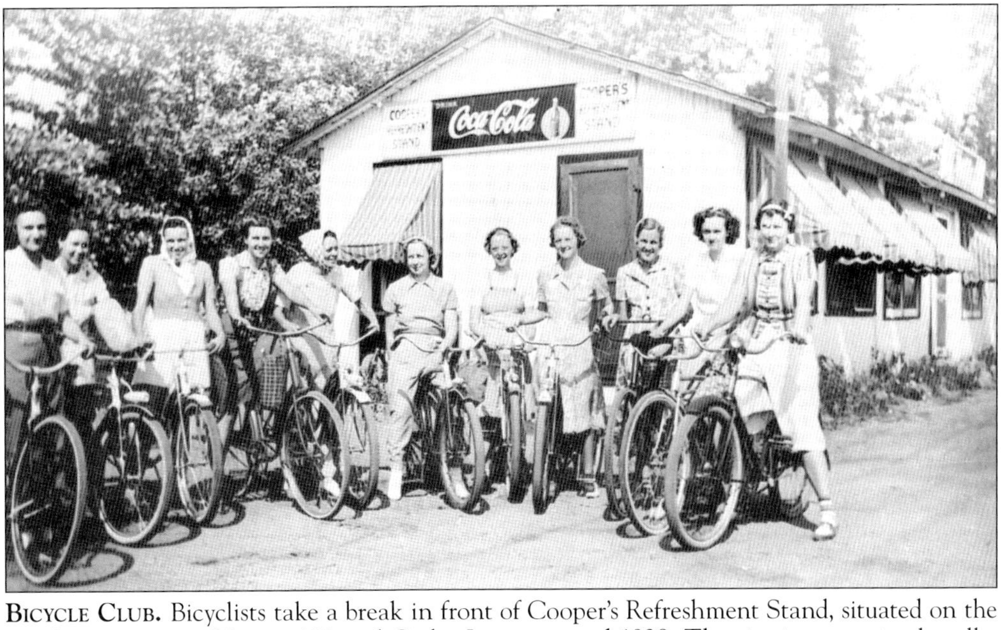

BICYCLE CLUB. Bicyclists take a break in front of Cooper's Refreshment Stand, situated on the northeast corner of Route 130 and Cedar Lane, around 1938. The site is now a jug handle. Pictured are, from left to right, Doris Donnelly, Iris Rainier, Margie Boldizar, Edna Burkhardt, Esther Denneler, Mary Jones, Helen Pullen, Lil Ridgway, Evelyn Donald, Peg Pierson, and Gladys Cooper. (Courtesy of Donald Cooper.)

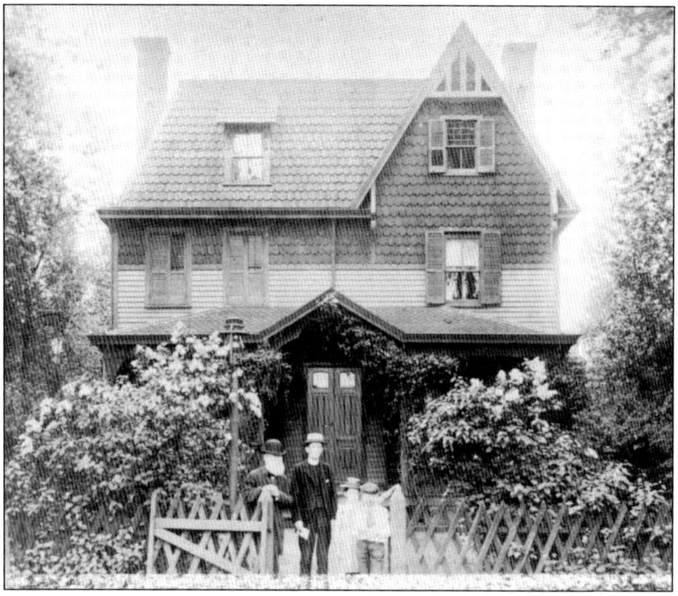

St. Stephens Rectory. Pictured in 1901 are the Reverend Samuel E. Hanger, his children, and his father. Living in the St. Stephen's Episcopal Church rectory, they appear to be leaving for church services. Built on the south side of East Third Street, the rectory is largely unchanged, although the large lilac shrubs and the interesting fence are no longer there. Reverend Hanger was rector from 1901 to 1913. The rectory is now privately owned. (Courtesy of Robert Panaro.)

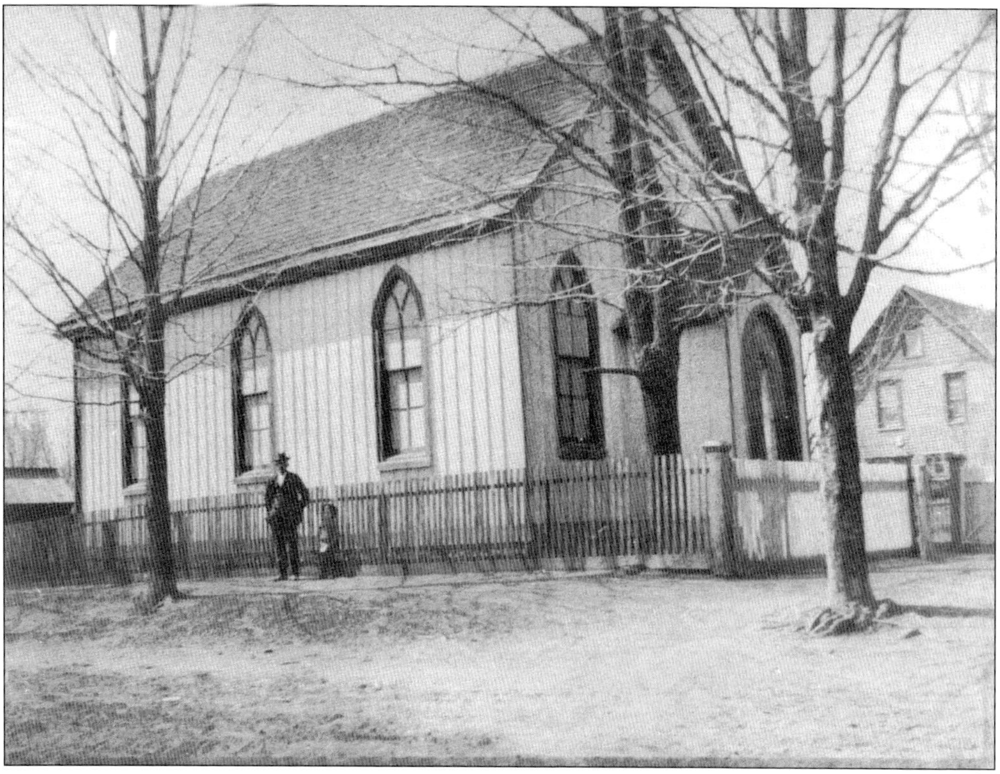

The Catholic Church. The first Catholic church in Florence was located on the southwest corner of West Second and Eyre Streets downtown. It was used until the late 1800s, when a large brownstone church was built to accommodate a larger congregation uptown. This little church was moved to the Florence Foundry property for use as a toolshed; today, it no longer exists. (Courtesy of Robert Panaro.)

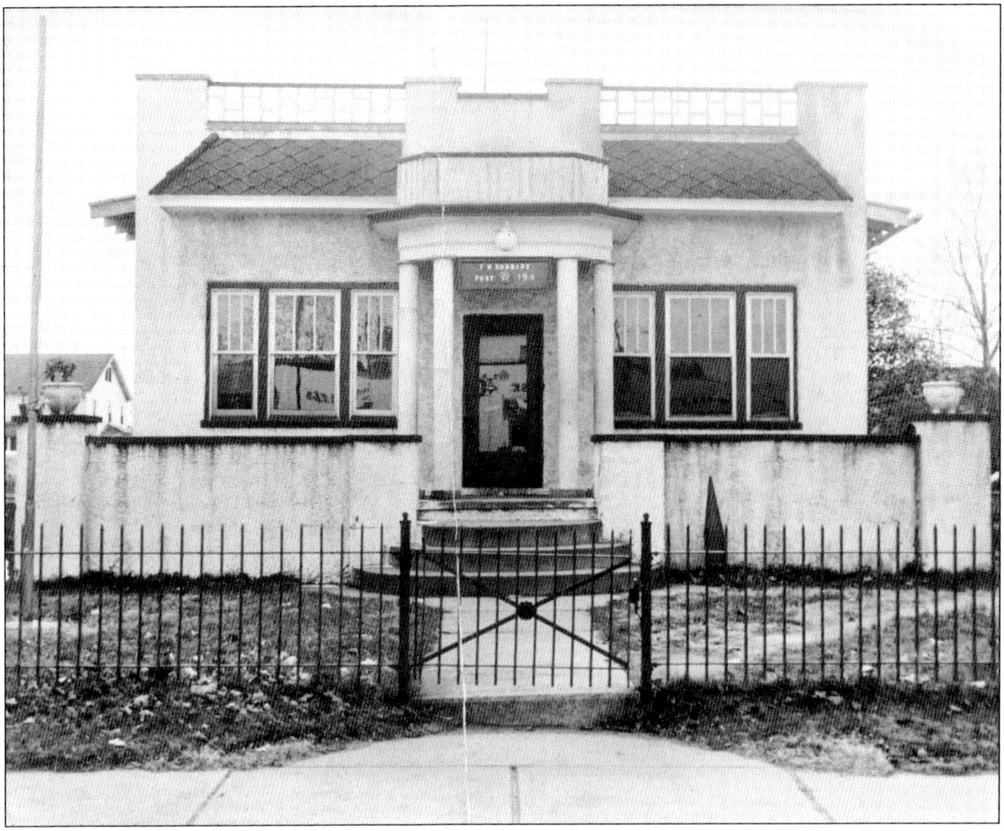

The American Legion. The American Legion Post 194 at 38 West Second Street was built after World War I. It was known as the "Dugout." The Legion then erected a building at Broad and Sixth Streets in 1950, when this little building became the CIO Union Hall until 1973. The CIO allowed use of the building as a "canteen" for local teenagers, with dancing and games. It is currently a day care center. (Courtesy of the Florence Historical Society.)

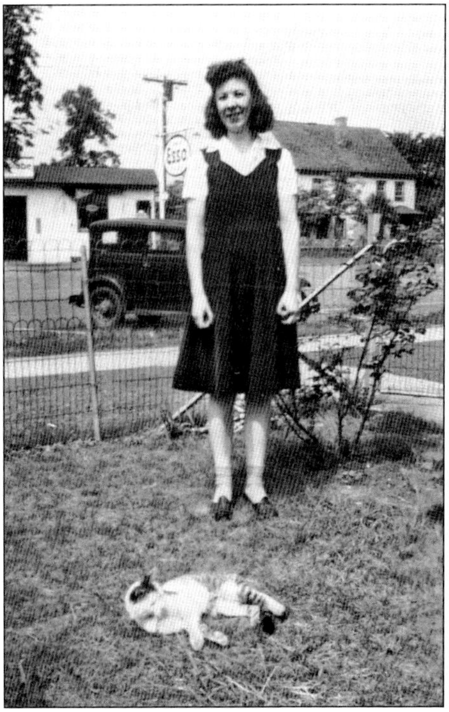

Carmela DiLullo. Carmela DiLullo stands in her front yard on the southwest corner of Front and Summer Streets in September 1943, with her cat Guido. Behind her is the Esso gas station that was owned at various times by Roy Nichols, Jim Ivins, the Foulks family, the Sayers family, and Herbert Fritchman. The large farmhouse across the street, which was owned by the Richardson family in its early years, was demolished in the 1960s. (Courtesy of the Florence Historical Society.)

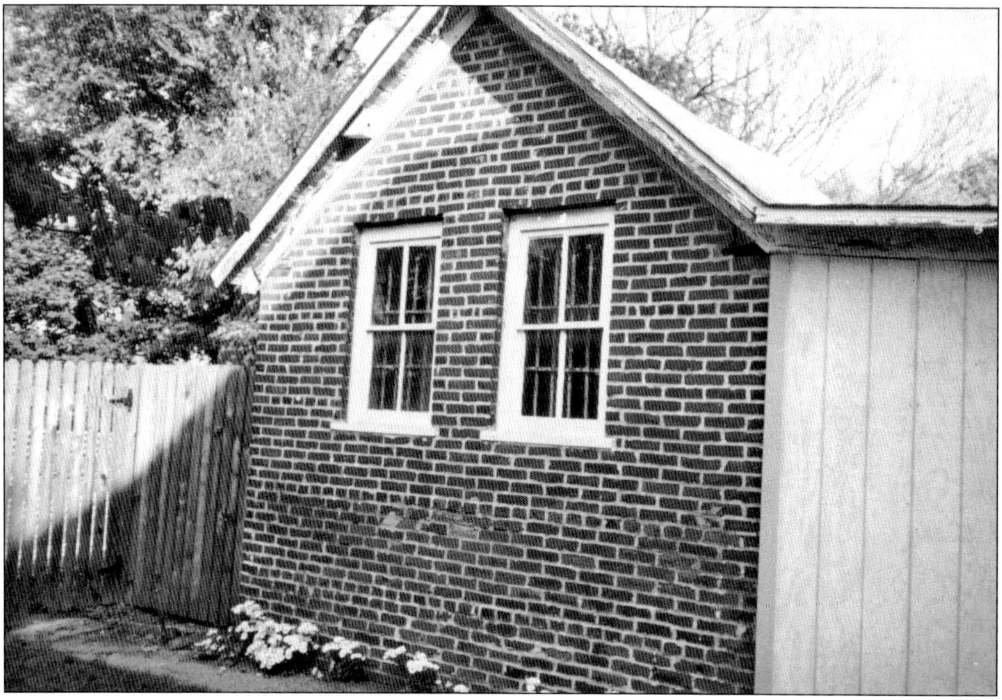

The Florence Jail. The first jailhouse in Florence was in the rear of 35 West Fourth Street. It is now a garage, but the bars are till on the windows. The only police officer in Florence at that time was John Mullen. On October 31, 1908, an escape was made by one of the foreign residents, who obtained a hammer and broke the lock on the door. (Courtesy of the Florence Historical Society.)

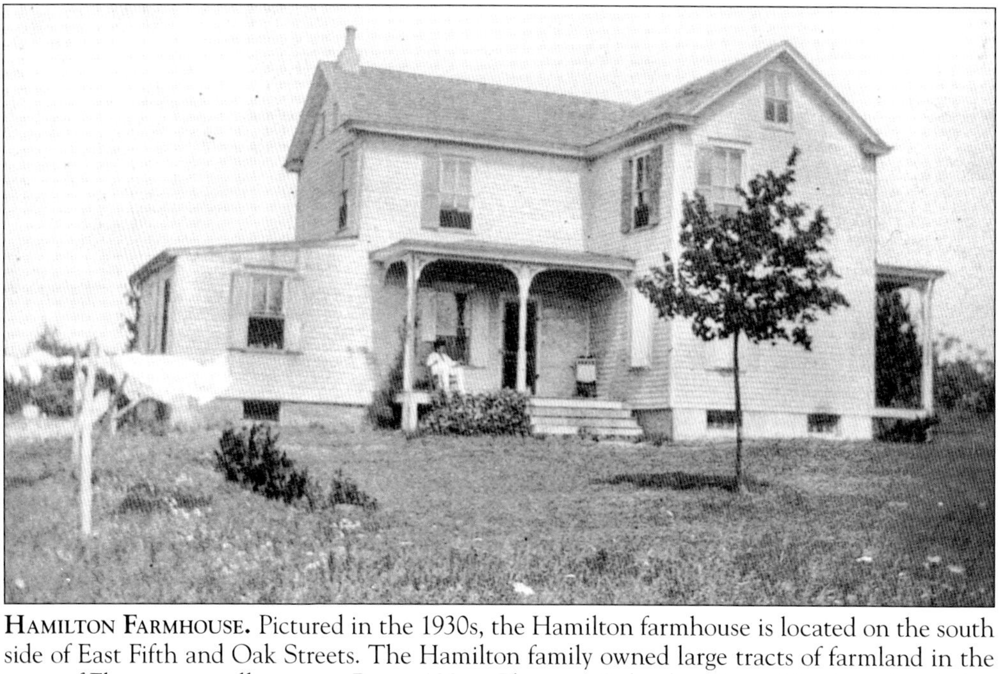

Hamilton Farmhouse. Pictured in the 1930s, the Hamilton farmhouse is located on the south side of East Fifth and Oak Streets. The Hamilton family owned large tracts of farmland in the town of Florence as well as across Route 130 on Florence-Columbus Road. This large family has been in Florence since before the 1800s. (Courtesy of Donald Cooper.)

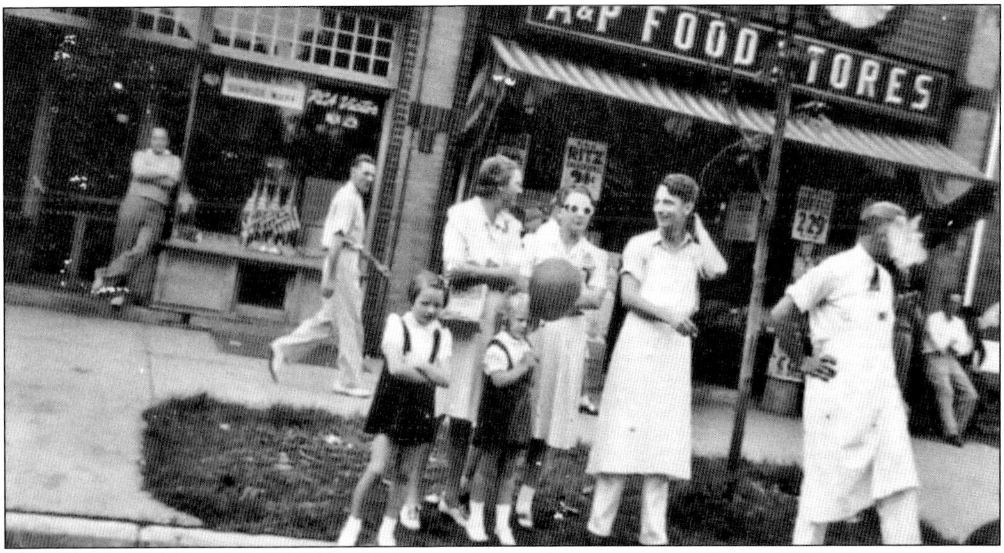

A&P MARKET. Florence residents love parades, and it appears in this c. 1940 photograph that even the employees of the A&P market have come out to enjoy the event. It later became Front Street Market in 1941, with Paul Conrey and Harry Fauver as owners. This row of stores is still in business at the south side of West Front Street. At various times, it included an Acme Market, a shoemaker, a five-and-dime store, post office, law office, an A&P market, the Florence Seafood store, an appliance store, a hardware store, and Front Street Market. (Courtesy of the Florence Historical Society.)

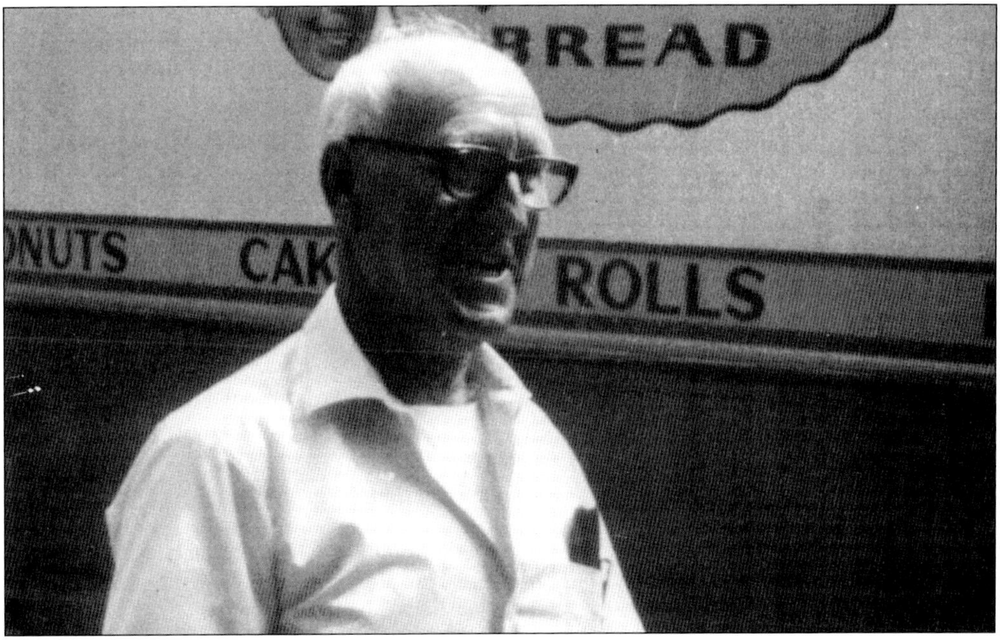

BERT THE BREAD MAN. Bert Mitchell from Clementon sold Freihofer bread and other baked goods in the Florence area during the 1940s and 1950s. Door-to-door delivery was common back then, when milk, fish, produce, clothes props, clothing, ice, coal, bread, and household goods were all sold by truck in the streets of town. Prevalent also in the 1930s were illegal beer wagons, and a snake oil salesman came once a year to ply his trade. (Courtesy of Doris Coates Jones.)

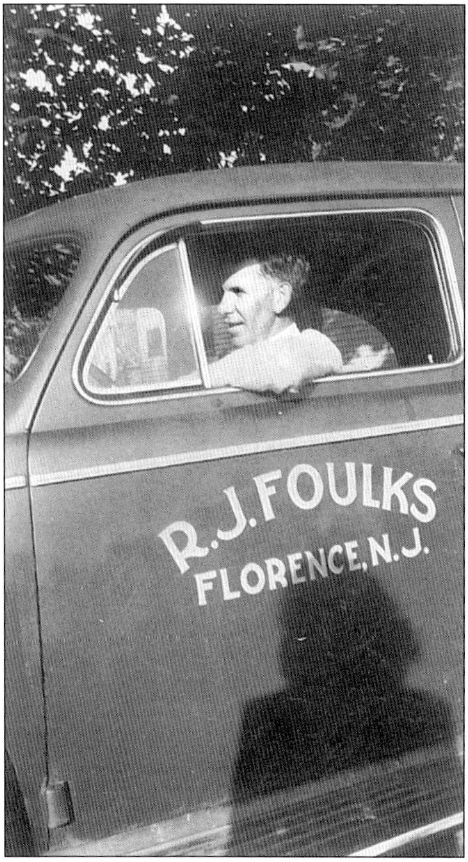

RAYMOND J. FOULKS. Raymond J. Foulks is pictured around 1940 delivering bread around town. He and his wife were proprietors of a store on Winter Street behind the Baird house. Their building was originally a carriage house for the Baird family. This store was a popular hangout for the schoolchildren, as it sold soda, ice cream, candy, and local drink Tak-A-Boost. (Courtesy of the Florence Historical Society.)

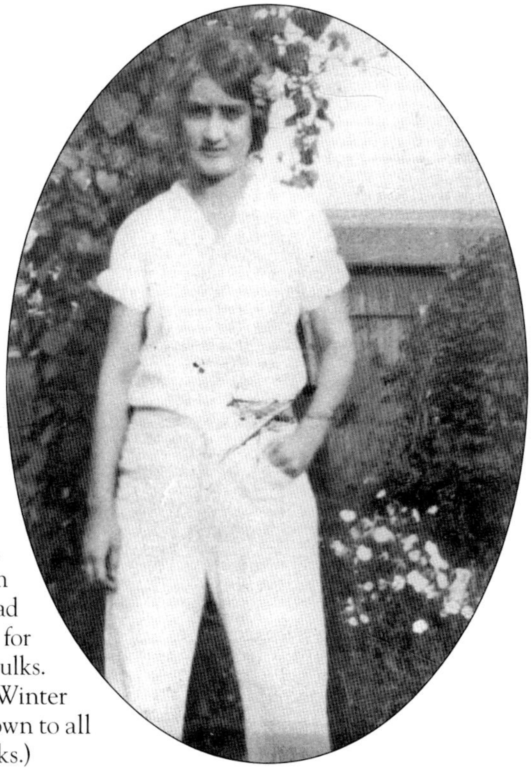

CLARA WOLFE FOULKS. Clara Wolfe Foulks, seen here at age 17, grew up on her parents' farm on Schuyler Ferry Road in the 1920s. They had a hothouse where vegetable plants were raised for sale. She married local bread man Raymond Foulks. Later, they were owners of a candy store on Winter Street between Front and Second Streets, known to all as Clara's. (Courtesy of Stuart and Julia Foulks.)

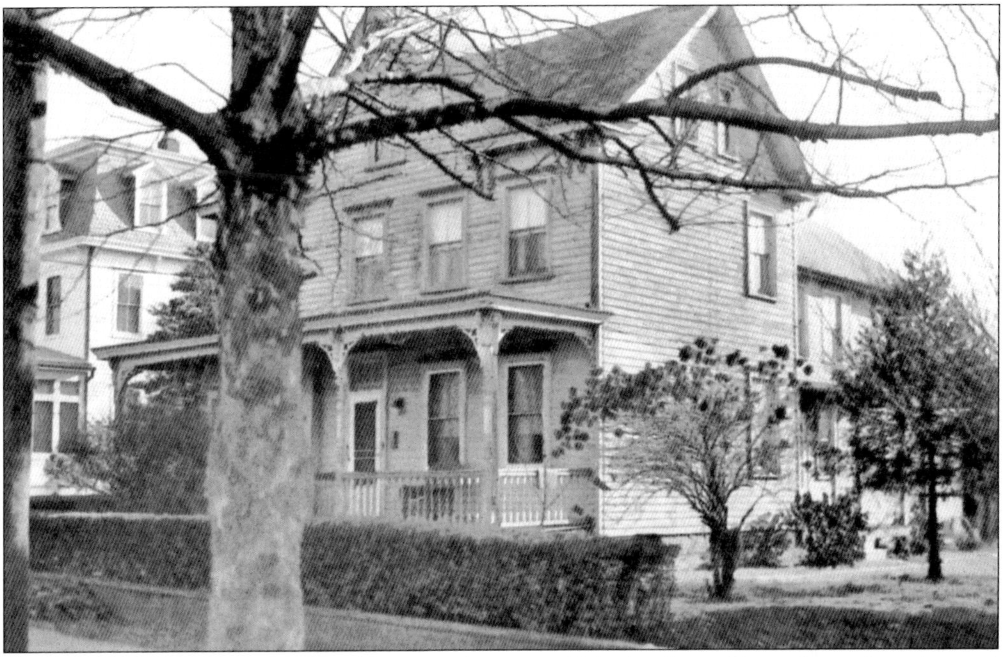

DOCTOR SHAVER'S OFFICE. This house in the second block of East Front Street has changed slightly over the years. Photographed in the 1940s, the porch and railing have since been removed, and picture windows have replaced the old windows in front. It later became the office of Dr. Kenneth Shaver. Since his death, other doctors have occupied the building, which still stands today. (Courtesy of Mary Tapper.)

GRANDFATHER BODINE. William Bodine is shown on his farm with his horse Allan around 1900. This appears to be on Olive Street, although an old map shows he had a farm in earlier years where the Von Thaden farm is located. He sold five different kinds of chickens as well as eggs and produce. Bodine family members were also prominent in the Florence Bank. (Courtesy of the Florence Historical Society.)

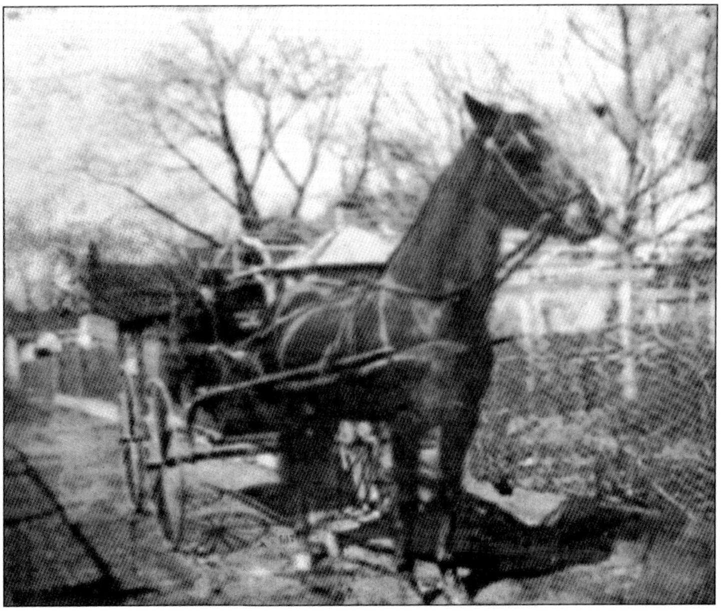

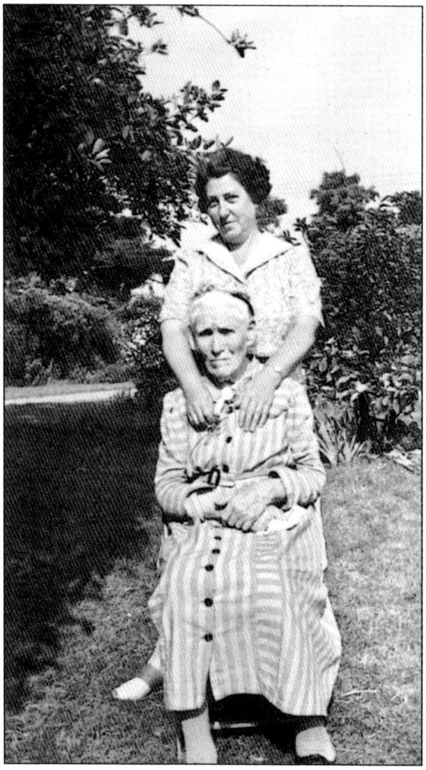

SARAH "SALLY" MARTER. Sally Marter shares a moment with Cora Brown in 1943. Matter had a large farm in Florence fronting on Schuyler Ferry Road and spanning the area all the way to West Sixth Street. Many children picked crops on her grounds to earn money during the Depression. Marter never married and died at the age of 90. She is buried at Coopertown Cemetery. (Courtesy of the Florence Historical Society.)

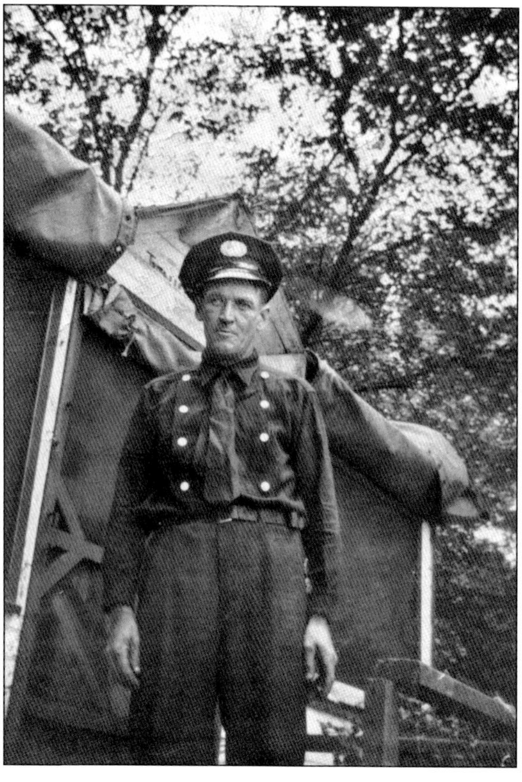

BILLY MOORE. Billy Moore is shown around 1930 in front of one of the cabins on Money Island, adjacent to Florence in the Delaware River. He was paid rent by vacationers for these cabins and took his clients across the river in his rowboat for their summer stays, subsequent to his father, Watson Moore, having the contract with Delaware River Sand Dredging Company in the 1930s. In January 1935, Billy fell through the ice in the river and was rescued by the Florence Township Beach Patrol. (Courtesy of the Florence Historical Society.)

Three

Business and Industry

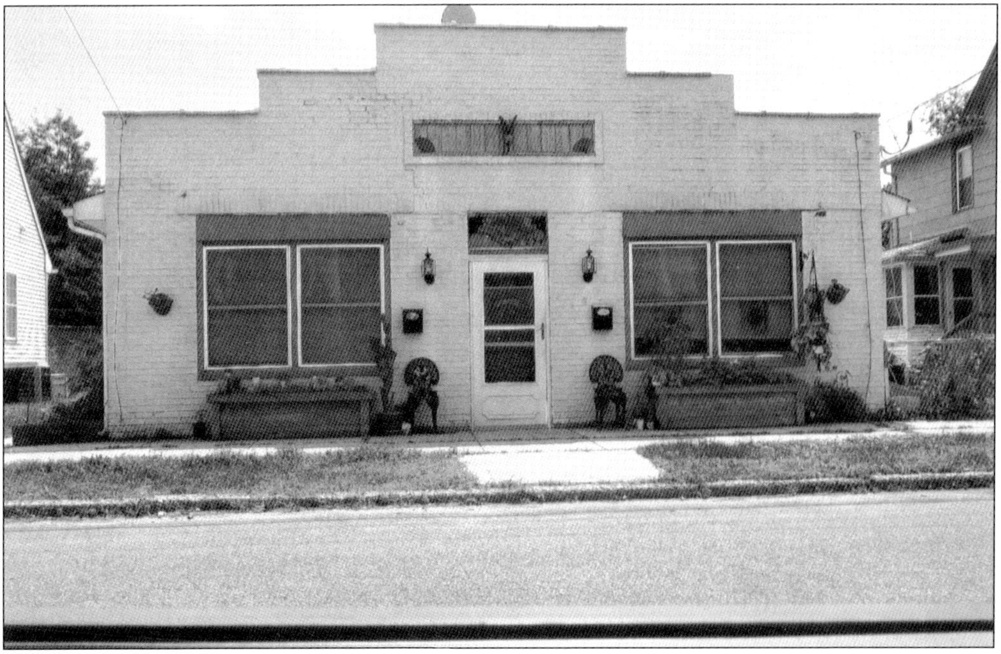

Dipsy Doodle. This little building was a popular hangout for students across the street from the high school on West Second Street during the 1940s and 1950s. Built around 1920, it had a jukebox for dancing and advertised a fountain and booth service. Patrons could buy ice cream, sandwiches, milk shakes, soda, and sundaes. The proprietor was Ed Markiewicz. The facade of the building is mostly unchanged today. (Courtesy of the Florence Historical Society.)

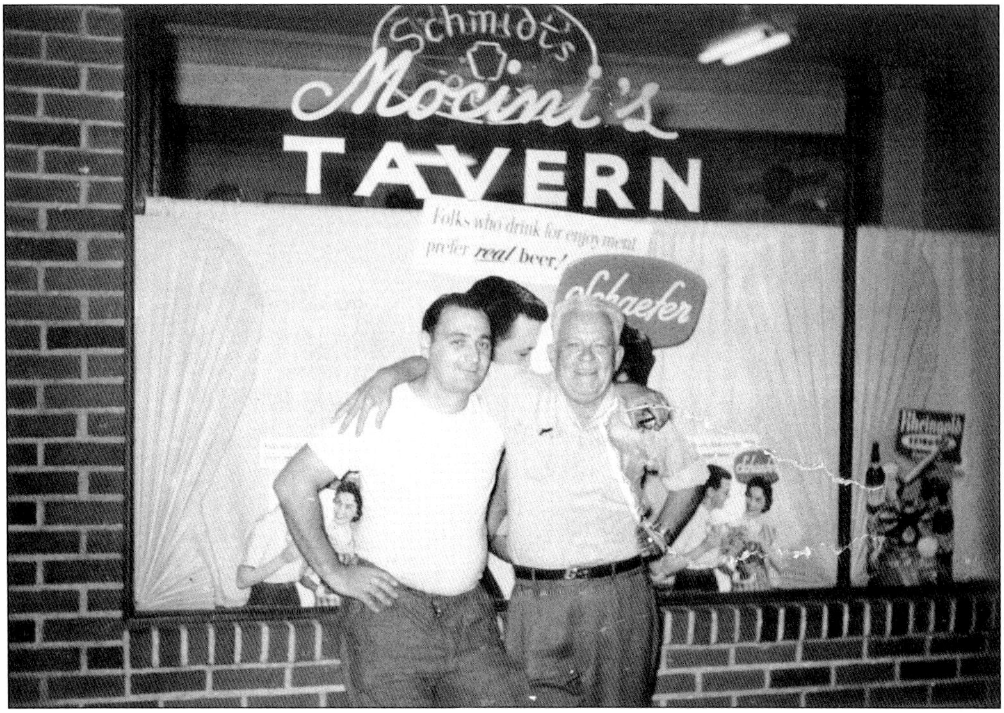

Mocini's Tavern. Andriano "Pabby" Mocini (left) stands with Alfred Green in front of his tavern downtown at the southeast corner of Second and Foundry Streets. This was formerly operated by Nick Puri before 1935. Nicknames for both boys and girls were common in Florence, and among Pabby's eight siblings were Olympio (or "Shanks"), David (or "Squeebles"), Amerigo (or "Micky"), and Irma or ("Mimu"). Also listed in the census were siblings Harry, Maria, and Clara. Pabby died in 2001 at the age of 76. (Courtesy of the Florence Historical Society.)

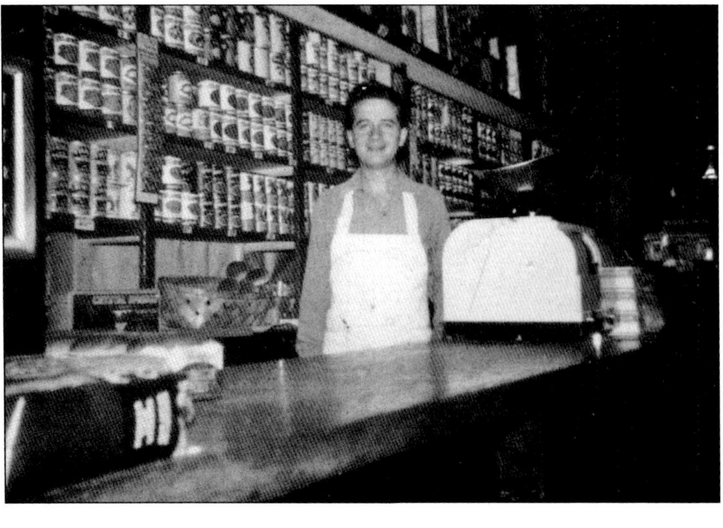

The Corner Market. Otello "Tots" Legnaioli stands ready to serve customers in his market at Second and Foundry Streets. Opened in October 21, 1949, it was heralded as Florence's newest and most modern self-service food store. Tots served as a medic with the US Army in Germany during World War II. (Courtesy of the Florence Historical Society.)

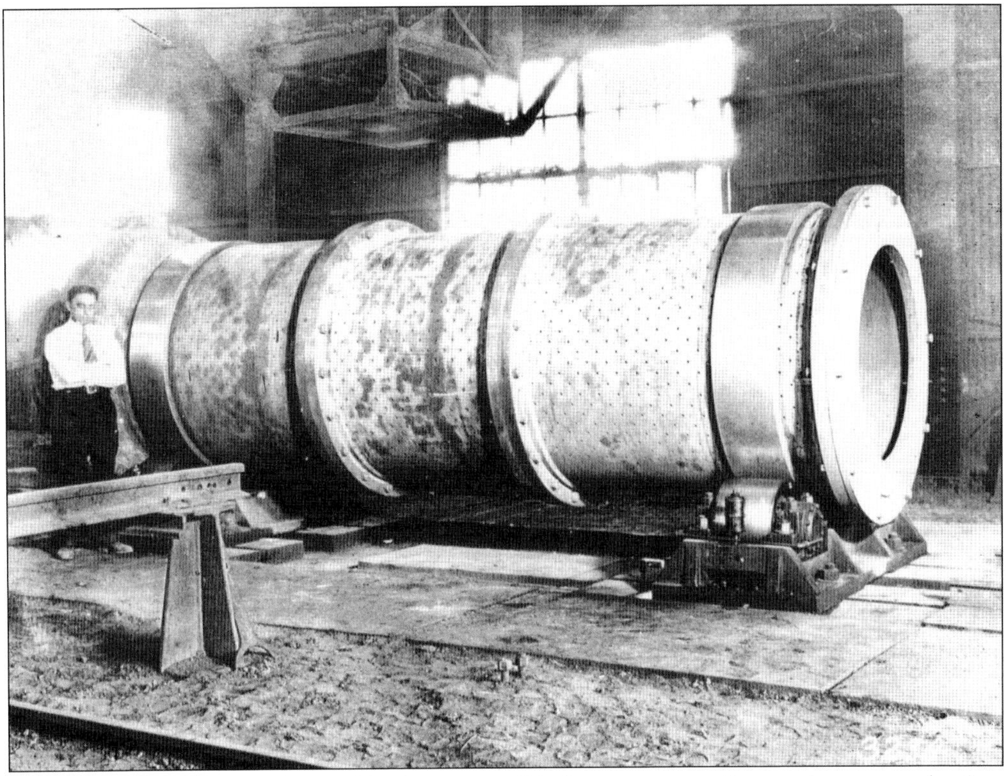

R.D. Wood Sand-Spun Pipe. Chief engineer Ed Camerota proudly stands next to the first 36-foot sand-spun pipe on June 19, 1929. The pipe measured approximately 12 feet long. Like in all early foundries in the country, the floors were made of wood and wood blocks. These pipes were commonly used in municipal water systems, and records of their use date back to 1829 in Philadelphia. (Courtesy of the Florence Historical Society.)

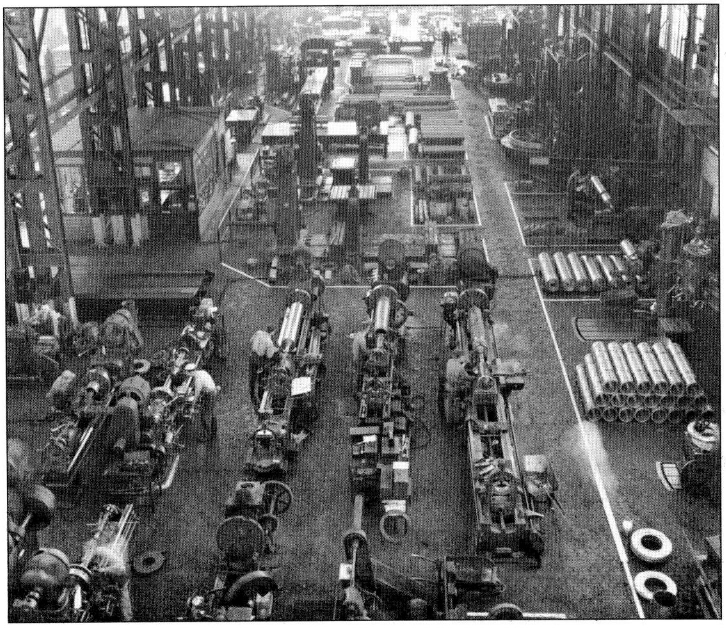

R.D. Wood Machine Shop. This overhead view of the machine shop in Florence gives a detailed picture of the kinds of machinery used in this large building. The workers are machining various items with lathes, horizontal milling machines, planer milling machines, vertical milling machines, and drill presses. The wood block and brick floors were common in these foundries. (Courtesy of the Florence Historical Society.)

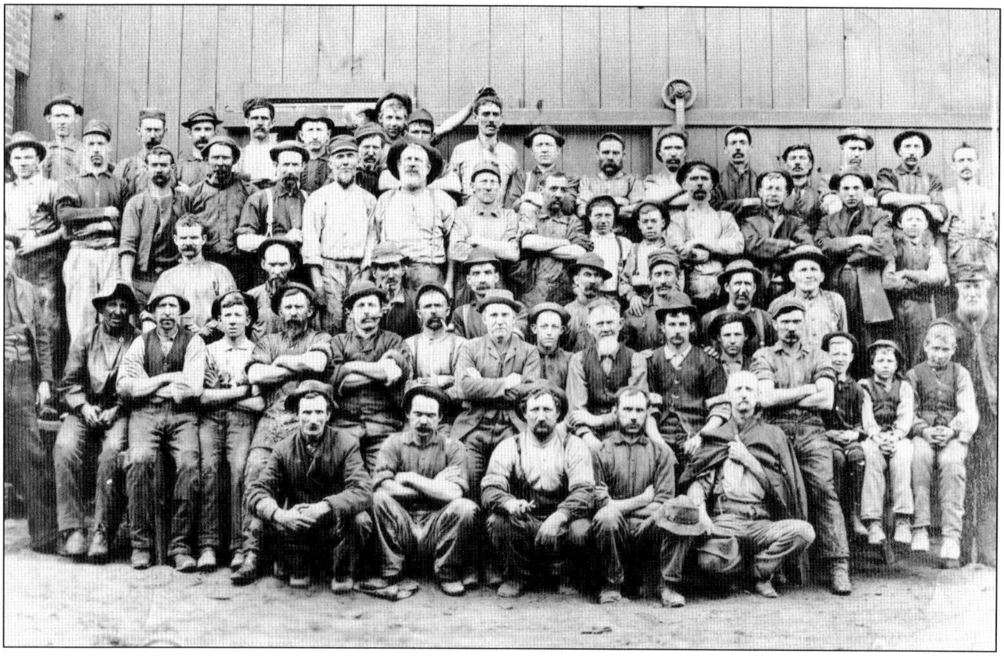

FLORENCE FOUNDRY LABOR GANG. Around 1905, one group of laborers for R.D. Wood Company is pictured at West Front Street. The small boys were also employees, before child labor laws were enacted. It was also common for children to bring their fathers' dinners to work in metal pails with lids. During its history, the R.D. Wood Company produced items for water and gas systems, parts for Baldwin locomotives, Mathews fire hydrants, and specialty items during World War II. (Courtesy of the Florence Historical Society.)

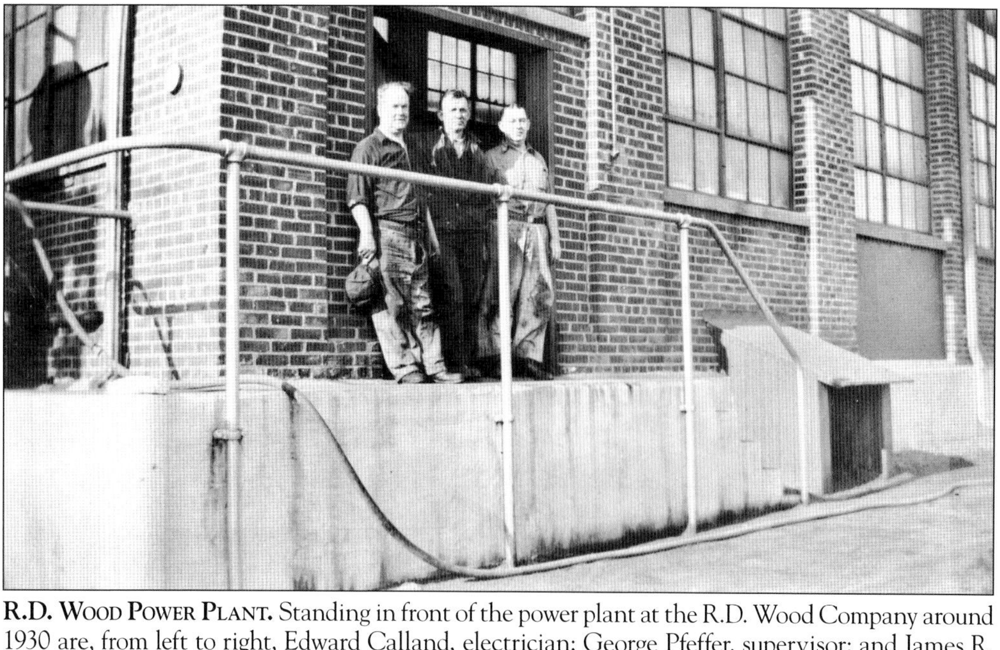

R.D. WOOD POWER PLANT. Standing in front of the power plant at the R.D. Wood Company around 1930 are, from left to right, Edward Calland, electrician; George Pfeffer, supervisor; and James R. Tapper Sr., electrician. After many years of operation since 1850, the plant closed its doors in March 2009. Most of the buildings have since been demolished. (Courtesy of Mary Tapper.)

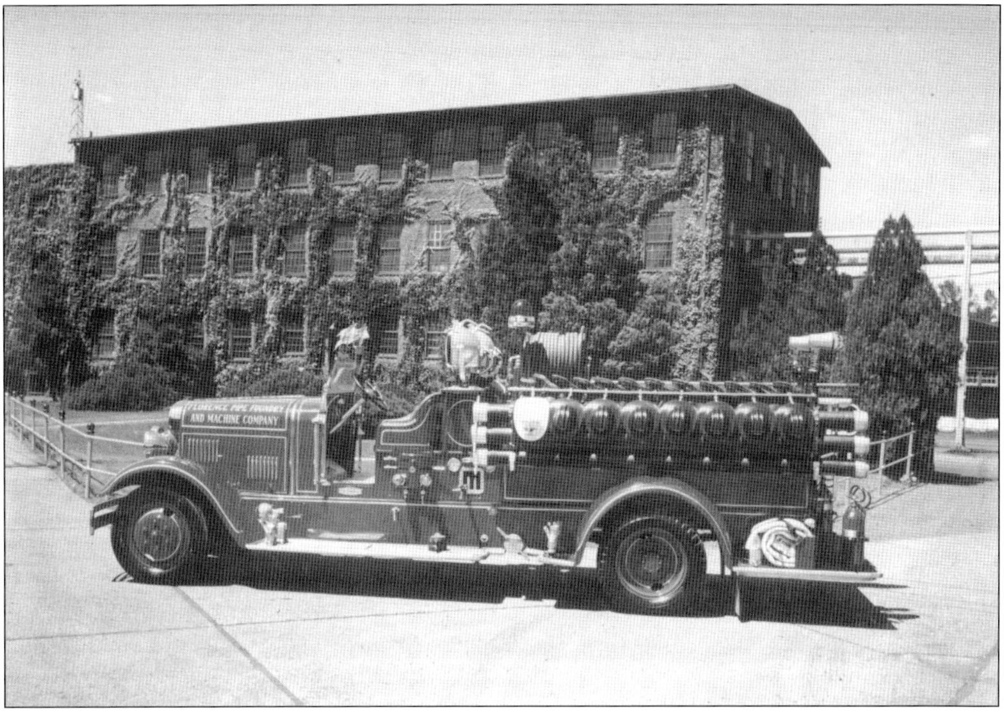

Florence Thread Company. A 1934 Seagrave fire truck stands in front of the Florence Thread Mill. Used last during the Florence Firehouse burning in 1972, the engine overheated, and the truck was retired from service. By 1928, the Florence Thread Company had moved to Riverside and the mill stood empty at the far end of the R.D. Wood property on West Front Street. (Courtesy of W. Allan Wood.)

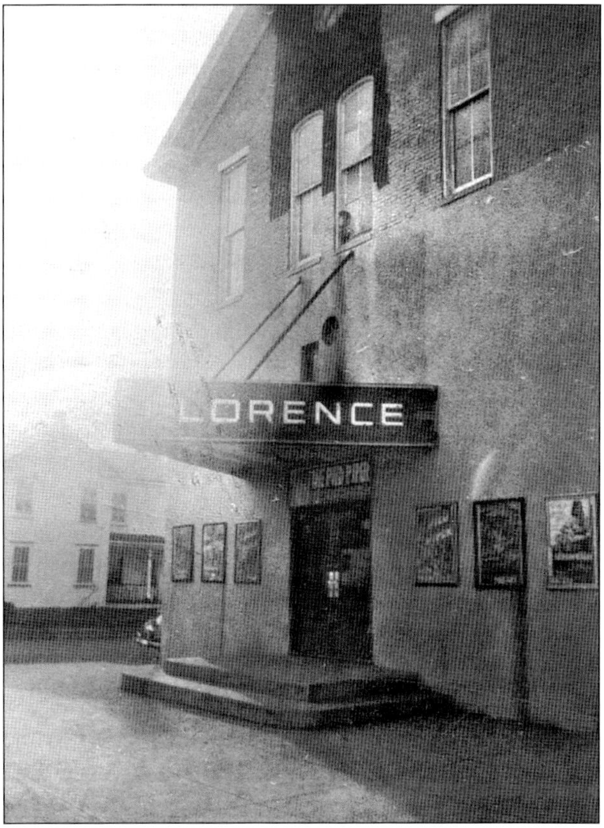

The Florence Movie. Pictured in December 1942, the Florence Movie was formerly Redmens Hall, and for some time, town hall. The second floor was also occupied by Gem Dress Factory in the late 1930s. During the 1940s and 1950s, free dishes were given to patrons each night until a set was eventually completed. The building is now Johnny's Gym (Florence Fitness) at the northwest corner of Second and Broad Streets. (Courtesy of Janet Griffith.)

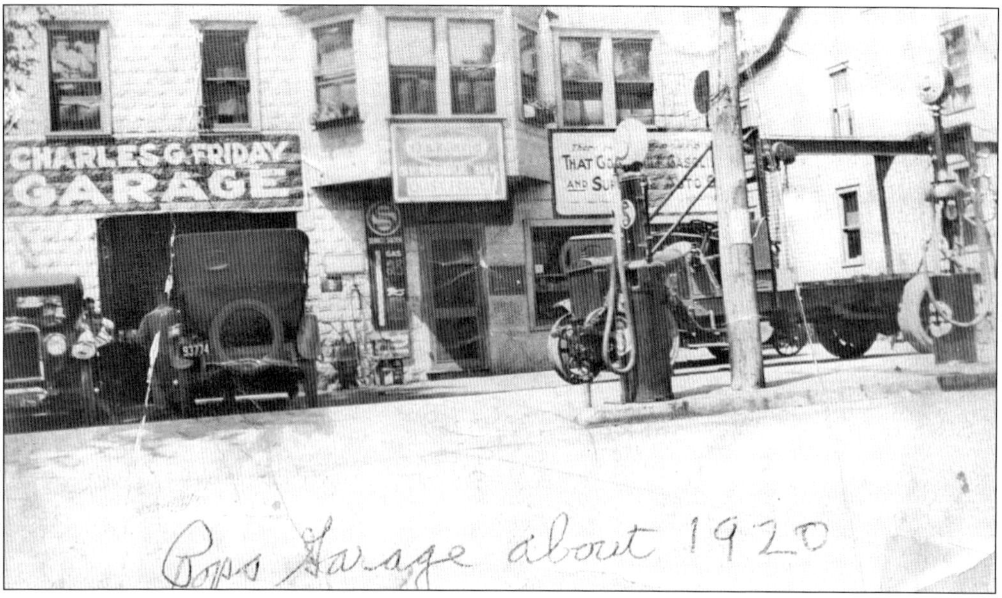

Friday's Garage. Charles G. Friday's garage, pictured around 1920, was located on the west side of Delaware Avenue in Florence Station. The building then became Wilson Chevrolet, before its move to Route 130 in 1949. Still standing, the building now houses private apartments. (Courtesy of the Florence Historical Society.)

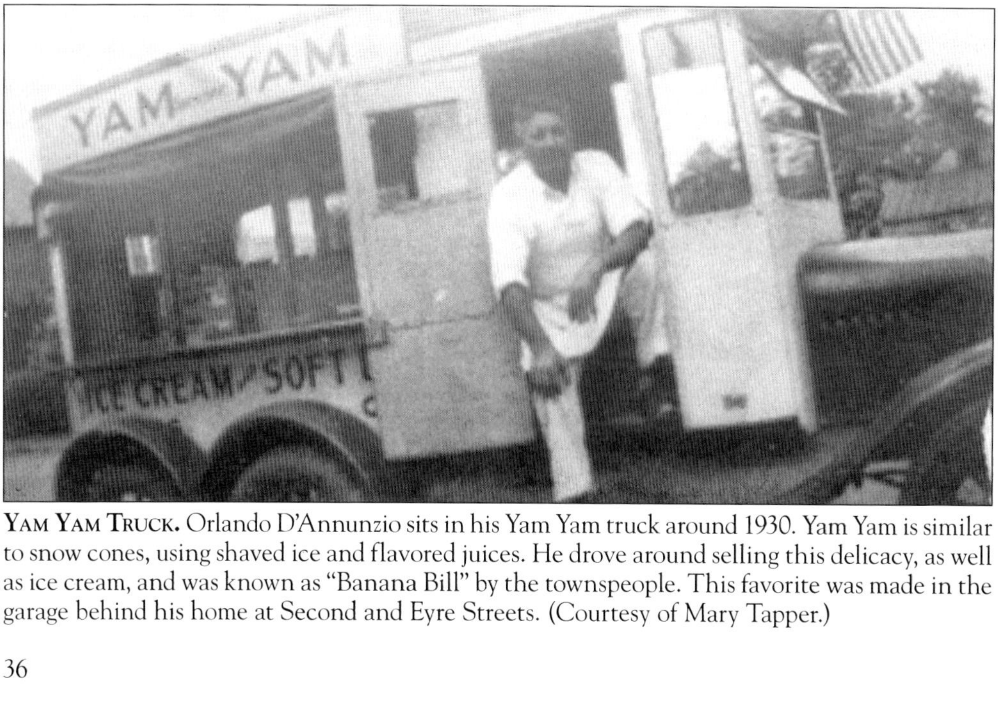

Yam Yam Truck. Orlando D'Annunzio sits in his Yam Yam truck around 1930. Yam Yam is similar to snow cones, using shaved ice and flavored juices. He drove around selling this delicacy, as well as ice cream, and was known as "Banana Bill" by the townspeople. This favorite was made in the garage behind his home at Second and Eyre Streets. (Courtesy of Mary Tapper.)

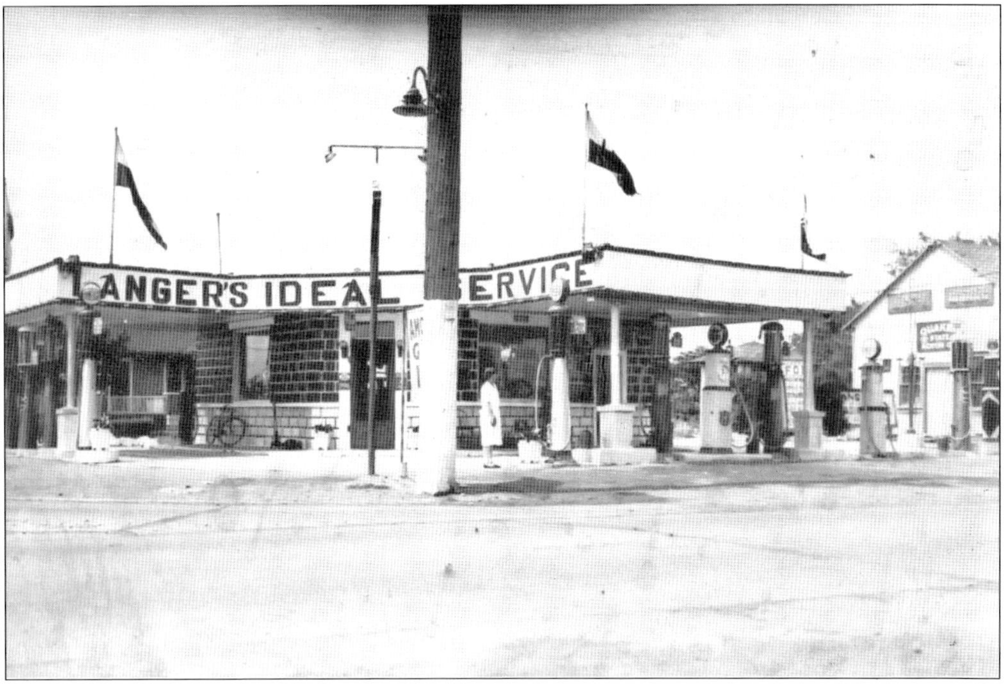

LANGER'S SERVICE STATION. Standing on the northeast corner of Route 130 and Delaware Avenue, Langer's Ideal Service Station is shown in 1928. There was also a luncheonette and a separate building used as a woodworking shop. This was torn down when Route 25 was widened. Next to the station is a service building, which was also demolished. (Courtesy of Jack Quig.)

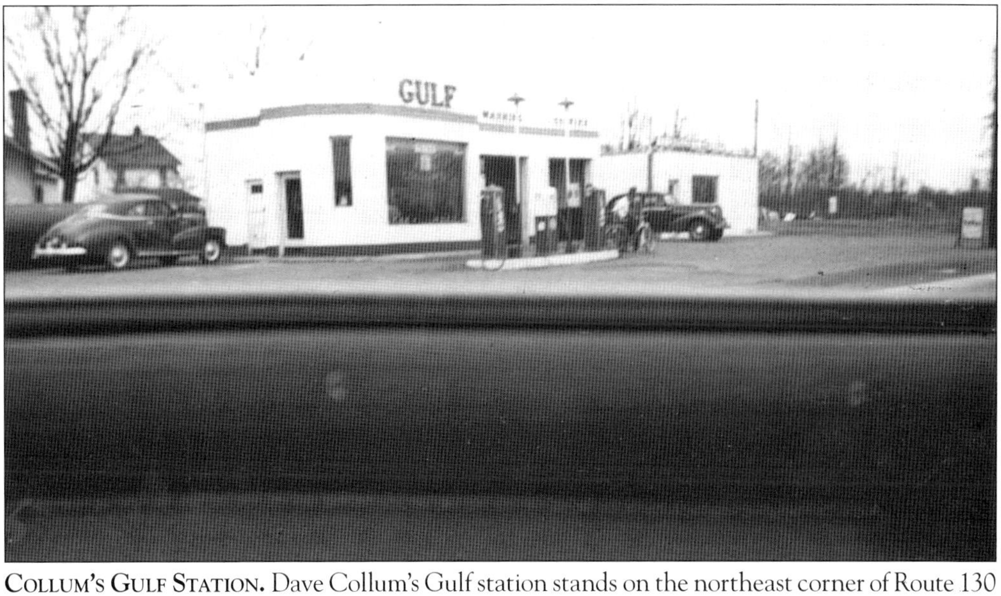

COLLUM'S GULF STATION. Dave Collum's Gulf station stands on the northeast corner of Route 130 and Delaware Avenue in the 1940s. Stories abound of the Midshipmen, a local band, practicing in the gas station at night and neighbors coming over and dancing in the parking lot. State troopers were called but only stayed to enjoy the gatherings. It continued to be a Gulf station under Barney Umstead's management in the 1950s and 1960s. A bank is now located on this property. (Courtesy of Donald Cooper.)

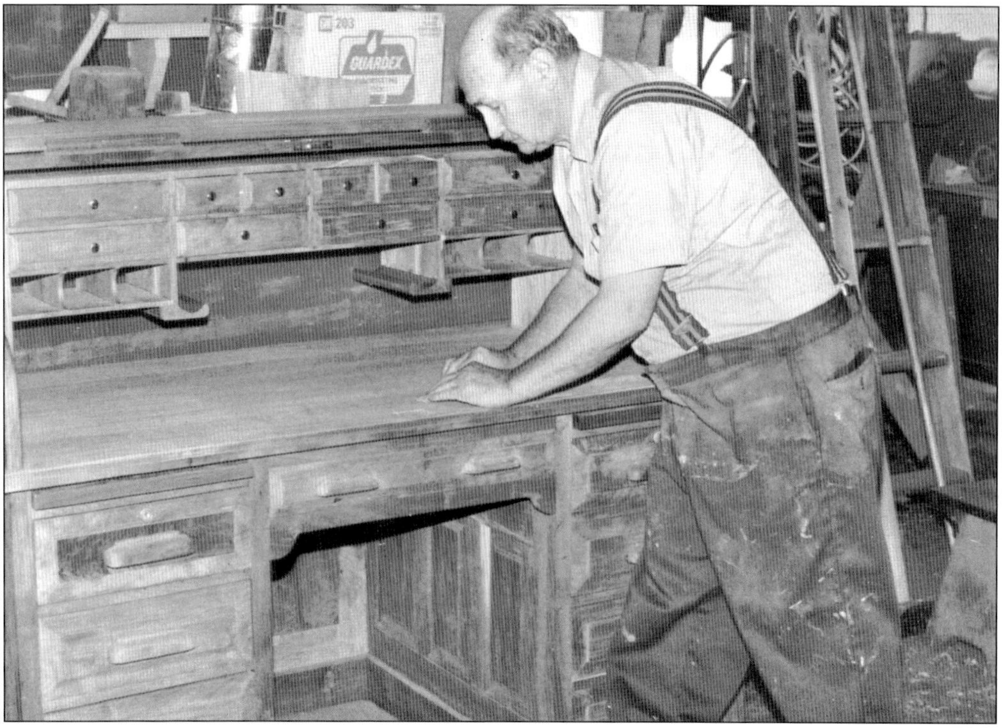

CLAUDE ANDERSON. Claude Anderson is shown in his workshop around 1960. He and Nick DiLullo established Andel Builders in the late 1950s and early 1960s. Many of the houses in the 300 blocks of East Fifth, Fourth and one side of Third Streets were built by them. Anderson also built several houses throughout Florence. Upon retiring from his regular job, he began a business building custom furniture and restoration of antique pieces, such as the doors of the Betsy Ross House in Philadelphia. (Courtesy of Marjorie Anderson.)

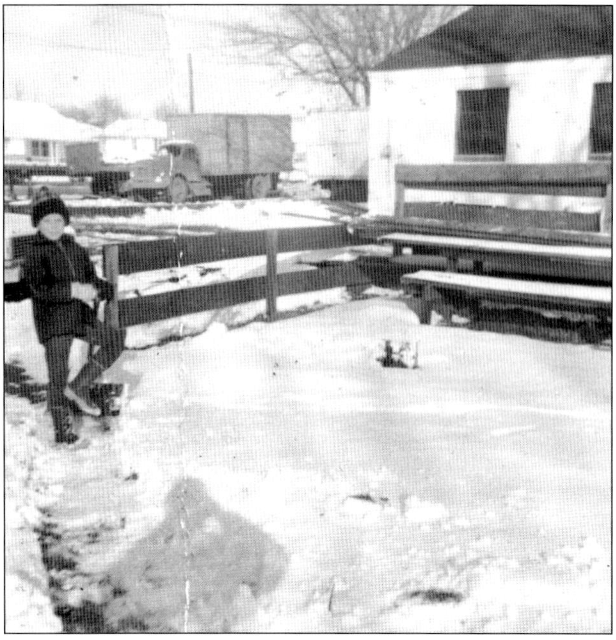

EVERETT TRUCKING. In 1970, Everett Trucking had a large operation on the south side of East Fifth Street near Walnut Street in Florence. Repairs were made to Florence Pipe Foundry trucks as well as other large rigs. This business was formerly Florence Motor Express. Joseph Bock Jr., son of Joseph Bock and Marion Everett Bock, is shown by the entrance gate. The buildings were demolished in 1998. (Courtesy of Marion Everett Bock and Joseph Bock Sr.)

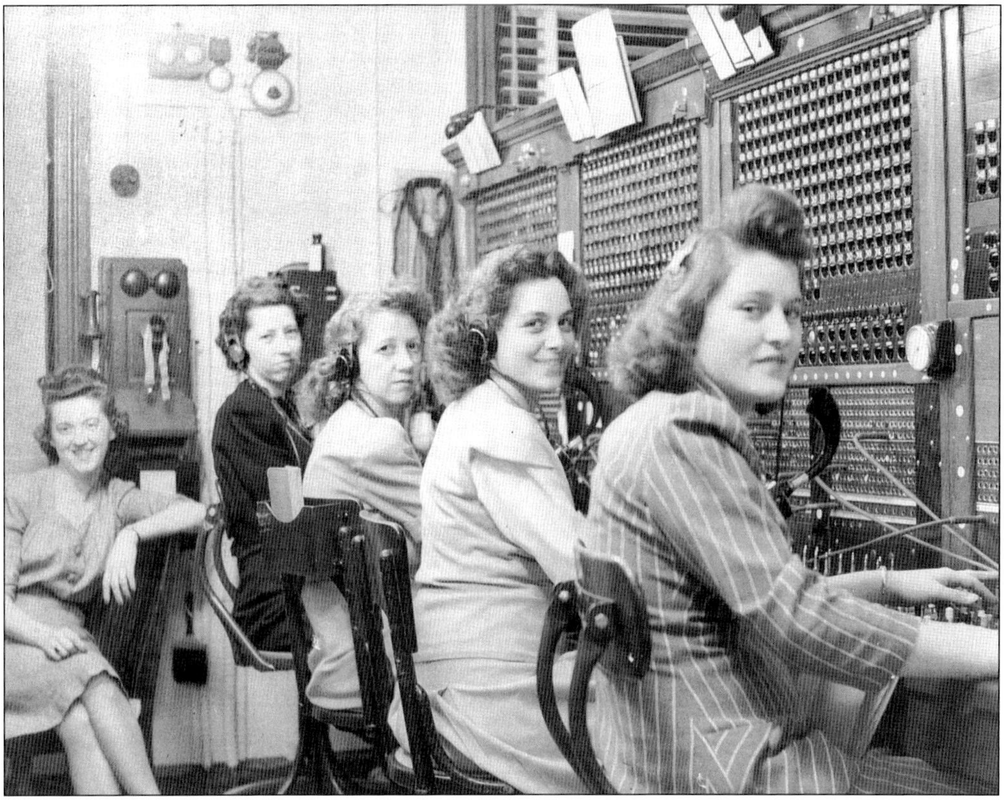

TELEPHONE SWITCHBOARD. Operators at the New Jersey Bell Telephone office in the 1940s are, from left to right, Rose Zdancewicz, unidentified, Mary Daniel, Lois Panaro, and Ann Argenti. In 1957, the exchange Hyacinth 9 replaced the Florence 7 numbers. In 1902, there were 10 subscribers. In 1909, the exchange was at 214 Broad Street. During that span of time, residents would pick up the phone, an operator would answer with, "Number, please," and a call would be requested. The operators usually knew the person speaking, and a hometown atmosphere prevailed. (Courtesy of Thelma Peacock Tilghman.)

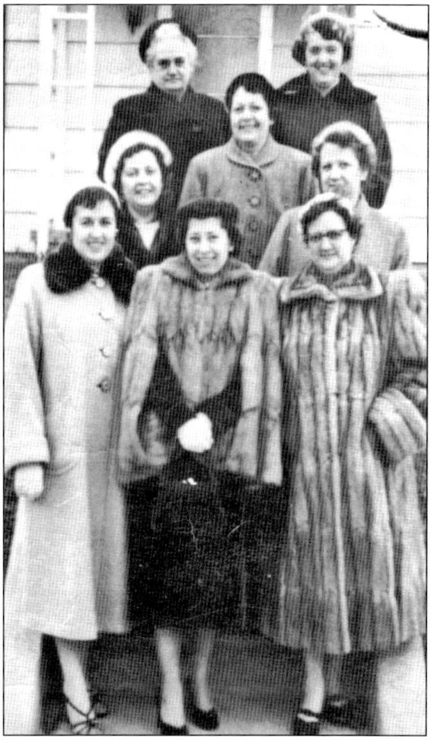

FLORENCE TELEPHONE OPERATORS. With the New Jersey Bell Telephone office in the first block of Broad Street on the east side, the operators handled calls manually before the dial system was implemented. The ladies shown in 1954 are (bottom row) Thelma Peacock Tilghman, Irma Brown, and Edna Heydorn; (middle row) Ann Kovacs, Esther Denneler, and Mary Daniel; (top row) a Mrs. Phillips and Rose Steiner. In 1963, the manual telephone service was replaced with the dial system. (Courtesy of Thelma Peacock Tilghman.)

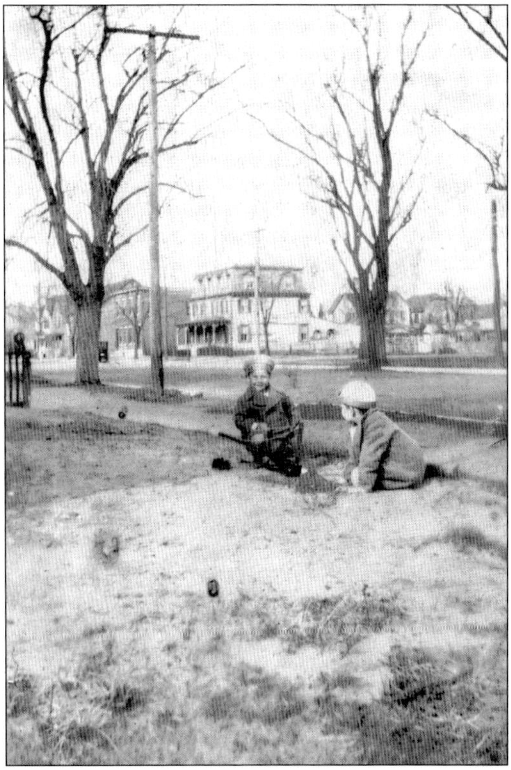

THE SITZLER CHILDREN. The Sitzler children play in front of their home near West Fourth and Broad Streets around 1925. This property would become Horner's Television, and it is now a professional building with a dentist and a foot doctor, Florence Foot Specialist. The house in the background with the mansard roof was once a taxi business. Next to it was the New Jersey Bell Telephone office. The empty lot on the east side of Broad Street became a row of stores in March 1954 after St. Stephen's Parish Hall was demolished in 1952. (Courtesy of Marjorie Anderson.)

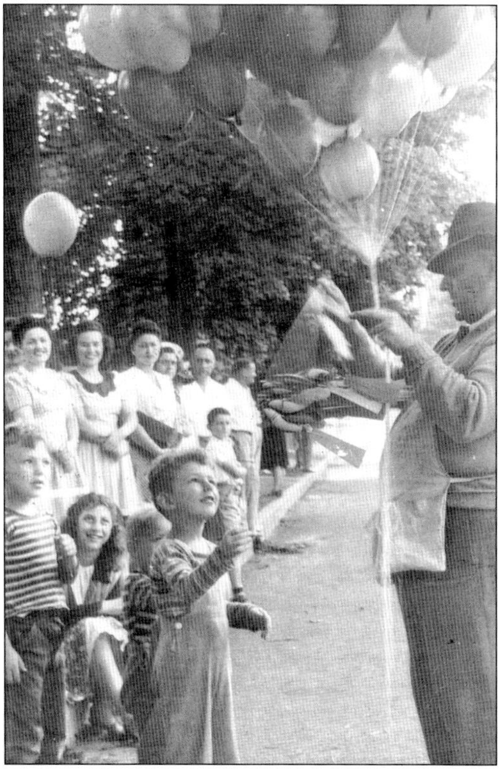

THE BALLOON MAN. In the mid-1940s, a local parade featured the popular "balloon man" in town. From left to right in the foreground with the balloon man are Paul Anderson, Hazel Cowan, and Norman Anderson. In the background are Ron Paglione, on the curb, and his father, standing directly behind. (Courtesy of Margie Anderson.)

Four

Service to Town and Country

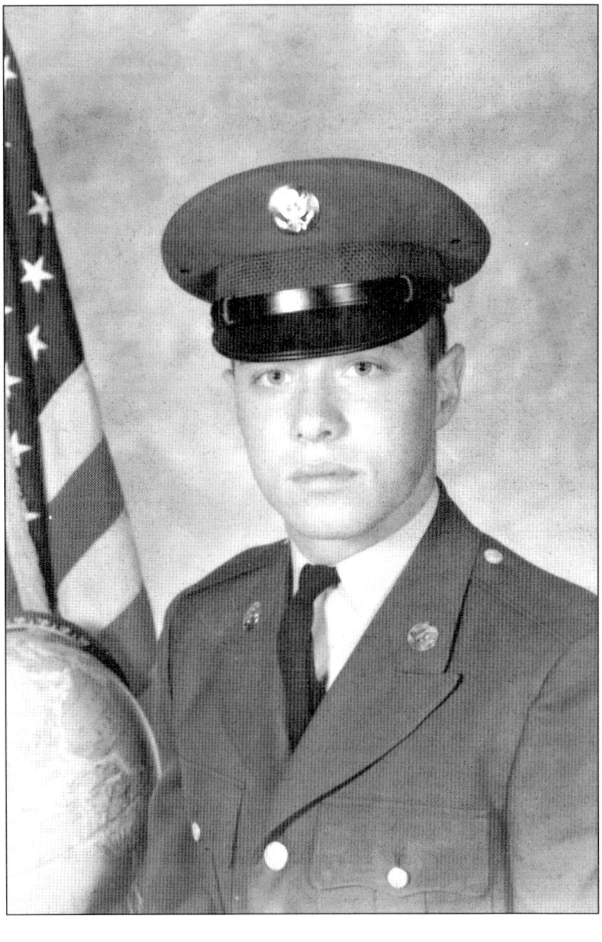

Ezra Budd Marter. Ezra (or "E.") Budd Marter III was a graduate of Florence Township Memorial High School, class of 1967. A sergeant in the US Army, he was killed in action on April 1, 1970, in the Quang Ngãi province of South Vietnam at the age of 22. He was survived by his parents, twin brother Jack, and sisters Nancy and Leslie. An athletic field is named after him on Old York Road in Florence, and his name is proudly affixed to the war monument at Front and Broad Streets. (Courtesy of the Florence Historical Society.)

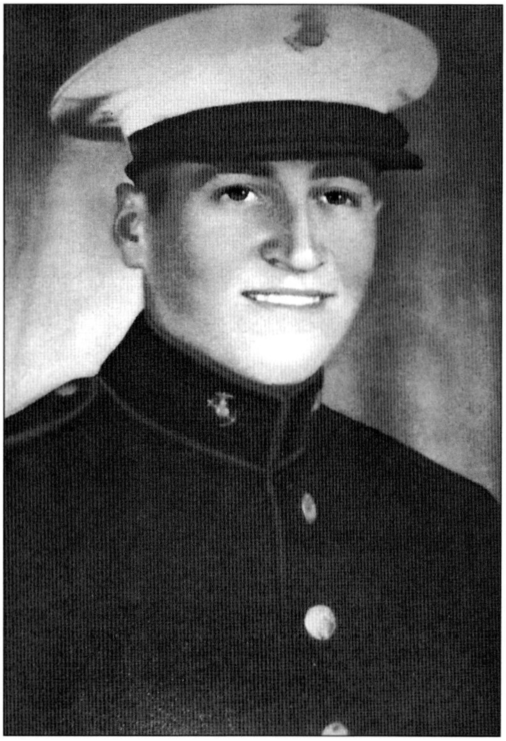

Nicholas P. Filipponi. Nicholas P. Filipponi lost his life at Iwo Jima in 1945 at the age of 23 while serving his country bravely in the US Marines. Son of Giovanni and Esterina Filipponi, he was one of seven children who grew up on Foundry Street in Florence. His brother Robert enlisted in the Navy at the same time and survived the war. Three sisters survive him—Mary Filipponi, Antonia DiRienzo, and Lena F. Flores. (Courtesy of Mary Filipponi.)

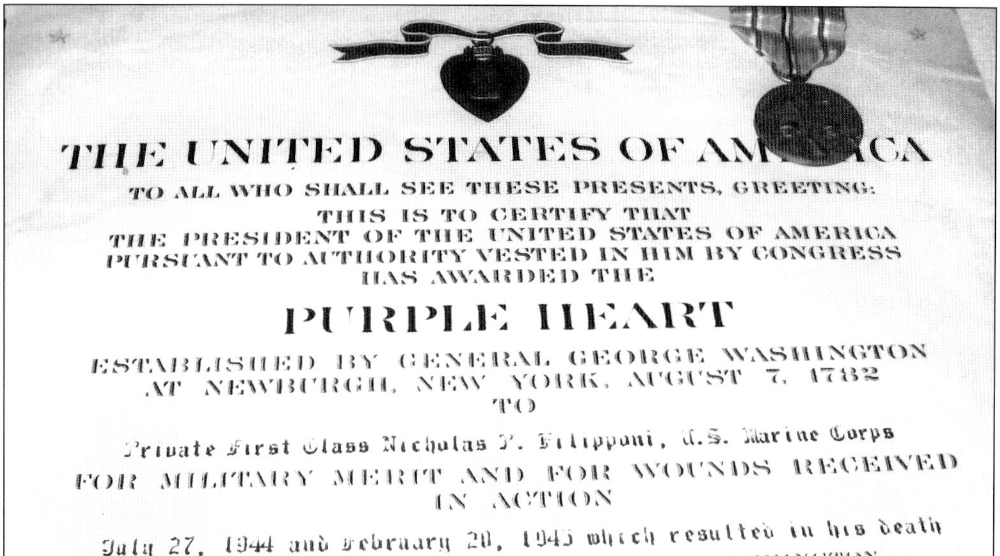

THE UNITED STATES OF AMERICA
TO ALL WHO SHALL SEE THESE PRESENTS, GREETING:
THIS IS TO CERTIFY THAT
THE PRESIDENT OF THE UNITED STATES OF AMERICA
PURSUANT TO AUTHORITY VESTED IN HIM BY CONGRESS
HAS AWARDED THE
PURPLE HEART
ESTABLISHED BY GENERAL GEORGE WASHINGTON
AT NEWBURGH, NEW YORK, AUGUST 7, 1782
TO
Private First Class Nicholas P. Filipponi, U.S. Marine Corps
FOR MILITARY MERIT AND FOR WOUNDS RECEIVED
IN ACTION
July 27, 1944 and February 20, 1945 which resulted in his death
GIVEN UNDER MY HAND IN THE CITY OF WASHINGTON
THIS 12th DAY OF April 1945

James Forrestal
SECRETARY OF THE NAVY

GENERAL, U.S.M.C.
THE COMMANDANT, U.S. MARINE CORPS

Filipponi's Purple Heart. A copy of Nicholas P. Filipponi's Purple Heart medal and certificate are proudly displayed at the Florence Historical Society. Awarded for his military merit and wounds received in action, it was signed by Pres. Franklin D. Roosevelt. (Courtesy of Mary Filipponi.)

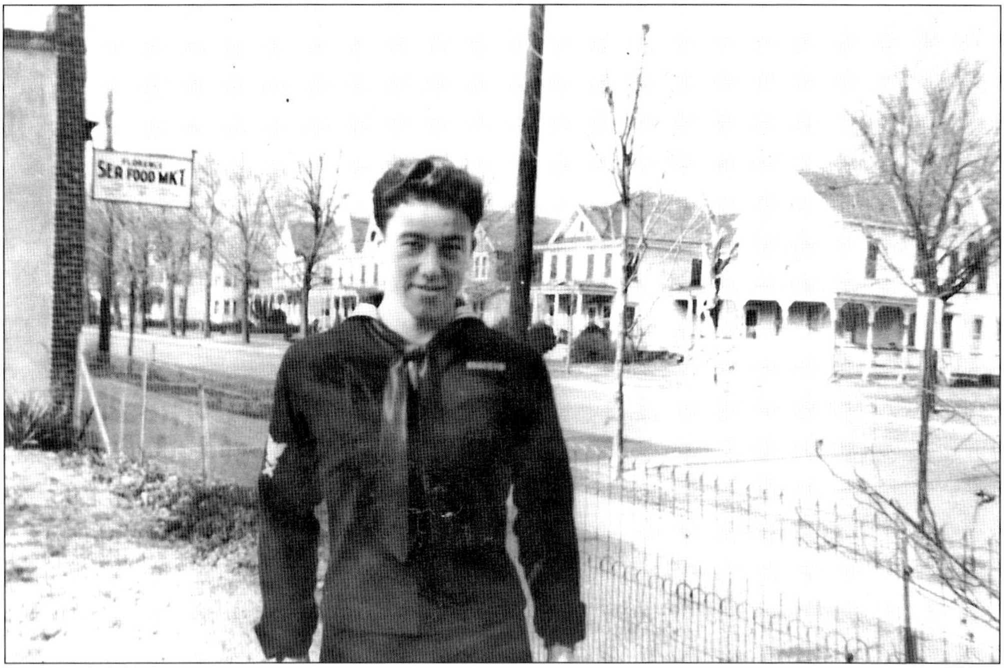

Nicholas J. "Nick" DiLullo. Nick DiLullo proudly poses in his side yard on the southwest corner of West Front and Summer Streets, which is now the parking lot for Casa Gangone Restaurant. He was a Navy veteran of World War II and a member of the Florence American Legion Post 194 for 63 years. Nicholas was also recipient of the Citizen of the Year award. His family came from Bristol in 1926, and his siblings were Carmela, Loretta, and Edith. He died in 2008 at the age of 86. (Courtesy of the Florence Historical Society.)

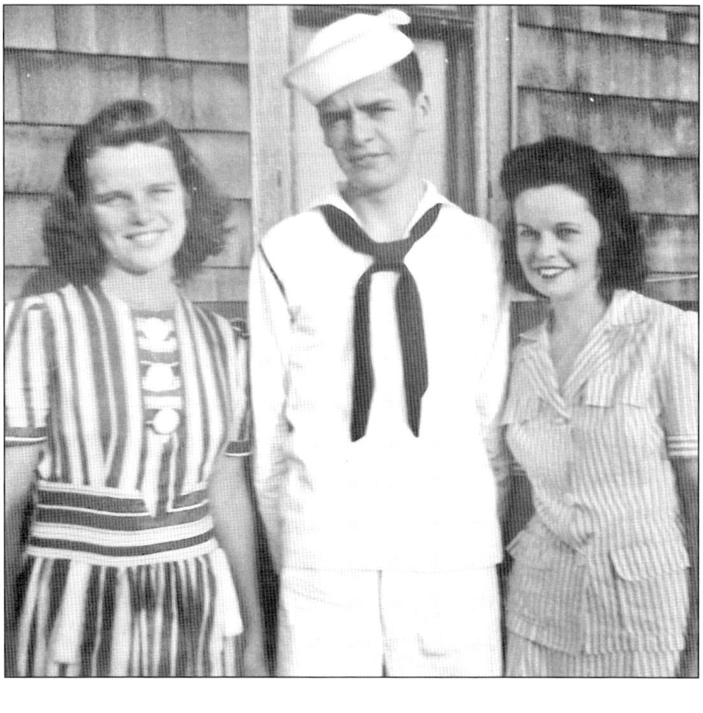

James E. "Jim" Dougherty. Home on leave from basic training in August 1943, Jim Dougherty stands with his sister Catherine (left) and Margaret "Peggy" Dougherty. He served in the Navy as radioman, and his ship transported Marines to their assigned destinations. Once when his ship landed at Saipan, he met Nicholas Filipponi from his hometown of Florence. Jim was born on June 29, 1925, married Muriel Sweetman in 1951, and died on February 14, 1979. (Courtesy of the Florence Historical Society.)

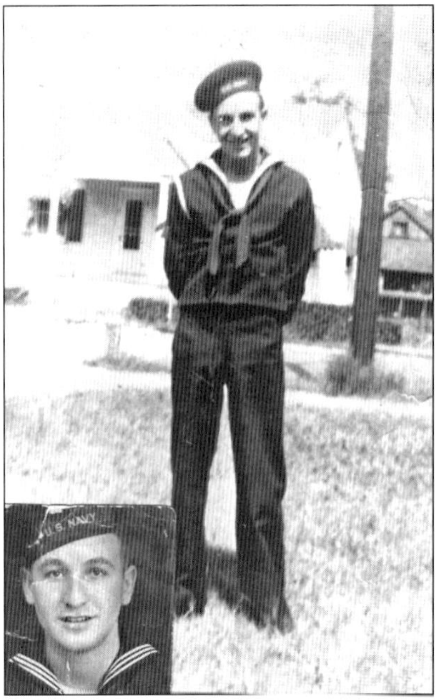

NELLO D'ANNUNZIO. Joining the Navy in World War II, Nello was assigned to the destroyer USS *Chevalier*. On October 6, 1943, the *Chevalier* and two other destroyers intercepted nine Japanese destroyers in the Solomon Islands. The *Chevalier* received great damage and sank. Fifty-four men were killed, including Nello. The *Chevalier* received three battle stars for World War II service. (Courtesy of Ed Noval.)

THE WISPERT FAMILY. George and Hannah Wispert enjoy a day at Gettysburg with their son William. George rode with the 1st New Jersey Cavalry at Gettysburg. An exploding shell tore his right arm off, which is apparent in the picture. The photograph was taken after 1865, but daughter Margaret is missing from the group, as she was born in 1875. Young William almost lost his life while playing near the Delaware River when a cave-in occurred. He was pulled from the pile of dirt just in time and revived by the town doctor. (Courtesy of Jim and Hannah Roache.)

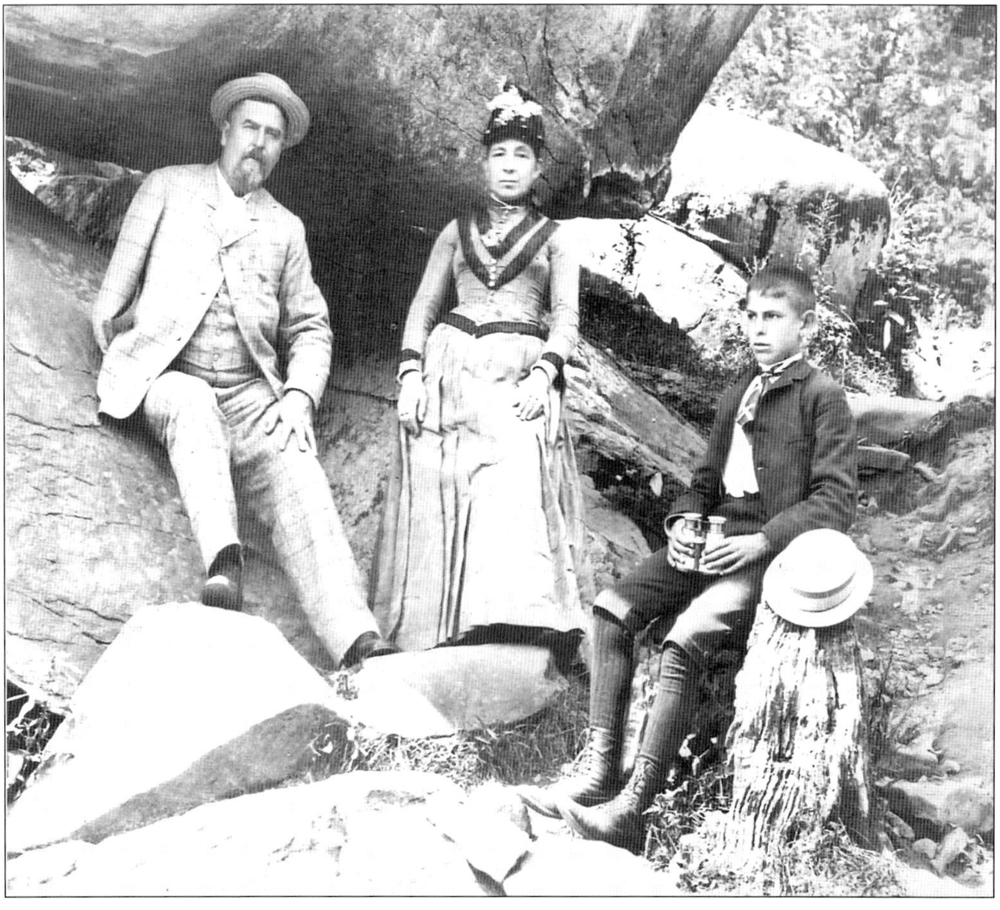

Doris Peake. Doris Peake proudly poses in her Gray Ladies uniform. Affiliated with the American Red Cross, the Gray Ladies met during World War II and as late as 1957. Gray Ladies worked under the supervision of camp hospital staff, and among their duties were reading, writing letters, playing games, and performing other small personal services for hospitalized members of the armed forces. (Courtesy of Charles Breingan.)

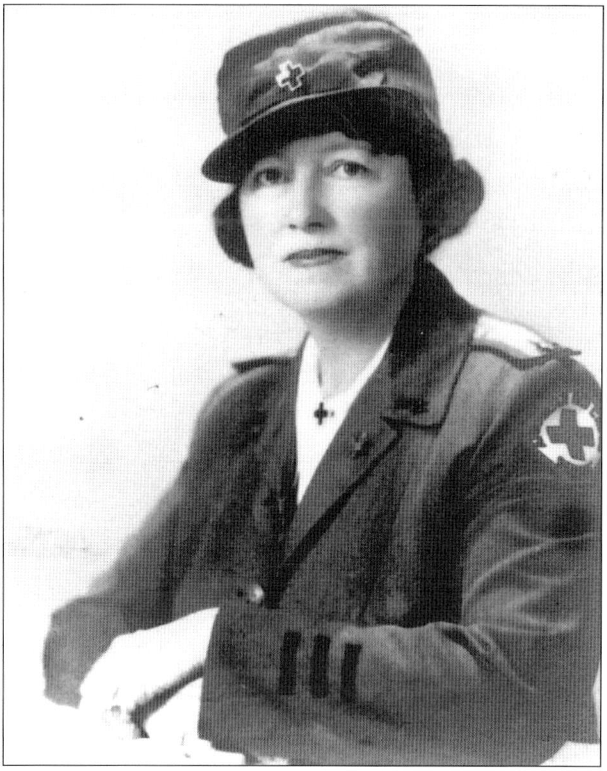

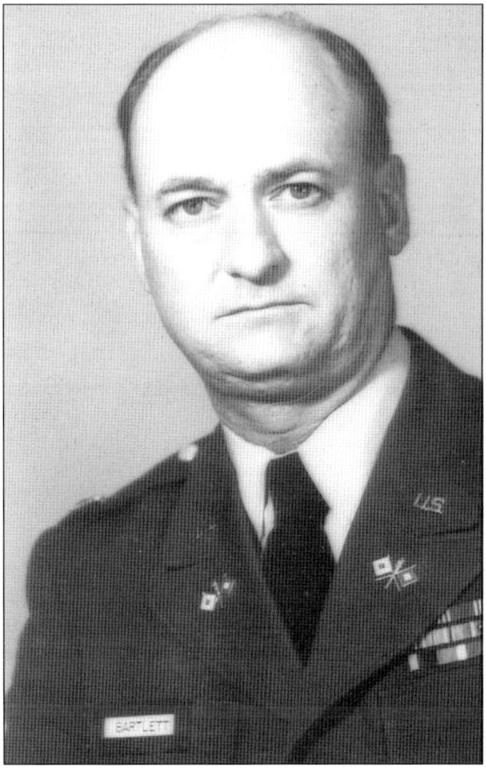

Elmer E. Bartlett Jr. Elmer E. Bartlett Jr., shown here in his US Army uniform, was Florence's most decorated soldier of World War I. He received the Distinguished Service Cross twice and Croix de Guerre among other decorations. His occupation was coremaker at Florence Pipe Foundry and Machine Company before retirement. Bartlett died in 1953 at the age of 63. (Courtesy of the Florence Historical Society.)

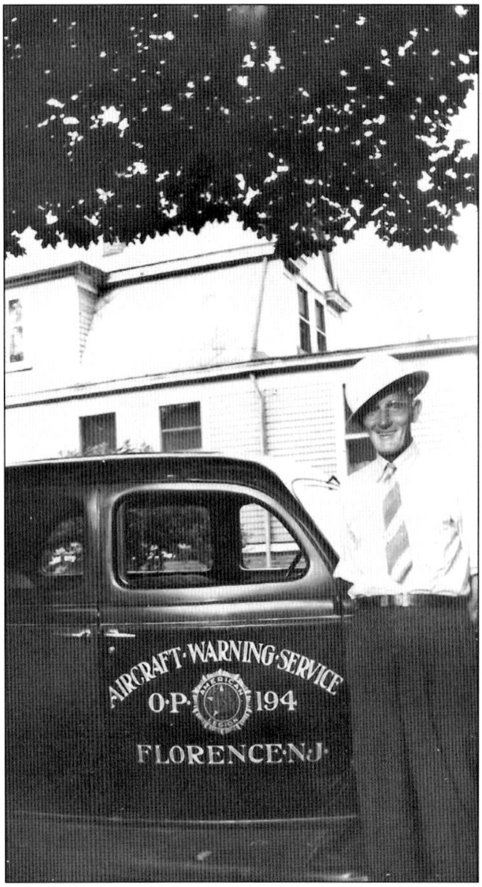

ALBERT GRIFFITH. Shown with the truck of American Legion Post 194 is Albert Griffith, chief observer of the Aircraft Warning Service during World War II. Classes in aircraft recognition service were held at the high school. Volunteers were requested to serve during evening hours. The program began in 1941, and the skies were watched 24 hours a day. (Courtesy of Janet Griffith.)

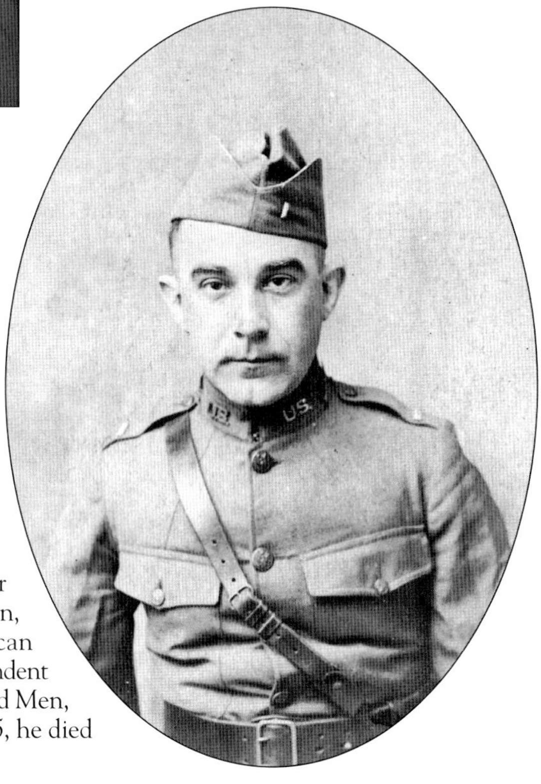

WILLIAM H. ABSALOM. Seen here in his World War I uniform, William H. Absalom served in the US Army. Upon his discharge, he distinguished himself as an active participant in politics with the Democratic Party. As a sports lover, he also was a member of the Florence Building and Loan Association, the Florence Fire Company No. 1, the Mohican Boat Club, Free and Accepted Masons, Independent Order of Odd Fellows, Improved Order of Red Men, and Loyal Order of the Moose. Born in 1885, he died on April 9, 1954. (Courtesy of Judith King.)

Frank Donald Green. Pvt. Frank D. Green, also known as F. Donald Green, was another Florence man who served overseas in World War II. He was issued the American Defense Service Ribbon, the Good Conduct Medal, Bronze Star for the Tunisian Campaign, a Bronze Star for the Sicilian Campaign, and an EAME (European-African-Middle Eastern) Campaign Medal. He served overseas from 1942 to 1944 and was honorably discharged in 1945. (Courtesy of Richard Glass.)

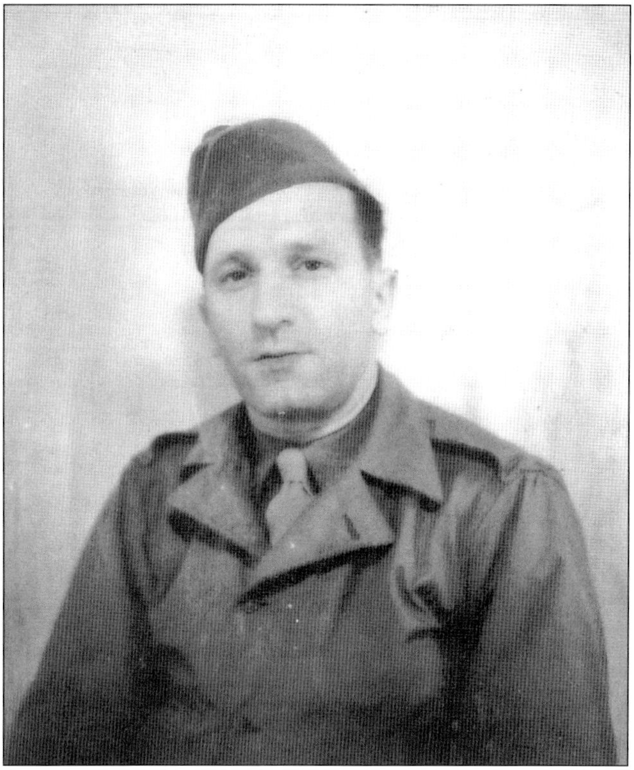

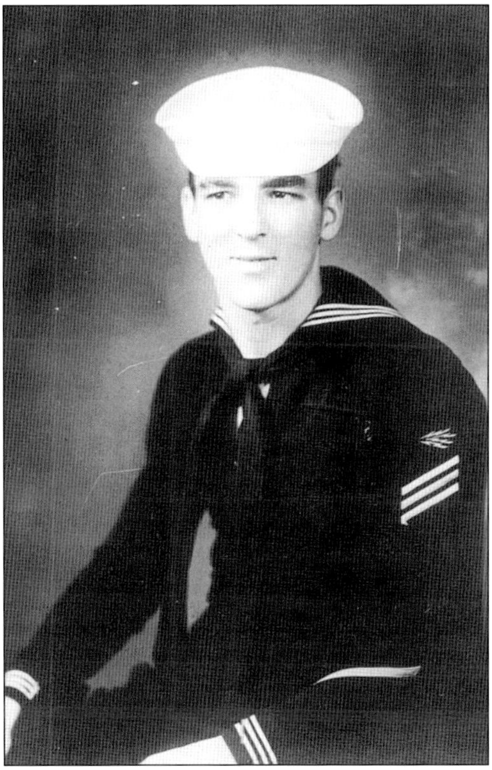

Richard Glass. Serving in the US Navy in 1953 was only a small part of Glass's service to his country. He also was in the US Coast Guard, the US Army, and the Seabees. Glass has continued to support servicemen from the town of Florence by volunteering for the construction of military monuments in several locations. His family traces many generations to the early days of Florence. (Courtesy of Richard Glass.)

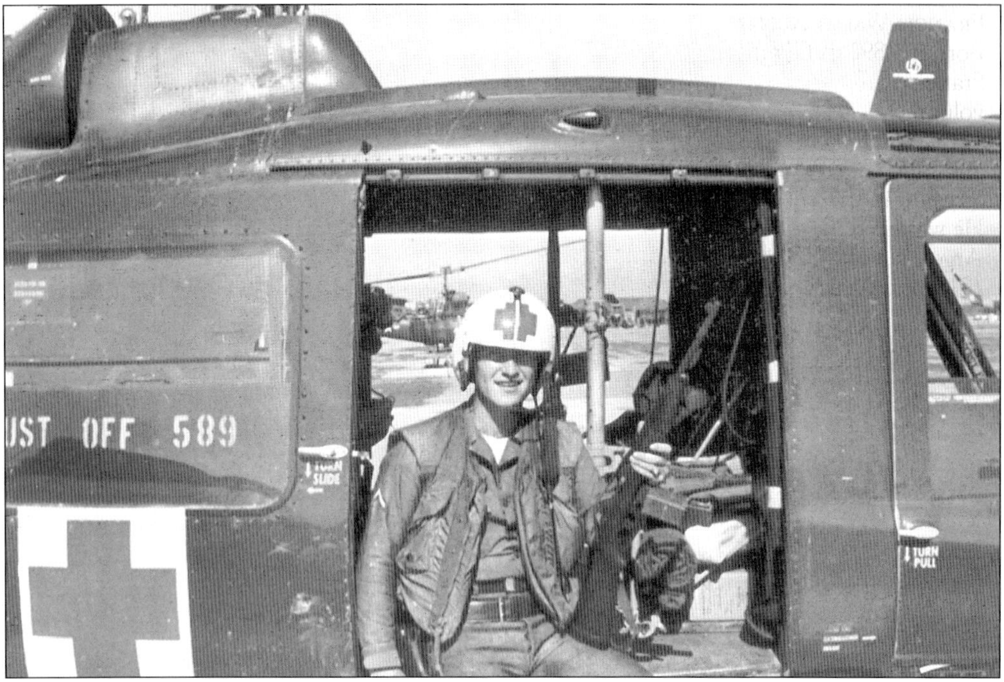

William "Billy" Hughes. Billy Hughes served in Vietnam in 1964 with a medevac unit. On one of his missions, he was shot and returned to the United States for treatment and recovery. He received an air medal, six oak leaf clusters for bravery in action, and the Cross of Gallantry. Billy now resides in Florida. (Courtesy of Doris Coates Jones.)

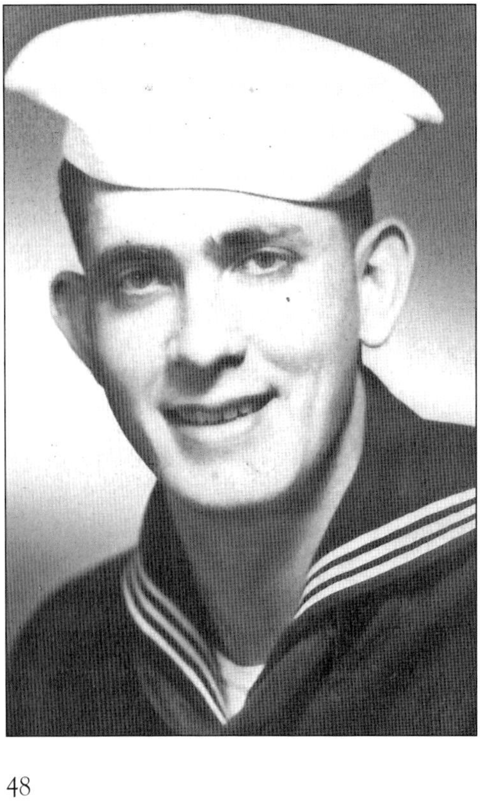

Stuart J. "Stu" Foulks Sr. Stu Foulks Sr. served his country with honor for four years in the US Navy. During the Korean War, he was a commissary clerk for over three years aboard the USS *Catamount* (LSD 17). As a youth, Stu helped his father, Raymond Foulks, deliver bread to homes around town. He was very proud that his ancestors fought for the Union at Gettysburg during the Civil War. (Courtesy of Julia Foulks.)

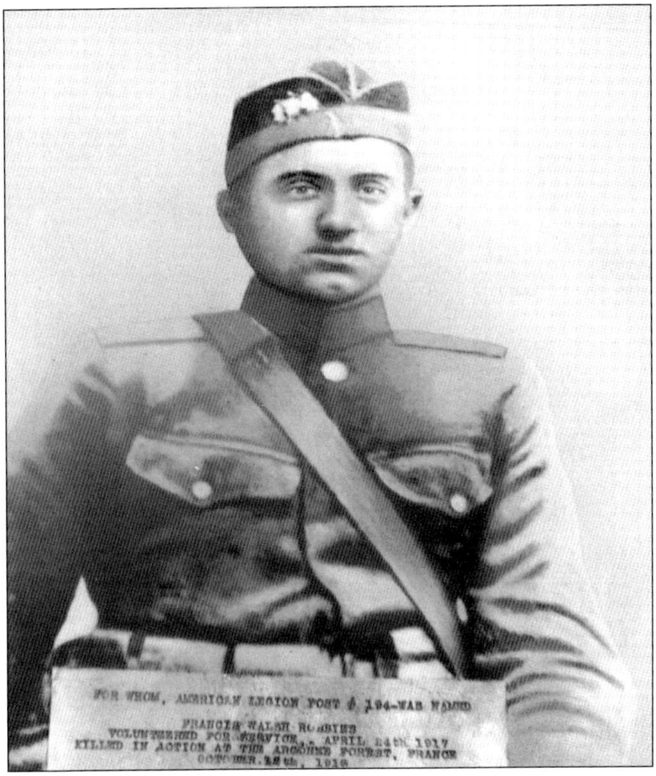

FRANCIS WALSH ROBBINS. Born in 1892 in Florence, Francis W. Robbins volunteered for service in 1917 during World War I and subsequently served as sergeant in the 114th Infantry. He was killed in action in the Argonne Forest, France, in 1918, and American Legion Post 194 in Florence was given his name. A brass plaque was erected by his mother, Loella M. Robbins, in St. Stephen's Church, honoring his service to his country. (Courtesy of Francis W. Robbins Post 194 American Legion.)

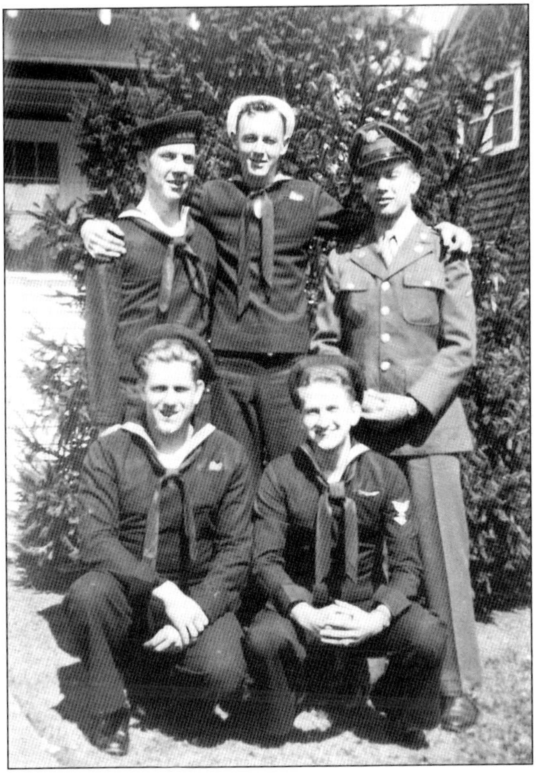

FIVE SERVICEMEN. Posing during World War II are, from left to right, (standing) Thomas Maloney, Robert Wilkie, and Frank Carlson; (kneeling) Russell "Icky" Roughton and Joseph Weber—all Navy men, except for one. They gathered at Frank Carlson's house on West Third Street next to Bill and Hazel Cowan's house for this picture. (Courtesy of Jim Maloney.)

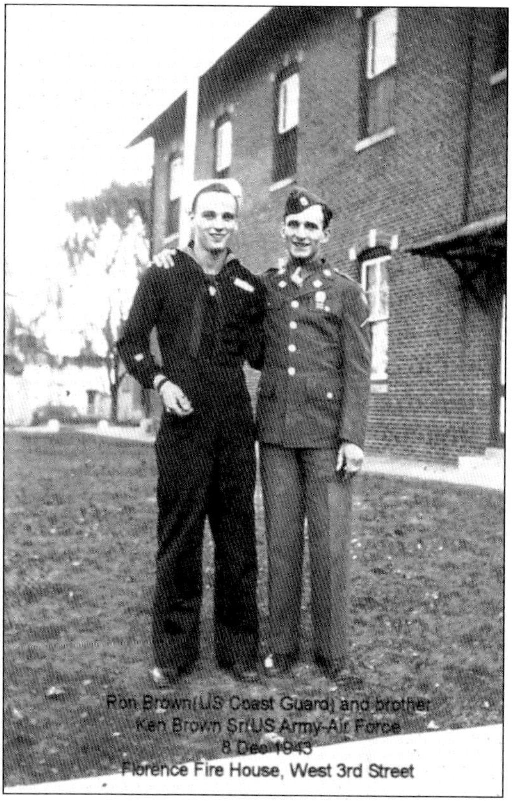

The Brown Brothers. Brothers Ron Brown of the US Coast Guard (left) and Ken Brown of the US Army Air Forces are on leave on West Third Street in Florence, not far from their home. Behind them stands the Florence Fire Company, which has changed little over the years. (Courtesy of Ken Brown.)

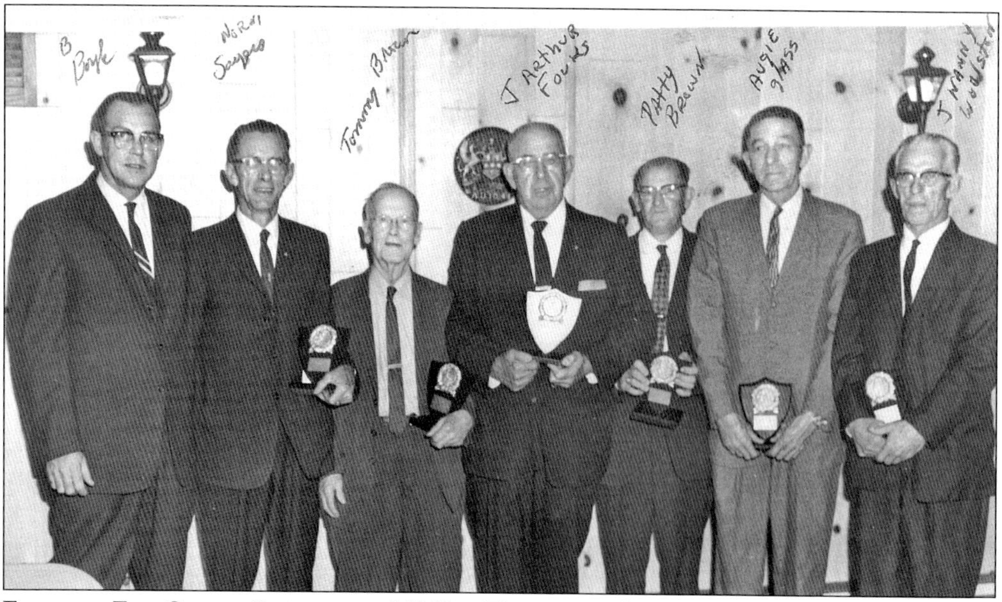

Florence Fire Chiefs. Posing around 1967 at Florence Firehouse No. 1 are past fire chiefs with their service plaques. From left to right are Bernard Boyle, Norman Sayers, Thomas Brown, charter member W. Arthur Foulks, Alfred "Paddy" Brown, August Glass, and John A. "Nanny" Woolston. While directing traffic during a fire call, Paddy Brown was killed by a hit-and run-driver in 1968. (Courtesy of the Florence Historical Society.)

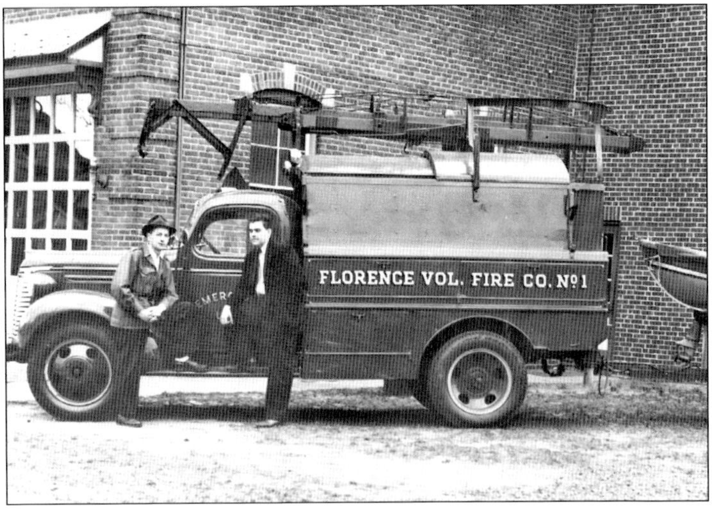

SQUAD TRUCK. In February 1950, the Florence Emergency Squad bought a c. 1936 Chevrolet truck with a rescue boat attached from Bell Telephone for $450. Richard Jones (left) and Ralph Foulks pose in front of the new acquisition. The firehouse also looks different since this was before the truck bays were added on the right. (Courtesy of Thelma Peacock Tilghman.)

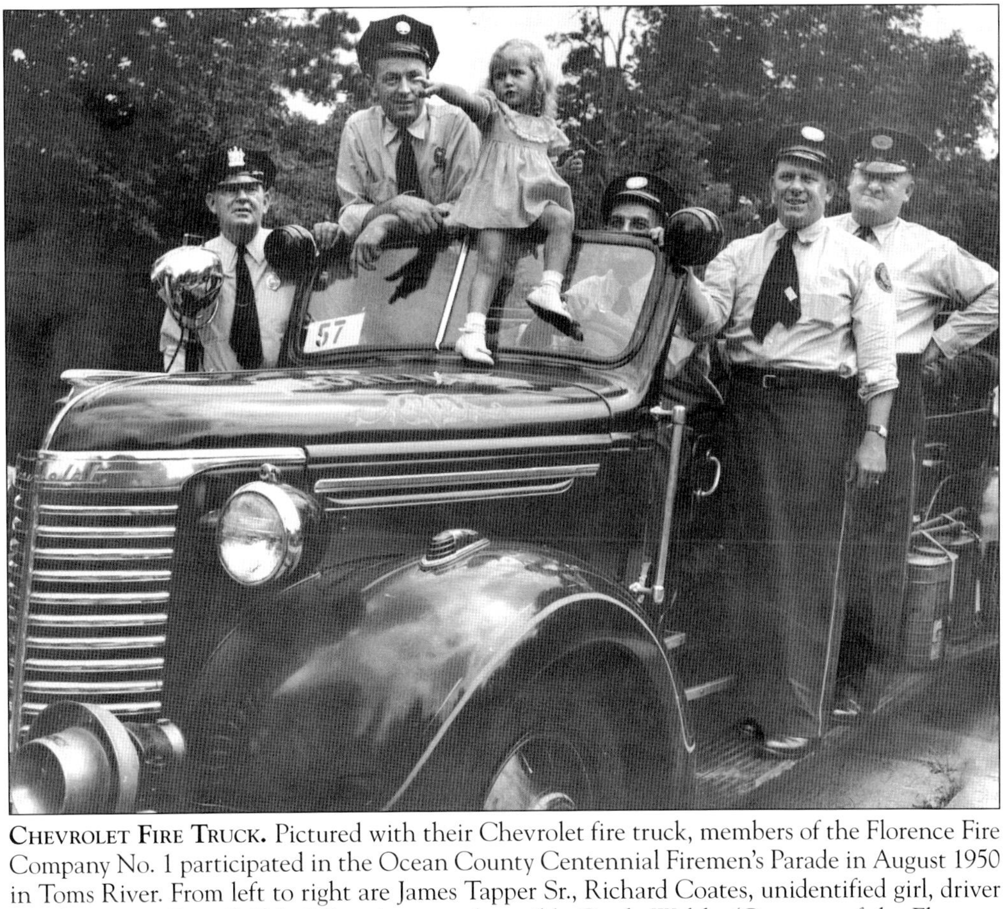

CHEVROLET FIRE TRUCK. Pictured with their Chevrolet fire truck, members of the Florence Fire Company No. 1 participated in the Ocean County Centennial Firemen's Parade in August 1950 in Toms River. From left to right are James Tapper Sr., Richard Coates, unidentified girl, driver Frank Rainier, Russell "Icky" Roughton, and possibly Grady Walsh. (Courtesy of the Florence Historical Society.)

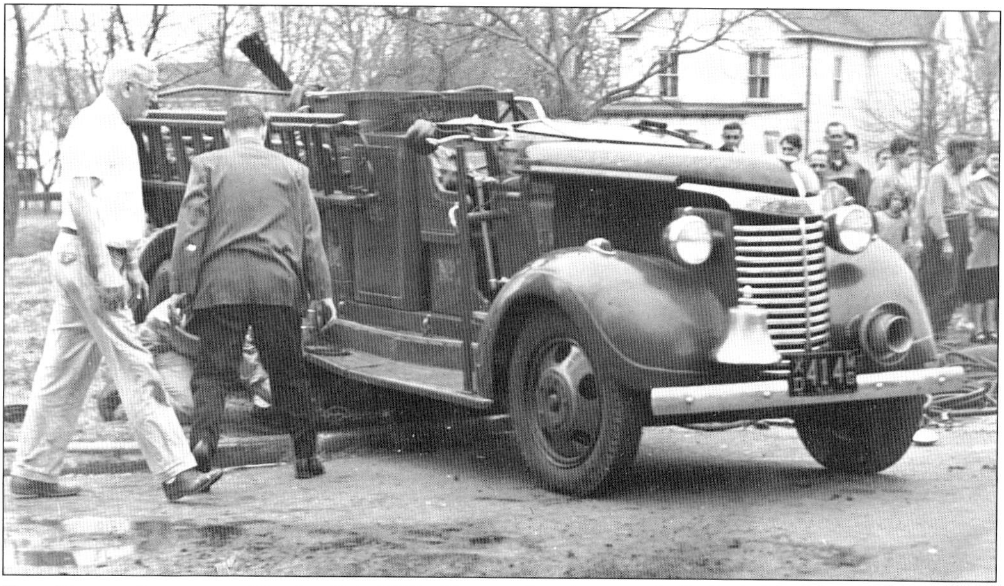

FIRE TRUCK ACCIDENT. On April 4, 1952, Chester Sutphin was killed while answering an alarm, when a collision overturned the fire truck. He was chief driver at the time and chose to report for fire duty instead of leaving for work. The truck has been righted in the picture, and John Barry (left) assists at the accident. Injured were J. Davis Wolfe and Edward Markiewicz. (Courtesy of the Florence Historical Society.)

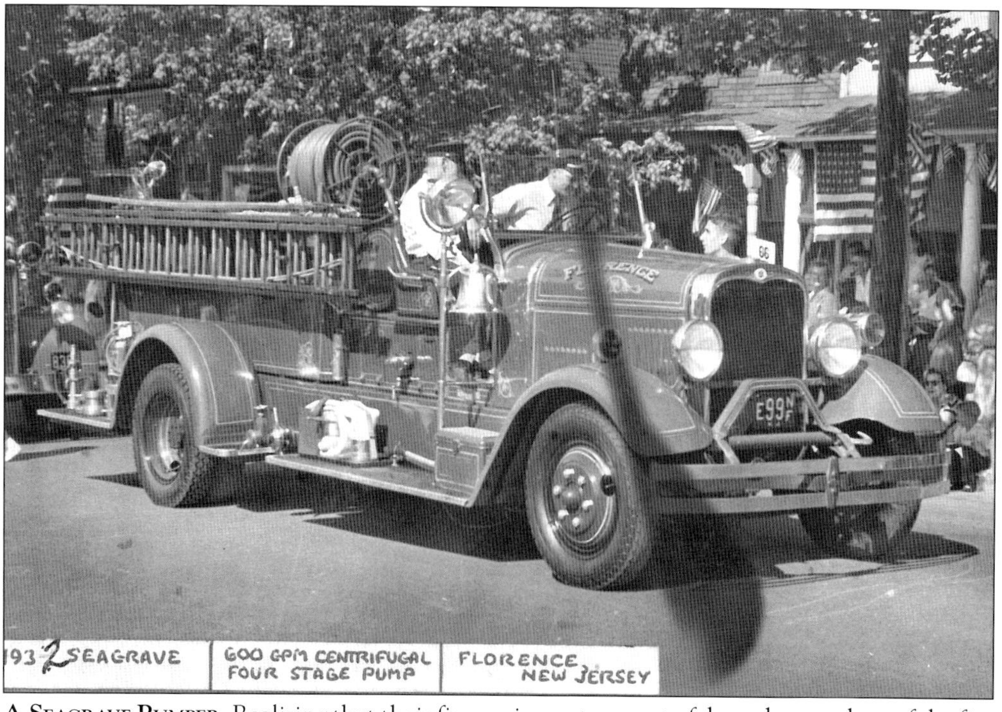

A SEAGRAVE PUMPER. Realizing that their fire equipment was out of date, the members of the fire company purchased a new Seagrave pumper, since the township water system had been installed. Funds were raised by holding cake sales, dinners, and carnivals. This picture celebrates the housing of the new truck. (Courtesy of Judith King.)

Five

Memorials and Celebrations

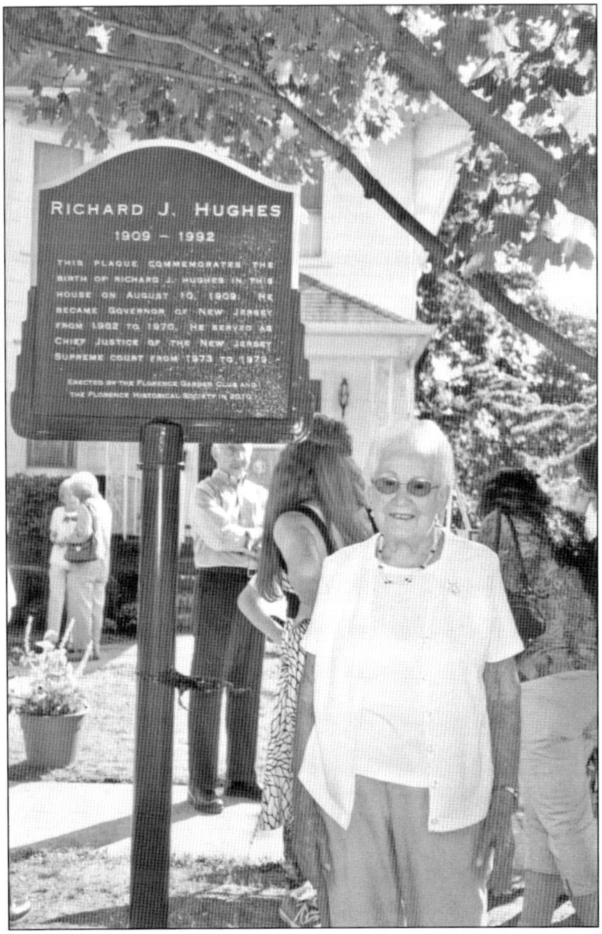

Hughes's Plaque. To honor Richard J. Hughes, who was born in Florence in 1909, the Florence Garden Club and the Florence Historical Society joined in the acquisition of a plaque erected in front of Hughes's former home on East Front Street in 2010. Hughes was the only individual who served as governor of New Jersey and chief justice of the New Jersey Supreme Court. Mary Tapper poses with the sign after the ceremonies. (Courtesy of the Florence Historical Society.)

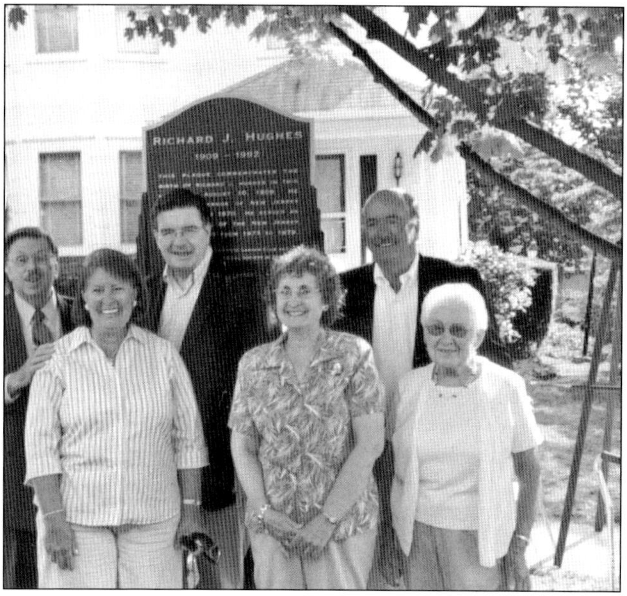

HUGHES'S COMMITTEE. From left to right, Richard Dennison, Deb Hartshorn, Judith King, and Mary Tapper pose in front of two of Governor Hughes's sons in 2010 after the dedication. Absent from the picture was committee member Jack Ulmer, who prepared refreshments at the Florence Methodist Church for this celebration. Also helping but not pictured were Mark King and Kim Roache, who drove over 200 miles to retrieve and deliver the plaque from the foundry in Pennsylvania. Florence Township is also thanked for erecting the sign. (Courtesy of the Florence Historical Society.)

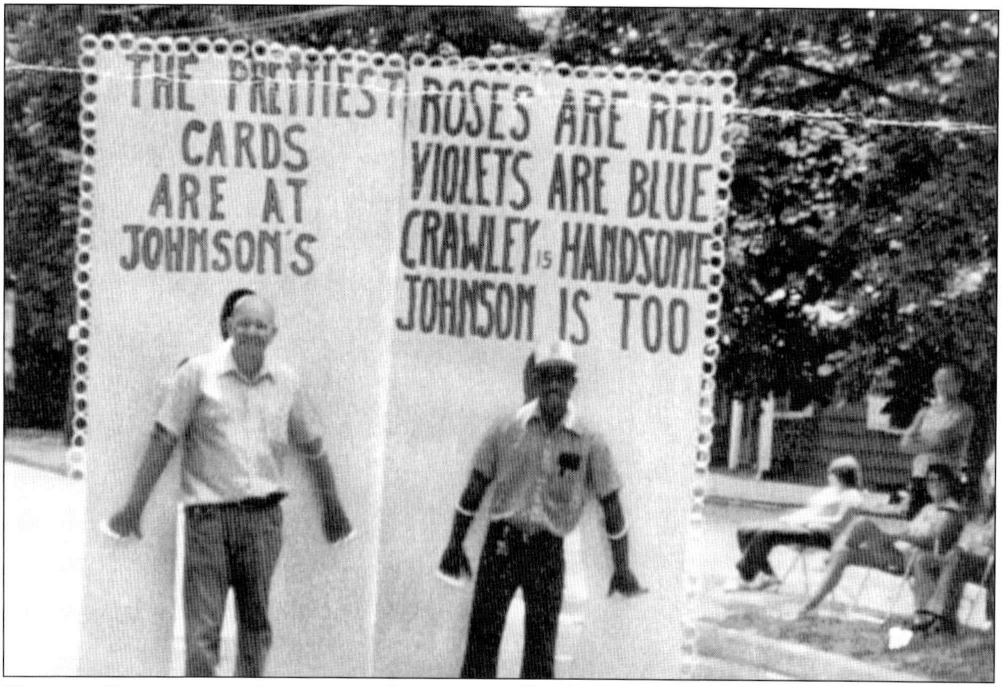

NILS AND DOC. One parade entry eagerly anticipated by the townspeople was the yearly presentation of Nils Johnson, owner of Johnson's General Store. His sidekick was always "Doc" Melvin Crawley. The parade was always held a week after Fourth of July as part of the Florence Township Patriotic Celebration. The day consists of ceremonies at local monuments, activities at the Water Works Field after the parade, band concerts, and fireworks in the evening. (Courtesy of the Florence Historical Society.)

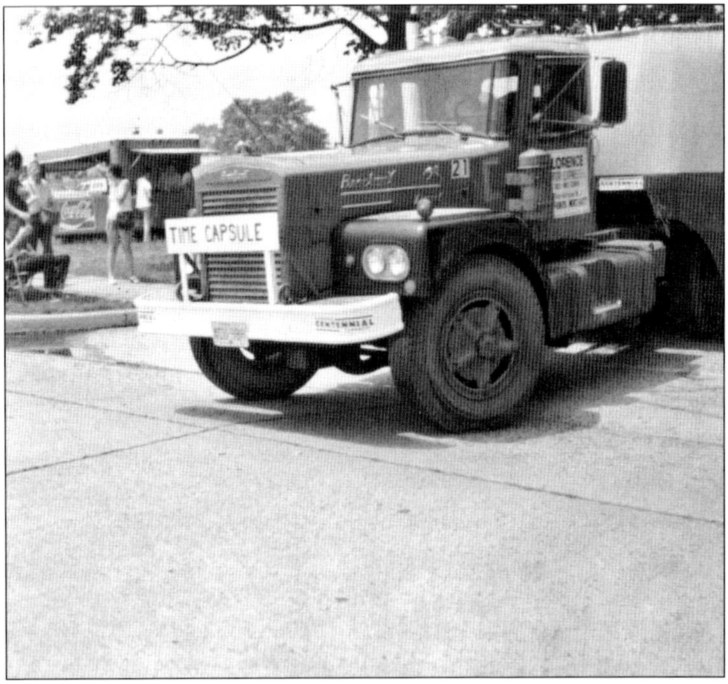

Florence Motor Express. In Florence's centennial parade in 1973, this truck, on loan from the Florence Motor Express (formerly Everett Trucking), towed the time capsule. Among other things, the capsule contained many family histories. The centennial marked 100 years since Florence formed its own government, independent of Mansfield Township. (Courtesy of Joe and Marion Bock.)

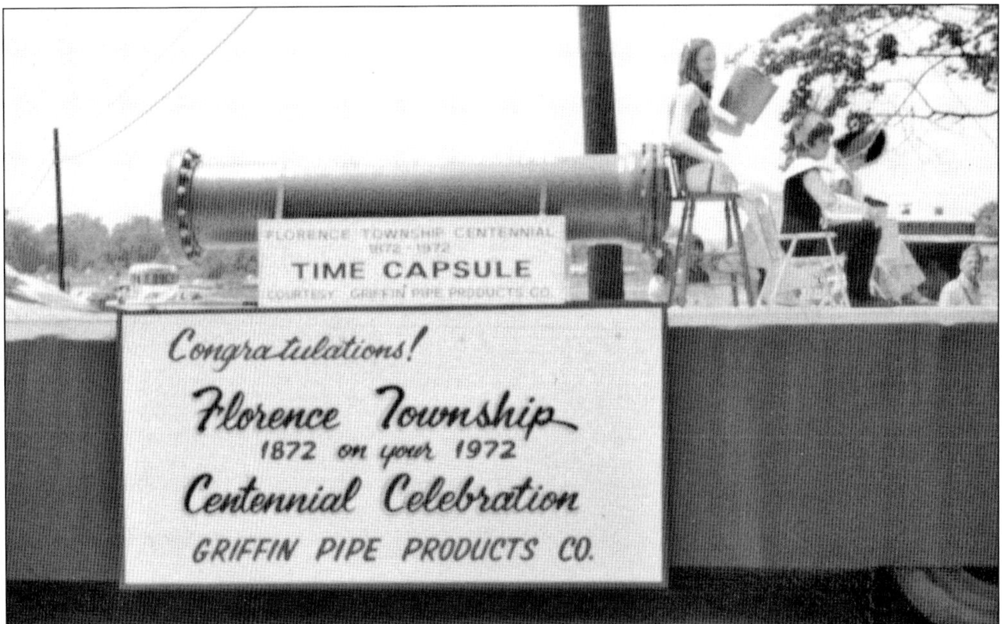

Centennial Time Capsule. The time capsule used in the 1973 centennial celebration was a section of pipe produced and donated by Florence's Griffin Pipe Company. It contained some family histories, a telephone directory and telephone, area-church Bibles, a Sears, Roebuck & Co. catalogue, an American flag, copies of the June 28, 1973, edition of the *Register News* (which ceased publication in 2015), and menus from local restaurants listing foods and prices. It was buried in front of the high school, which is now the Riverfront Middle School. (Courtesy of the Florence Historical Society.)

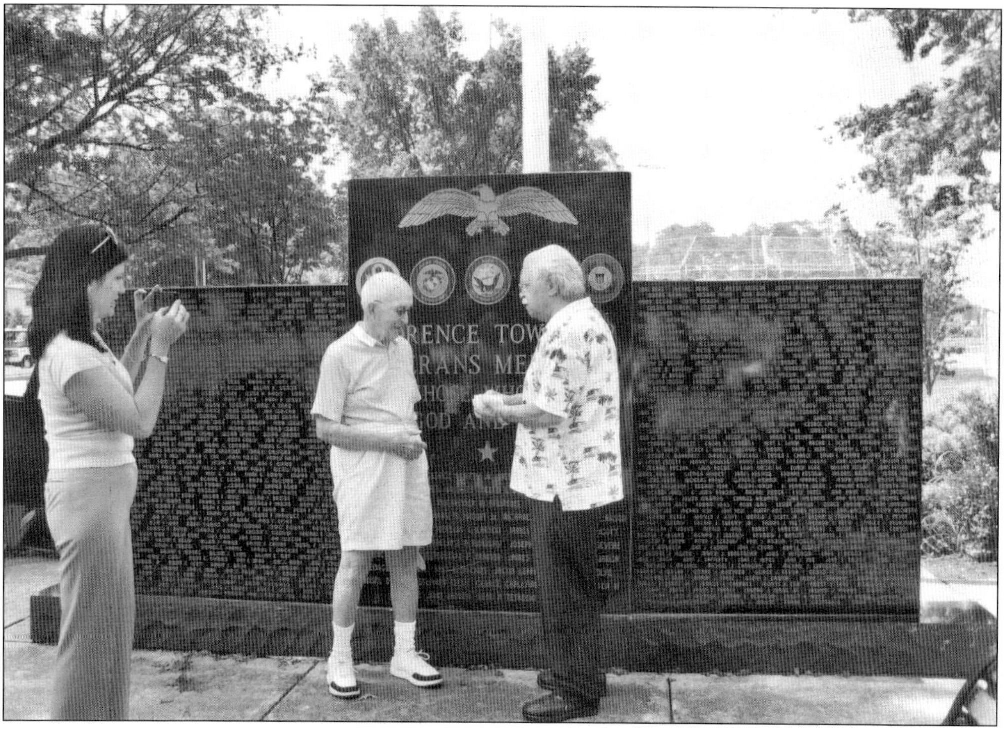

MOHICAN BOAT CLUB MEDAL. Standing in front of the veteran's monument on Broad Street are photographer Jeannie Sullivan (left), medal recipient Charles "Scoots" Adams (center), and medal presenter Charles Pitzo. As the last living member of the Mohican Boat Club, Adams is receiving a medal that Pitzo retrieved from an antique shop in south Jersey and decided to return to Florence. The medal was inscribed in 1919 to J. Milton Absalom, a World War I Army veteran and boat club member. (Courtesy of the Florence Historical Society.)

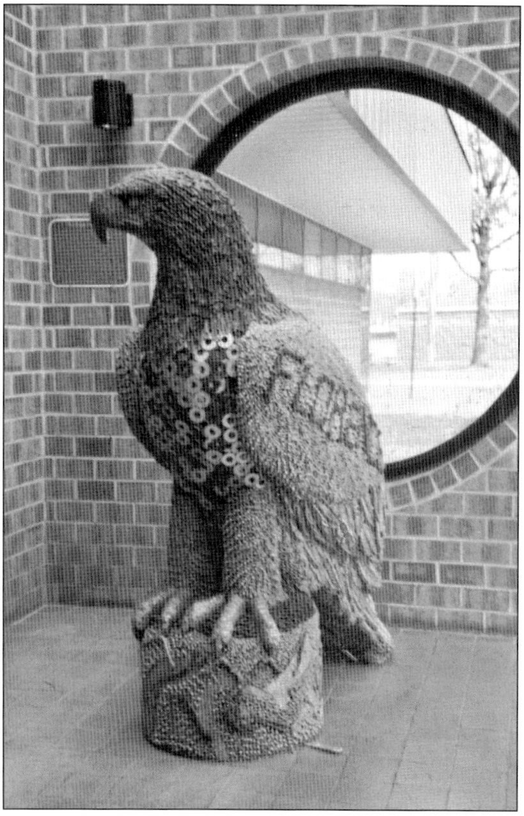

EAGLE TRIBUTE. Named *Captain of Industries*, this eagle was made by Florence Station artist Gary Bukowski as a tribute to the industries that supported Florence Township and employed its residents for over 100 years. Its feathers are made of nuts, bolts, screws, washers, nails, and antique wrenches. One side has "Florence" spelled out with Florence pipe, while the other side has "Roebling" spelled out with Roebling cable. (Courtesy of the Florence Historical Society.)

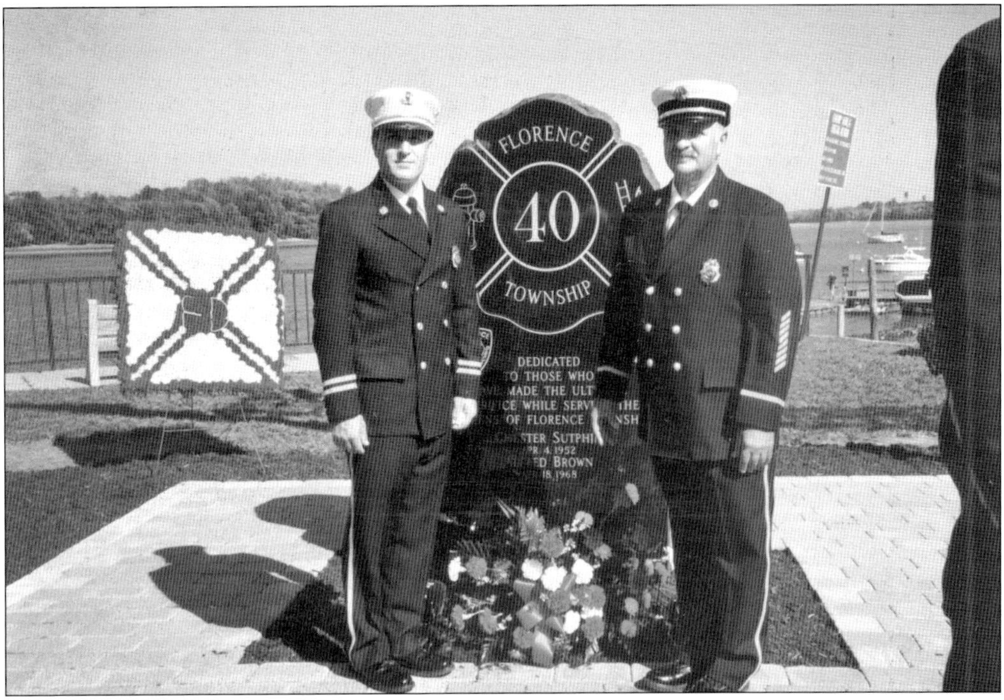

Firefighter Ceremonies. Unveiling of the firefighters' monument at Clark Carey Volunteer Memorial Park at the township wharf was an auspicious occasion in September 2002. Albert Jacoby and son Albert Jacoby Jr. proudly pose in their uniforms. Landscaping for this area was also furnished by Jacoby Sr. and his son. The aerial truck in the background flies the American flag, which has been a local tradition at patriotic ceremonies in town. (Courtesy of Mary Tapper.)

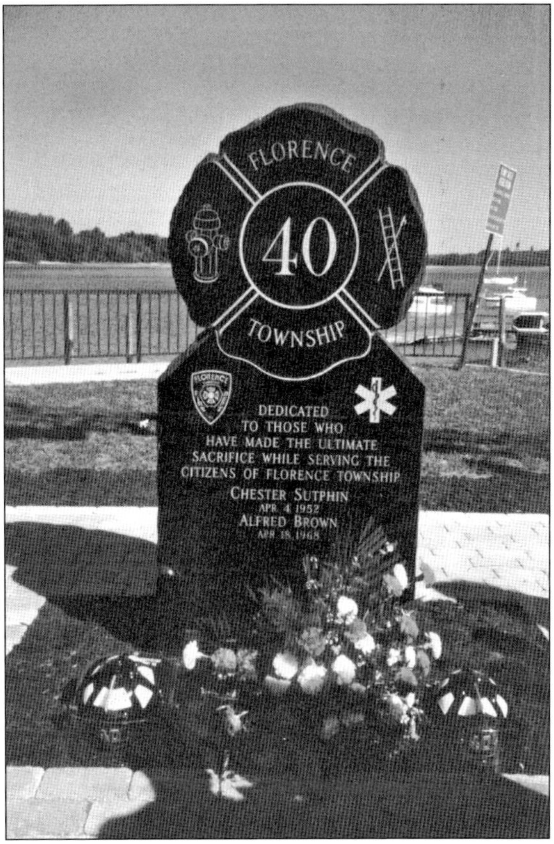

The Firefighters' Monument. On September 28, 2002, this monument was placed at the township wharf in honor of firefighters who died in the course of their duty. It was erected by the Florence Township Fire Department, and pavers were sold to support the cost of this stone. (Courtesy of the Florence Historical Society.)

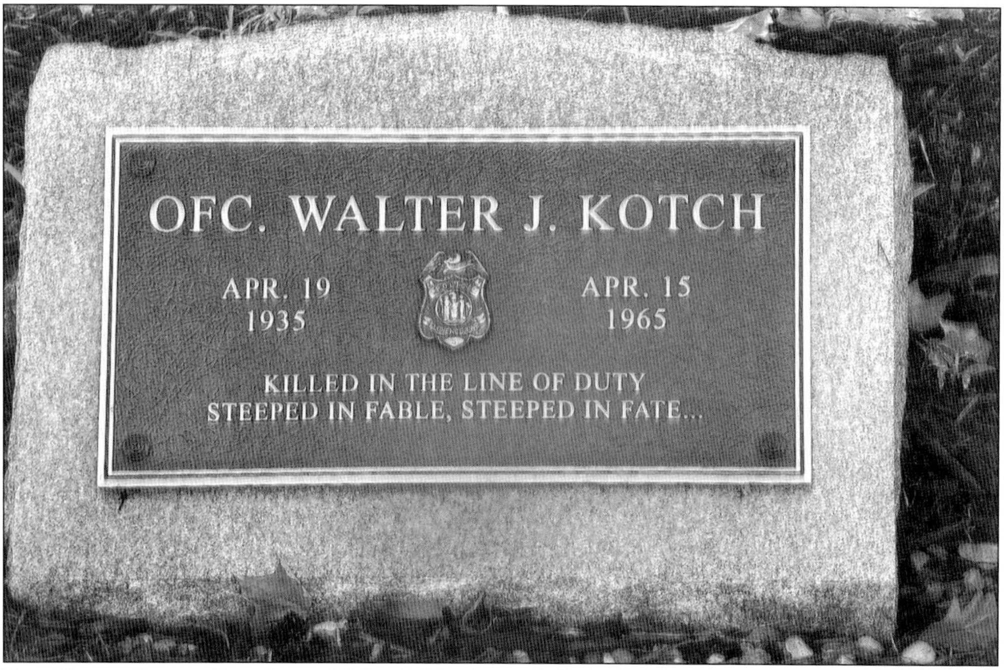

THE KOTCH STONE. Patrolman Walter J. Kotch was killed while escorting a funeral procession at Route 130 and Cedar Lane on April 15, 1965. There was no traffic signal at that time. This stone at the Municipal Building on Broad Street marks his passing, and a memorial service is presented each year for family and friends at this site. (Courtesy of the Florence Historical Society.)

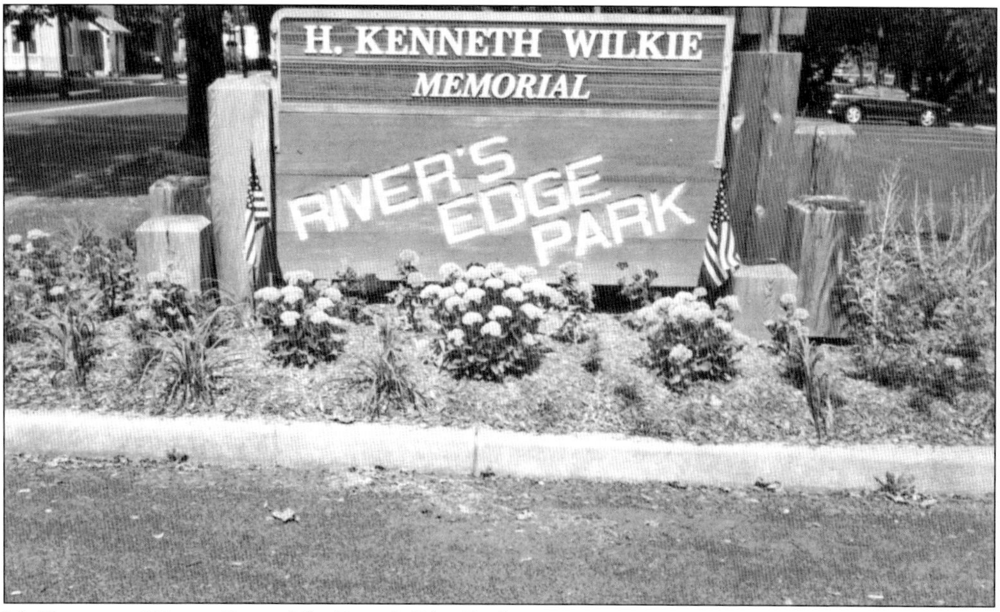

H. KENNETH WILKIE PARK. The River's Edge Park on West Front Street was rededicated in honor of H. Kenneth Wilkie, past mayor of Florence for 20 years. He was instrumental in obtaining the property from Griffin Pipe, and the dedication ceremony took place on May 25, 1991. This property was formerly known as the R.D. Wood mansion property, and the park is the site of weddings and other special occasions in town. (Courtesy of the Florence Historical Society.)

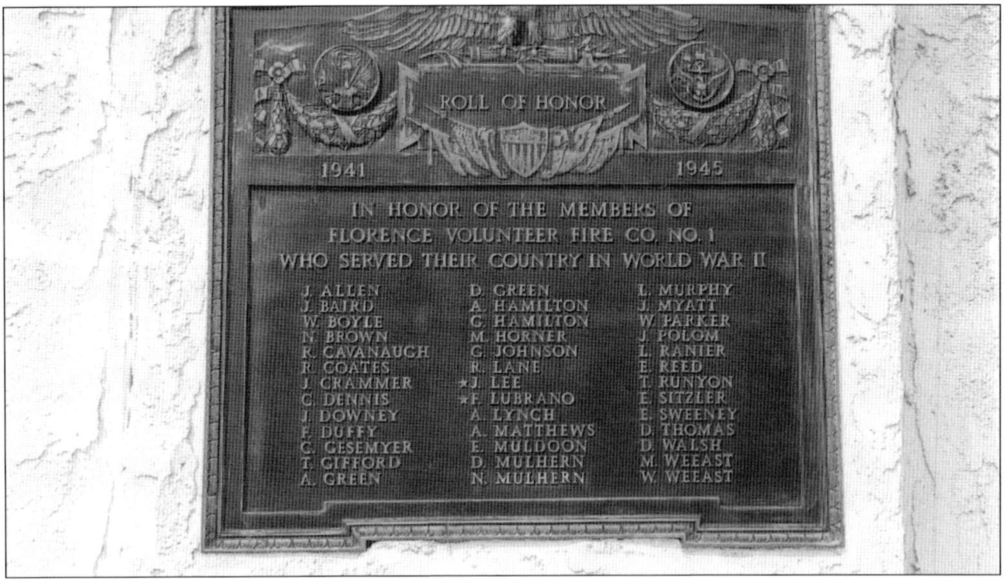

FIRE COMPANY ROLL OF HONOR. This plaque honors members of the Florence Volunteer Fire Co. No. 1 who served their country in World War II. It is located on the front of the old West Third Street firehouse. This building is now the home of the Florence Museum and Historical Society and the meeting place for the Florence Garden Club. (Courtesy of the Florence Historical Society.)

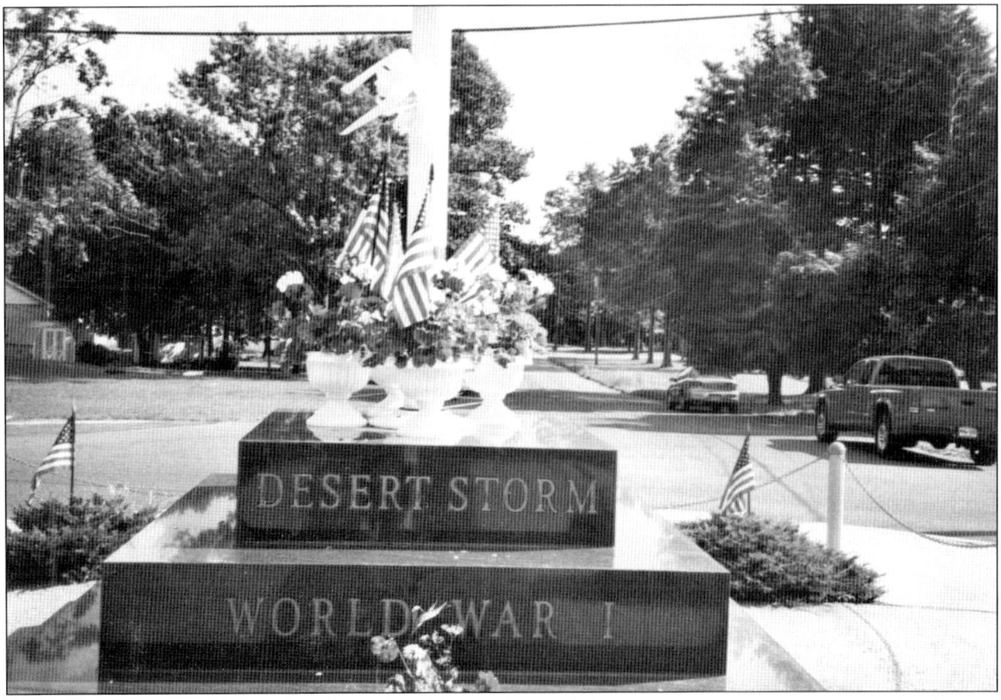

FIFTH STREET MONUMENT. Dedicated on December 7, 1991, this monument was erected to honor those veterans who made the supreme sacrifice during World War I, World War II, the Korean War, the Vietnam War, Operation Desert Storm, and Operation Iraqi Freedom. Located at the top of East Fifth Street intersecting Oak Street, the spot once held one of the Florence water towers, which was torn down in September 1991. (Courtesy of the Florence Historical Society.)

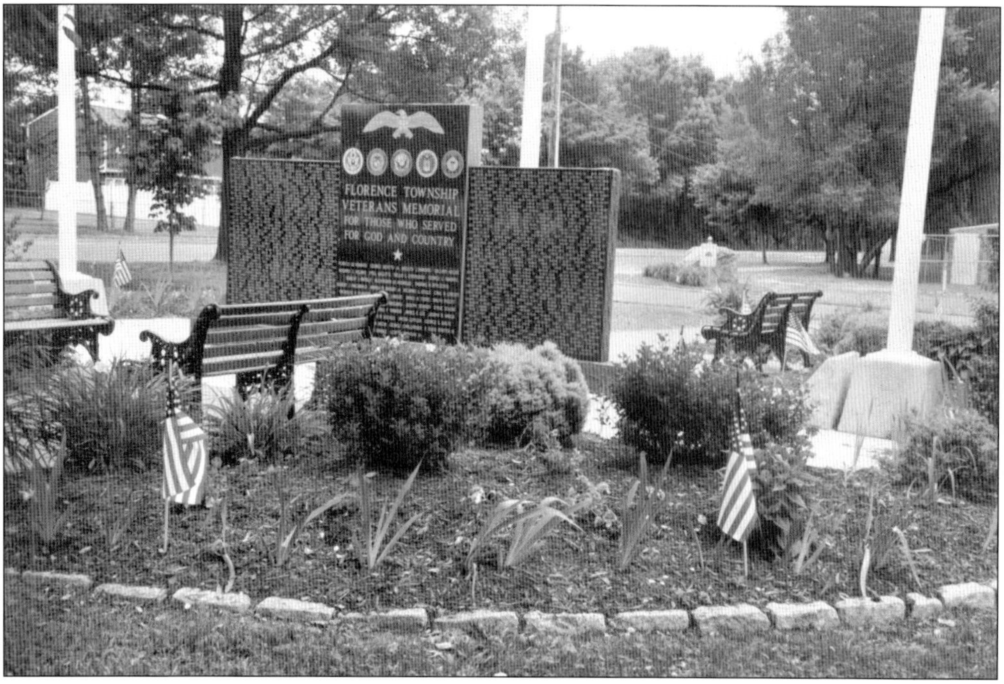

The Veterans' Memorial. The Florence Township Veterans' Memorial is located on Broad Street near the Municipal Building. It lists the names of all residents who have served "for God and Country" and was built to honor them and their efforts to protect this country. Names are also etched over the entire back of this monument. (Courtesy of the Florence Historical Society.)

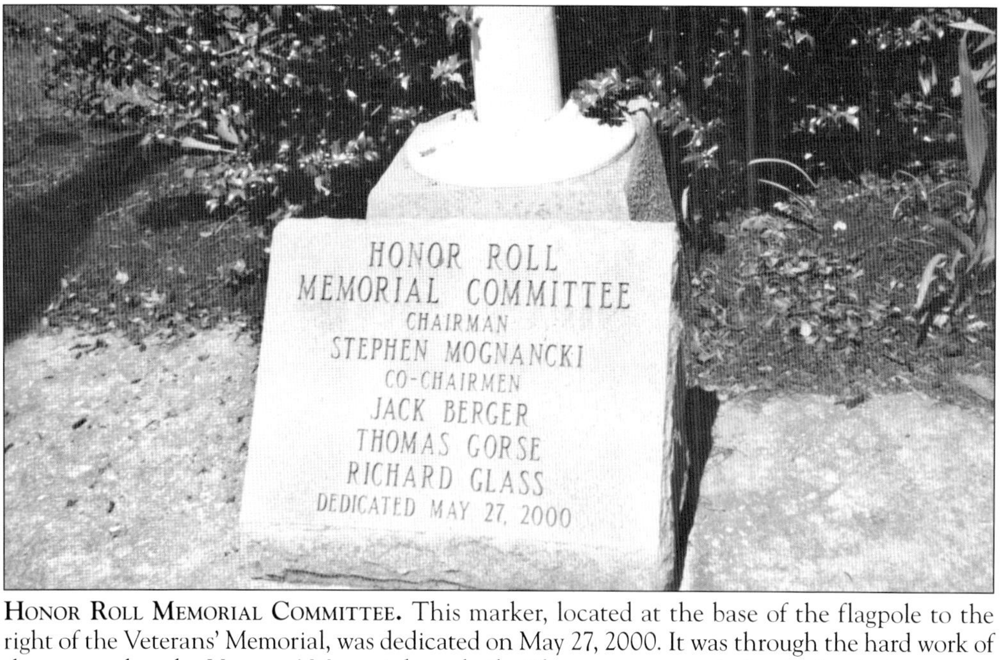

Honor Roll Memorial Committee. This marker, located at the base of the flagpole to the right of the Veterans' Memorial, was dedicated on May 27, 2000. It was through the hard work of these men that the Veterans' Memorial was built. These men not only fought for their country, but also fought to honor and thank Florence's residents who have served so valiantly to protect Americans' freedom. (Courtesy of the Florence Historical Society.)

ARTHUR FOULKS JR. Honored for his heroism in April 1949, Arthur Foulks Jr. receives a proclamation from Mayor William Berry in 2011. Foulks saved four boys from drowning in the Delaware River and was subsequently awarded the Carnegie Medal for Heroism. A rescue boat and motor were then dedicated to Foulks by the newly formed Florence Emergency Squad. (Courtesy of the Florence Historical Society.)

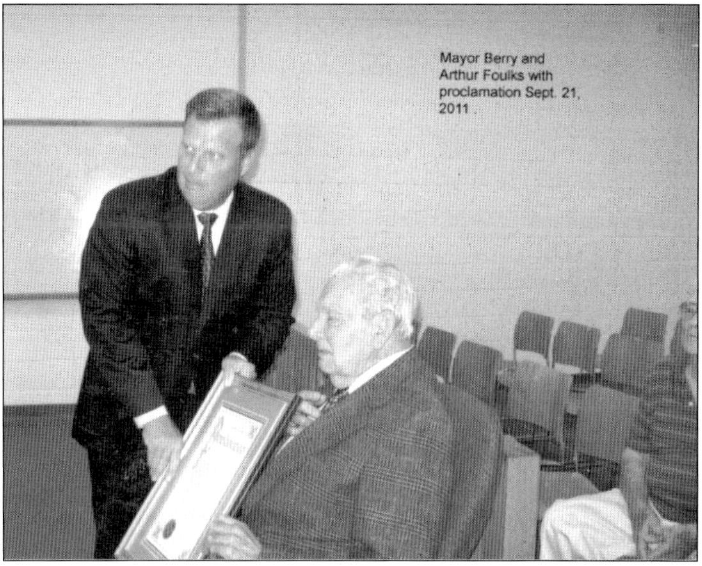

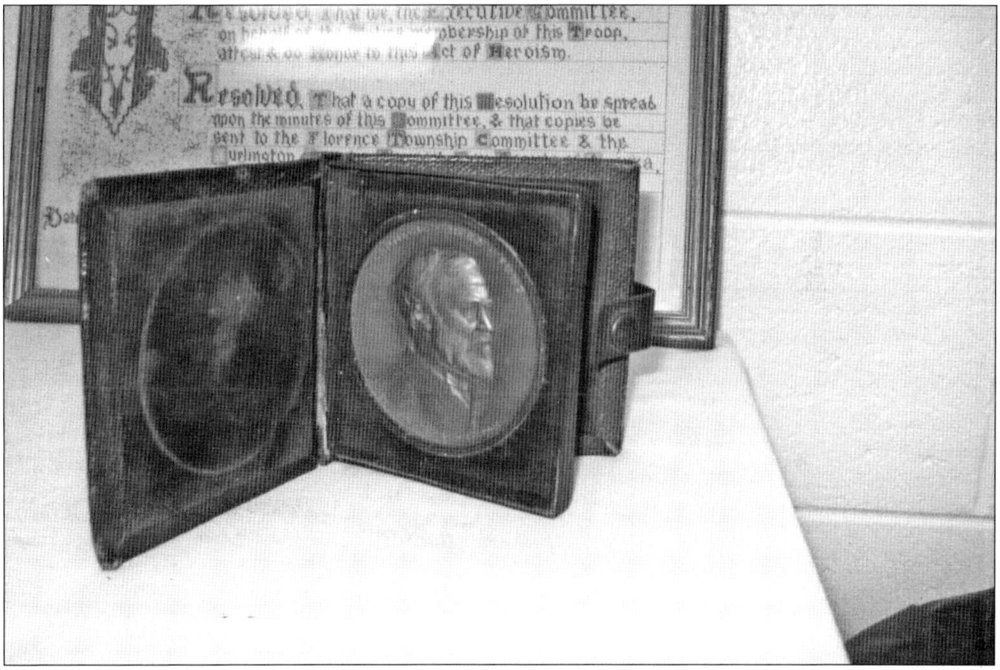

CARNEGIE MEDAL FOR HEROISM. Displayed in the Florence Museum at the old Third Street firehouse is the Carnegie Medal awarded to Arthur Foulks Jr. in 1949. Foulks graciously donated the medal after his recognition by the township mayor in 2011, as well as a commendation by the Boy Scouts of America to Arthur and his brother Ralph, who was also involved in the rescue. (Courtesy of the Florence Historical Society.)

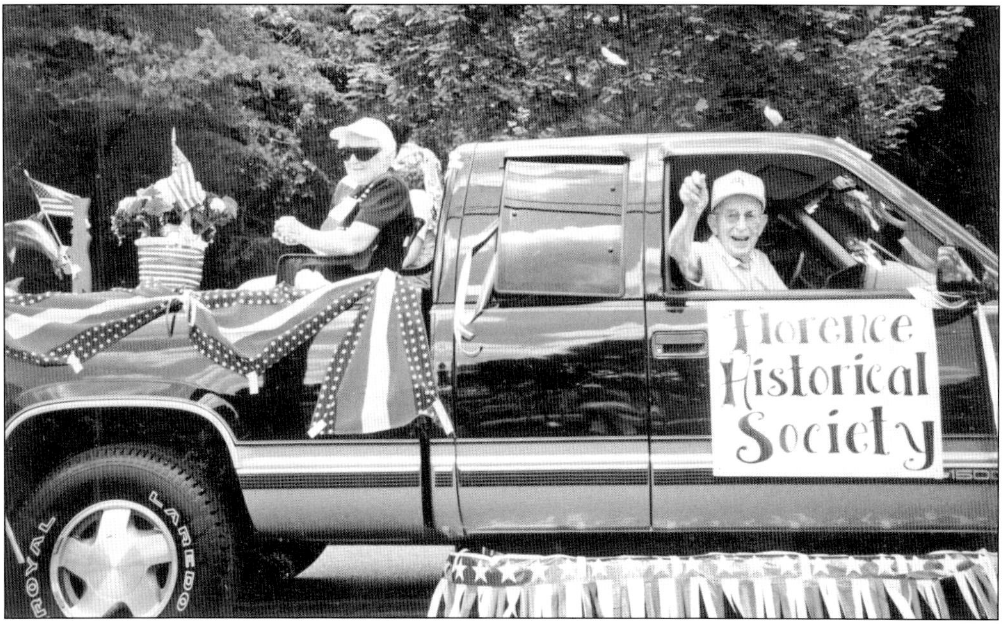

A Parade Float. The Florence Historical Society float passes the reviewing stand during the Patriotic Day parade in July 2005 at Florence. The society has been in local parades since 1997. Shown is a truck driven by Albert "Smokey" King. In the rear are Mary Bombelli Tapper and Judith Wilson King (on the far side) tossing candy to the crowd. Waving to the spectators is Charles "Scoots" Adams. (Courtesy of the Florence Historical Society.)

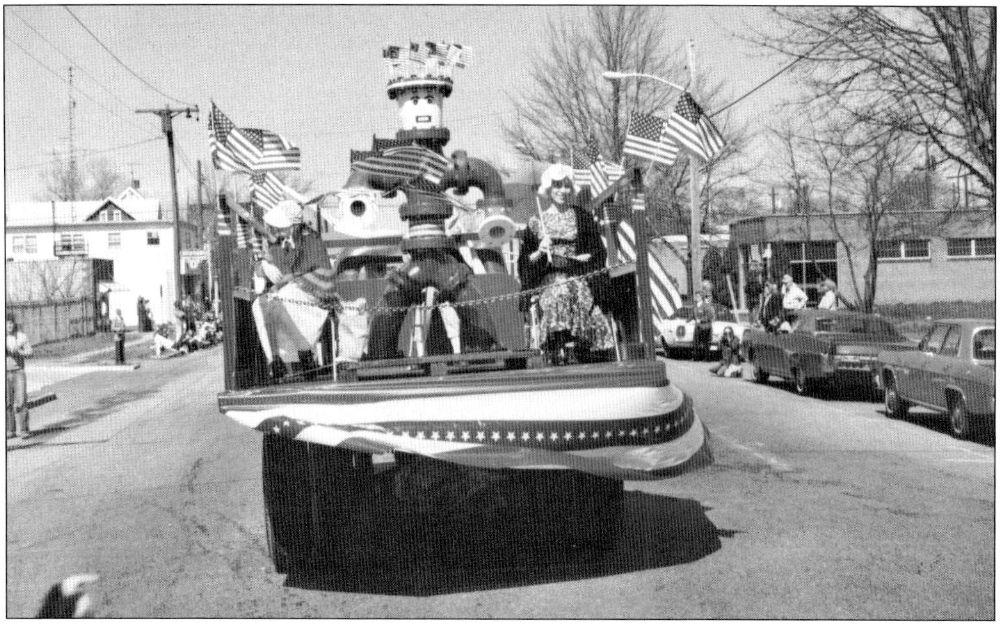

Griffin Iron Man. As part of the Florence Township bicentennial parade in 1976, Griffin Pipe entered a float with *Iron Man* as its feature. On the right is Loretta Carnival, and to the left is Jennifer Smith. Others on the float included Dean Carnival and David and Zachary Hraber. *Iron Man* is now in Edgewater Park on property of Rhawn Flange and Machine Company. (Courtesy of Joyce Maloney.)

Six

PEOPLE

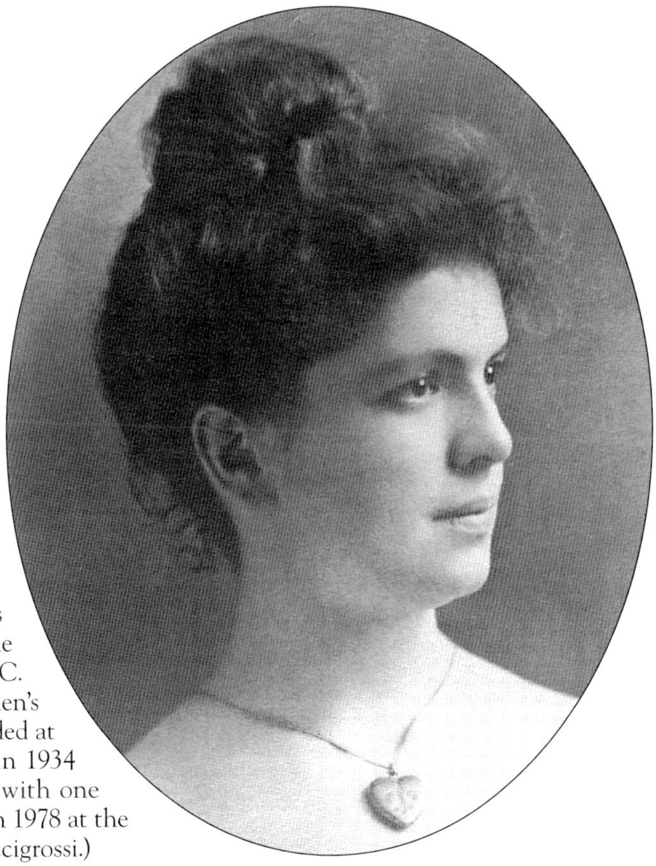

ELIZABETH FEWKES. This beautiful c. 1901 picture is of Elizabeth Christy, who was approximately 18 years old at the time. She secretly married Alfred C. Fewkes in June 1914 at St. Stephen's Episcopal Church, and they resided at 200 Broad Street. Alfred died in 1934 at age 55, leaving her a widow with one daughter, Nella. Elizabeth died in 1978 at the age of 87. (Courtesy of Mary Buccigrossi.)

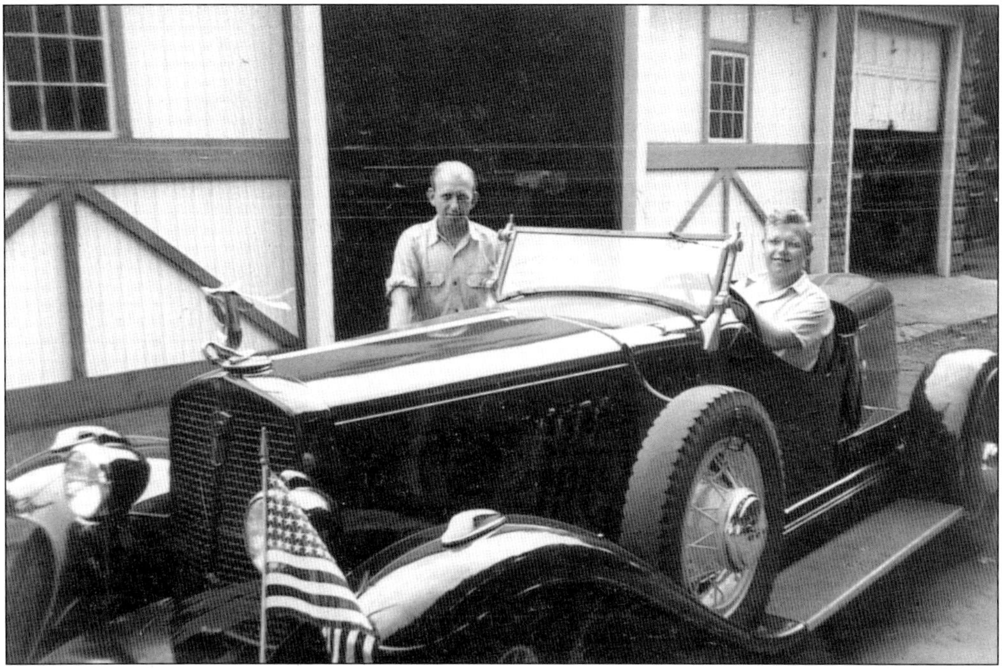

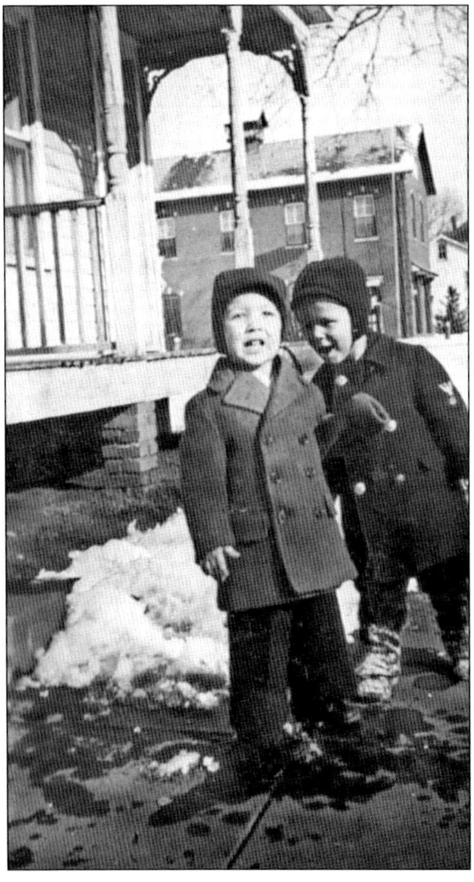

HAMILTON'S CAR. William Hamilton sits at the wheel of a boat-tailed speedster that he and his father, Presley Hamilton, built in 1947. Presley ran a bus company, and the garages in the background housed his buses on the street behind the Boulevard in Florence. The speedster was similar to the Cord and the Auburn, and had a 1931 Studebaker front end with an eight-cylinder Pierce-Arrow engine. (Courtesy of Donald Cooper.)

THE BROWN BROTHERS. Ron (left) and Ken Brown stand near their house on the corner of West Third and Spring Streets in the early 1930s. In the background is Florence Firehouse No. 1, now home to the Florence Historical Society. Ron later joined the US Coast Guard, and Ken later joined the US Army Air Forces in 1943. (Courtesy of Ken Brown.)

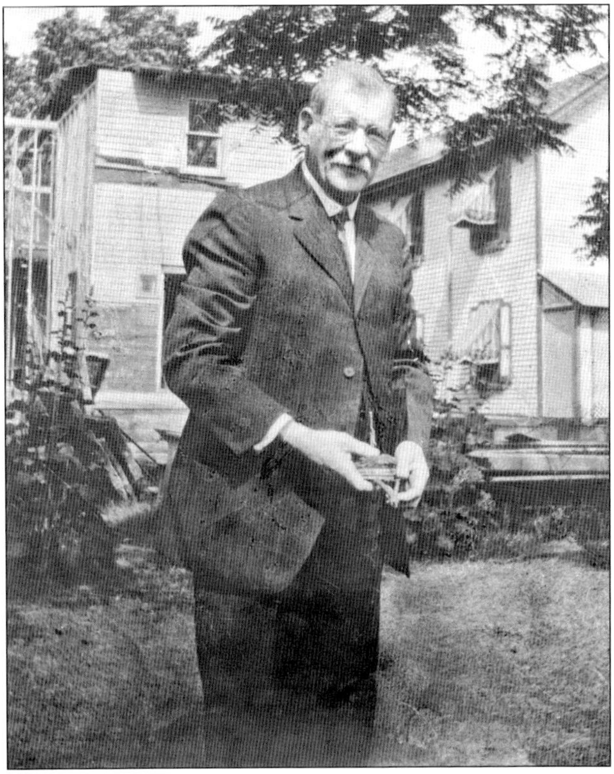

John Peacock. Justice of the Peace John Peacock poses in his backyard on Front Street around 1920. He was employed at the Florence Pipe Foundry and Machine Company for more than 30 years. Recently engaged in the real estate and insurance business, he also enjoyed the distinction of serving the township in every municipal office and was active for many years in county politics. Peacock died in 1924 at the age of 64. (Courtesy of Thelma Peacock Tilghman.)

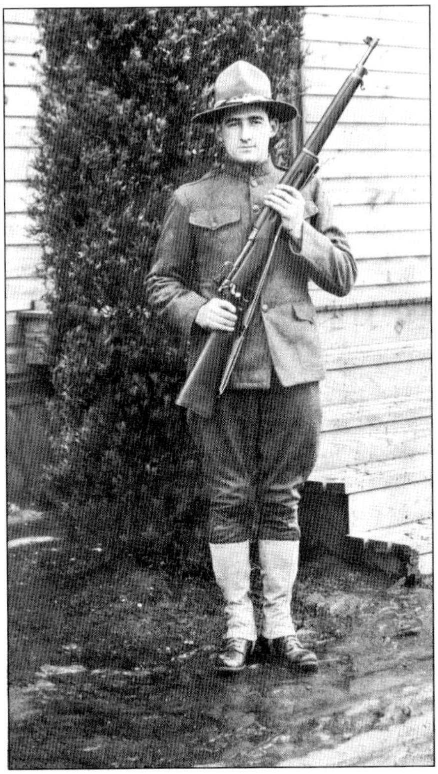

Frank Peacock. Proudly posing in 1918 at Camp Dix in New Jersey, Frank Peacock, age 22, served his country in the US Army with many other Florence boys. The Army uniform would change somewhat by World War II, with puttees being abolished and the hat redesigned. (Courtesy of Thelma Tilghman.)

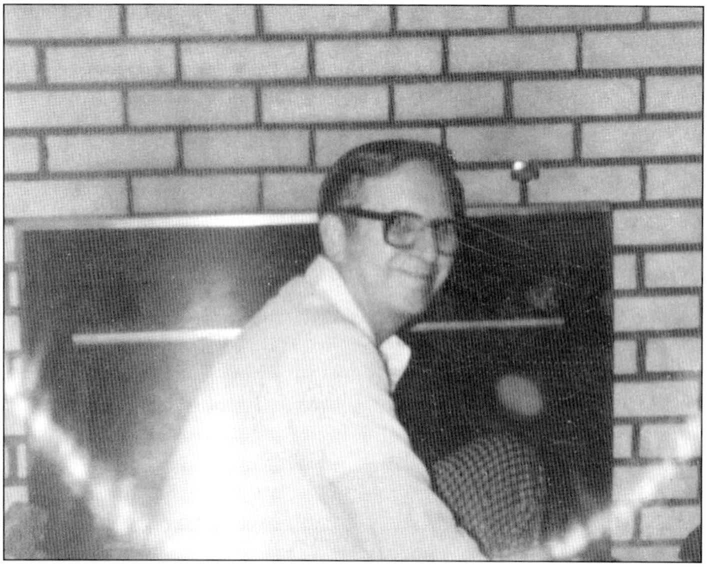

Dr. Harold E. Morris. Dr. Morris came to Florence as a general practitioner in 1958. After partnering with Dr. McCay, he opened his own practice on Delaware Avenue in October 1964. He and his wife, Ruth, raised two sons and a daughter in Florence. Dr. Morris died in 1985 at the age of 56. (Courtesy of Ruth Morris.)

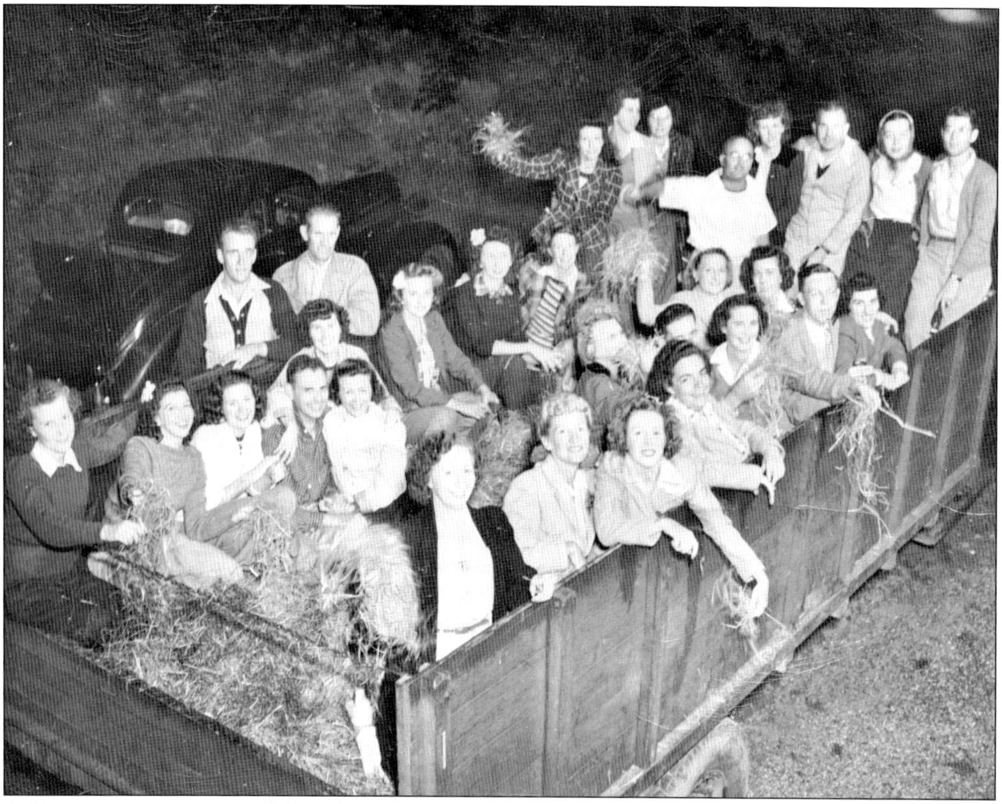

A Florence Hayride. Although it is unknown where this hayride took place, there are some Florence locals from the 1940s. The first lady on the left side at the end of the wagon is Mary Moro; she later married Carl Lubrano. The second and third ladies to the right are Mary Buccigrossi and Barbara Hulehan. The third lady on the side of the wagon, in the lower end of image is Melva Spotts, and Parker Mullen is first on the left in the back row by the cab. (Courtesy of Marge Angelini.)

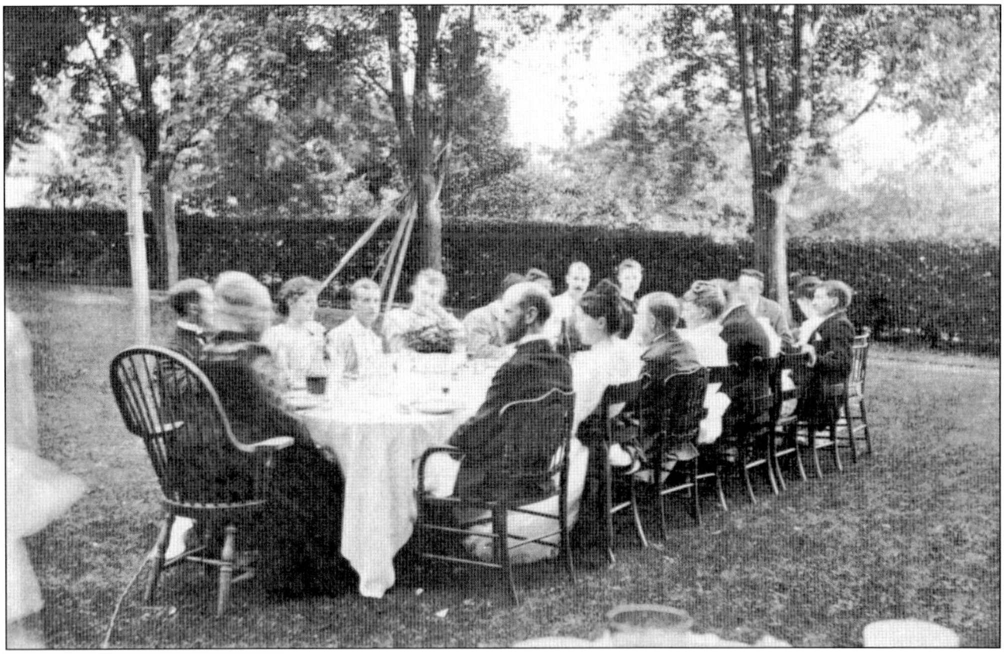

A Neilson Picnic. Known as Heart's Ease, this large Victorian house on East Front Street was built by William D. Lewis, an ambassador to Spain, for his daughter Sarah Neilson. A very prominent Main Line family from Philadelphia, the Neilsons had a party for their 50th wedding anniversary that was attended by guests arriving from Philadelphia on a special Pullman train to celebrate. The home still stands today, divided into halves for two families. This photograph, dated 1890, depicts a formal family picnic on the grounds. (Courtesy of the Burlington County Historical Society.)

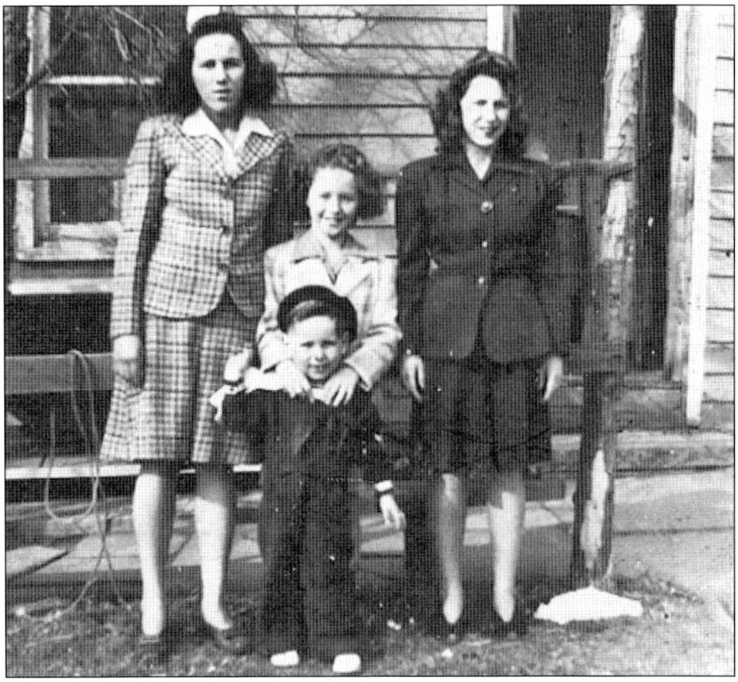

The Farah Family. Sisters Lillian Chumar (left) and Geraldine Dittman pose with their niece Georgine Fritchman and nephew Charles Farah in the early 1940s, on the side of the Farah household. Located at 214 Spring Street, this house is rumored to have been a nightclub in the 1920s. These relatives are part of the extended Warner family of four brothers and four sisters. (Courtesy of Geraldine "Dink" Warner Dittman.)

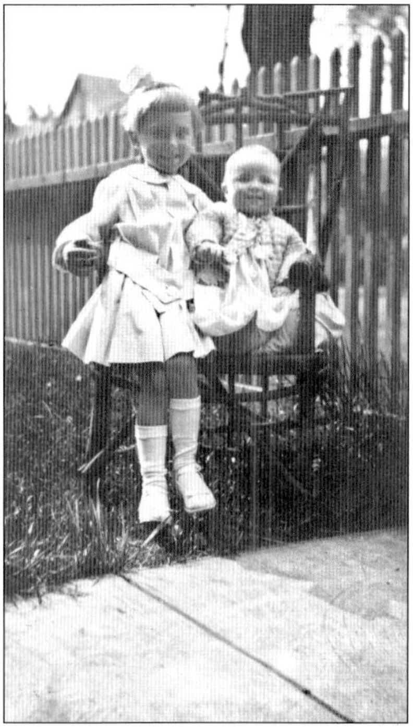

THE WILLIAMS FAMILY. Betty Williams and her brother John enjoy the backyard swing at their home on 612 West Third Street around 1918. Their father, Winsor Williams, was justice of the peace in town and not only performed marriages, but also heard court cases involving inebriated citizens and child support. John died at the age of 92 in 2010. (Courtesy of Carol Swift.)

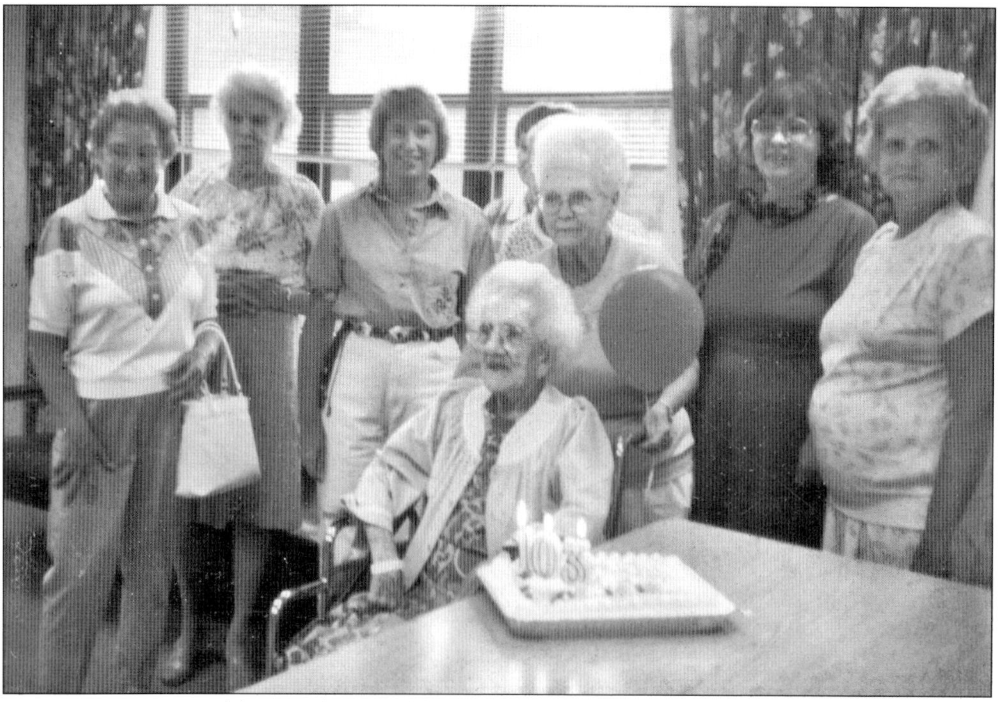

ALETHEA FOULKS. Celebrating her 103rd birthday around 1995, Alethea Foulks (seated) is joined by her friends, from left to right, Mary Tapper, Helen Fauver, Dorothy Bowers, Olie Jenkins (partly obscured), Dorothy Eaton, Rev. Patricia Wentworth, Linda Szathmary, and Marion Bock. Alethea died the next year, at the age of 104. She was the oldest member of the Florence United Methodist Church at the time. (Courtesy of the Florence Historical Society.)

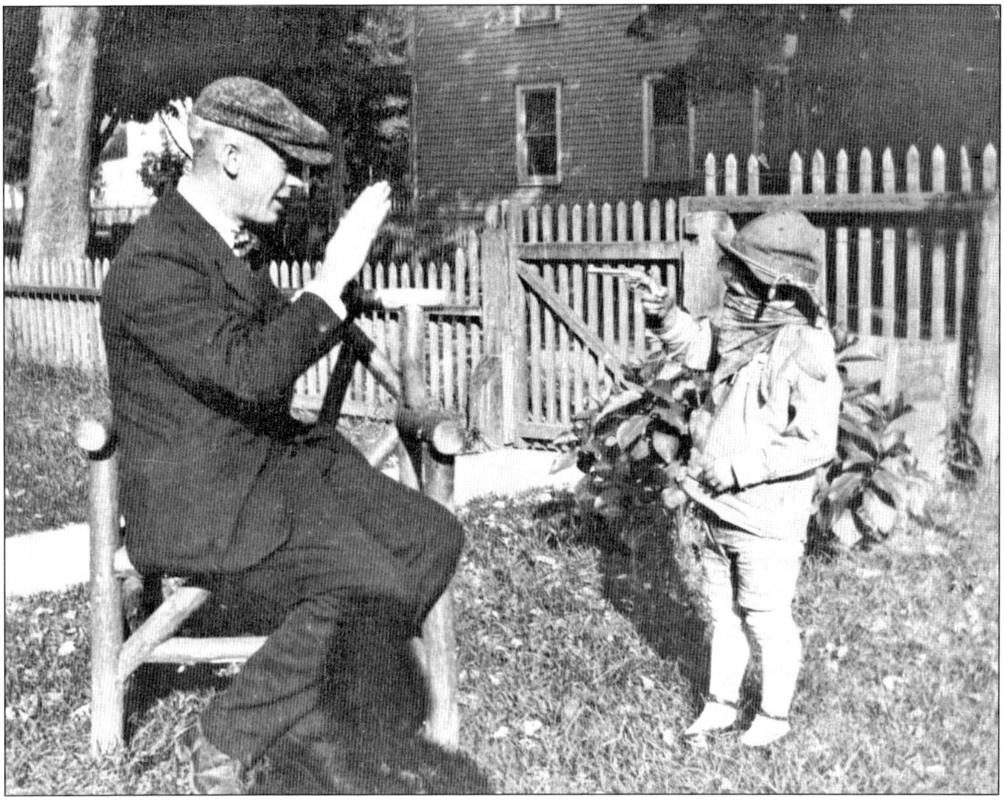

Rosamond Aikins, Bandit. Pictured in their backyard on the Boulevard around 1920, Rosamond Aikins "gets the drop" on her uncle Russell Aikins. The most popular movies at the time featured cowboys and Indians, and most children had toy guns to re-create the weekly serials shown at the movie house. (Courtesy of the Florence Historical Society.)

Aikins Hunting Party. A squirrel-hunting party headed by H. Rudgus Aikins with his sister Rosamond takes place on the Boulevard in Florence around 1925. It was common in those days for children to have BB guns, as they were taught proper usage and given safety lessons. Aikins later became a wood-shop teacher at Florence High School until the late 1960s. (Courtesy of the Florence Historical Society.)

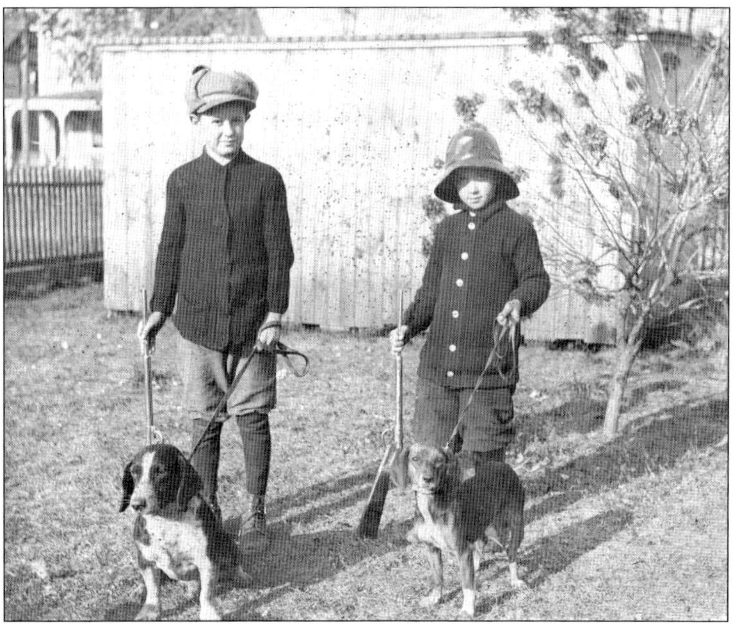

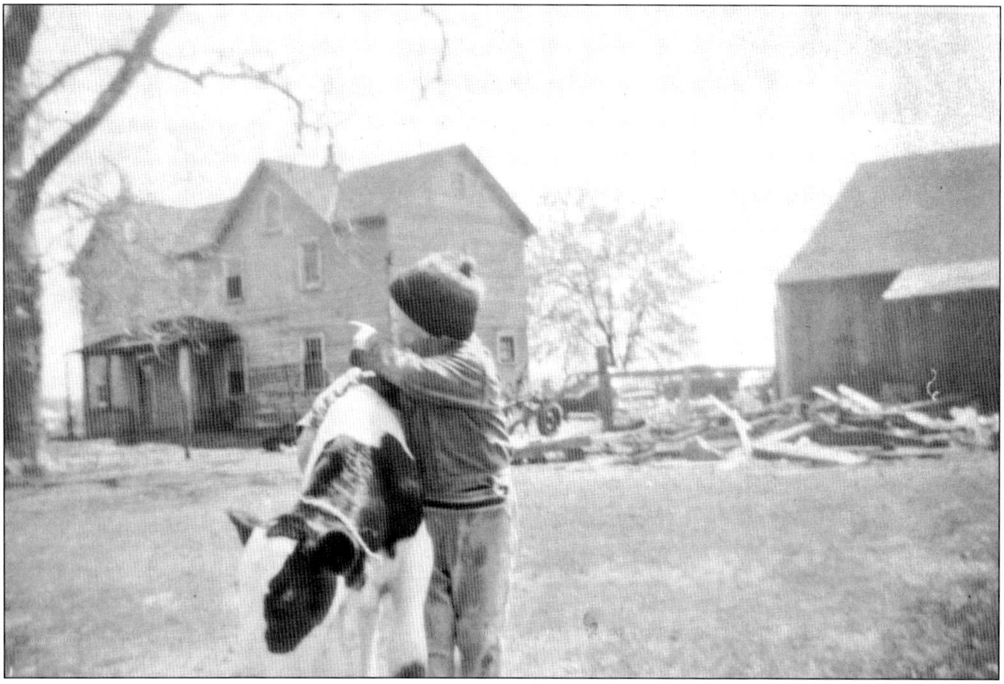

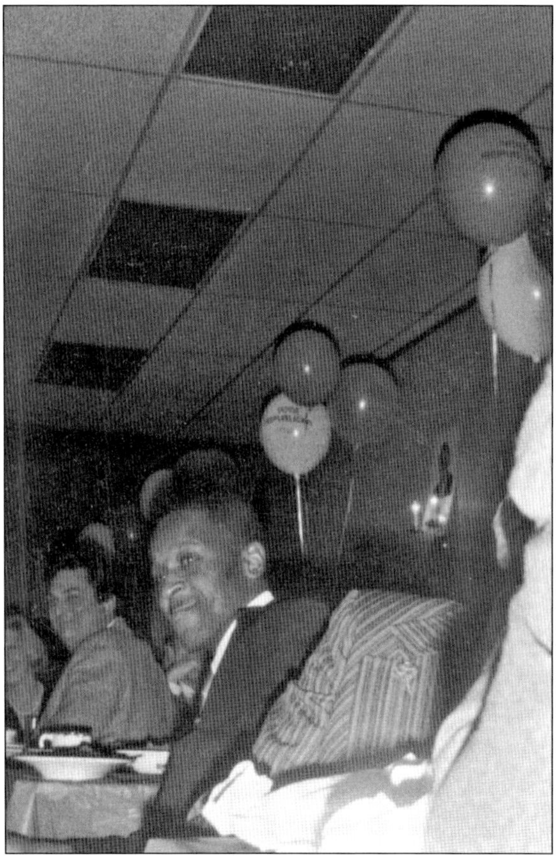

The Foundry Farm. Young Robert DuBell stands in the front yard of the Foundry farmhouse on West Fifth Street, where his father raised crops and livestock. This farm was in operation as early as 1907; in 1935, it also included Shahan's Coal Service. During the Depression, lots were provided for foundry employees to raise vegetables near the salt hay field at Woodlawn Avenue. The farmhouse fell into ruin in the mid-1960s, and the farmland is now the Oak Mill Development. (Courtesy of the Florence Historical Society.)

Melvin "Doc" Crawley. Doc Crawley celebrates his retirement in 1989. He was honored by the Lincoln Society of Florence at a testimonial dinner. Doc worked for the township for 30 years and is now a well-known and gregarious member of the community. He and Nils Johnson marched in costume at Florence parades for many years, to the delight of spectators. Doc still serves as a doorman at Dennison Funeral Home. (Courtesy of the Florence Historical Society.)

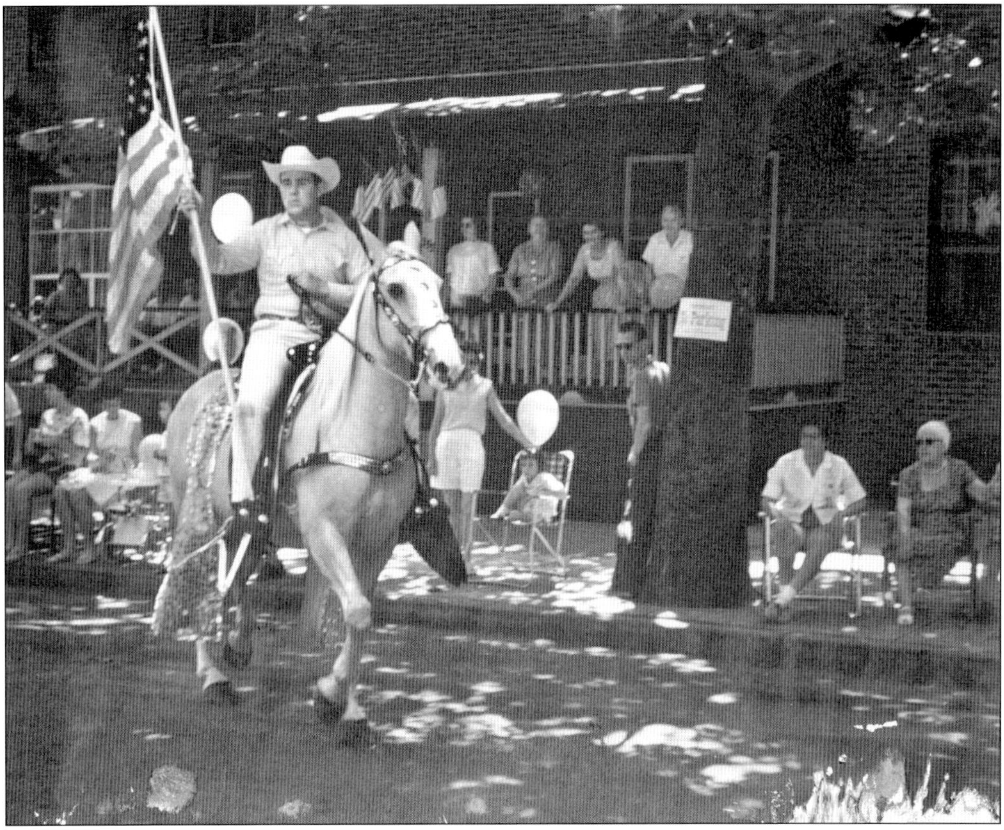

Joseph McHugh III. Joseph McHugh III, son of Florence's municipal judge McHugh, proudly rides his palomino horse in a Fourth of July parade in Florence around 1960. Also riding with him at different events were Albert King, Barry Schafle, and brothers Gerald, Brad, and Hilyard Simpkins. Joseph had his own insurance business until his death in 2011. (Courtesy of the McHugh family.)

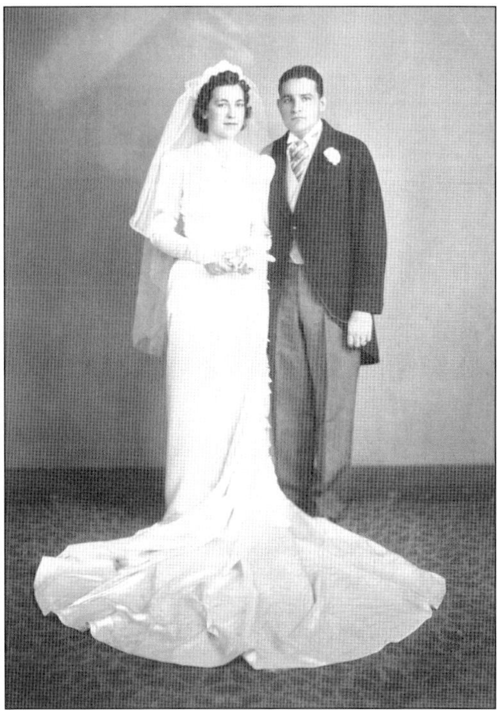

Joseph McHugh Jr. This beautiful c. early 1940s wedding photograph features Joseph McHugh Jr. and Emma Elizabeth LeJambre. Joseph was a non-lawyer municipal court judge during his 32 years on the bench in Florence. He became police recorder in 1947 and municipal magistrate in 1950. Joseph and his wife were graduates of Bordentown High School, and he later attended Rider College. At the time of their wedding, Joseph was employed at the Florence Pipe Foundry and Machine Company. (Courtesy of the Florence Historical Society.)

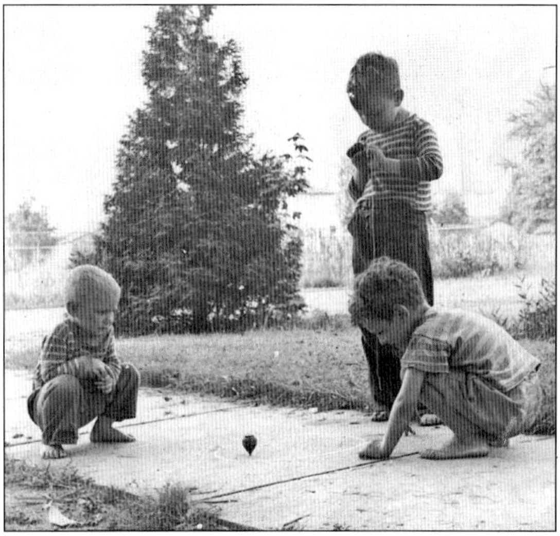

THE ANDERSON FAMILY. Paul Anderson (left), Edward Anderson (stooping), and Norman Anderson (standing) play "spin the top" near their house at Fourth and Broad Streets around 1944. Today, the empty lot has a professional office building on the spot. (Courtesy of Marjorie Anderson.)

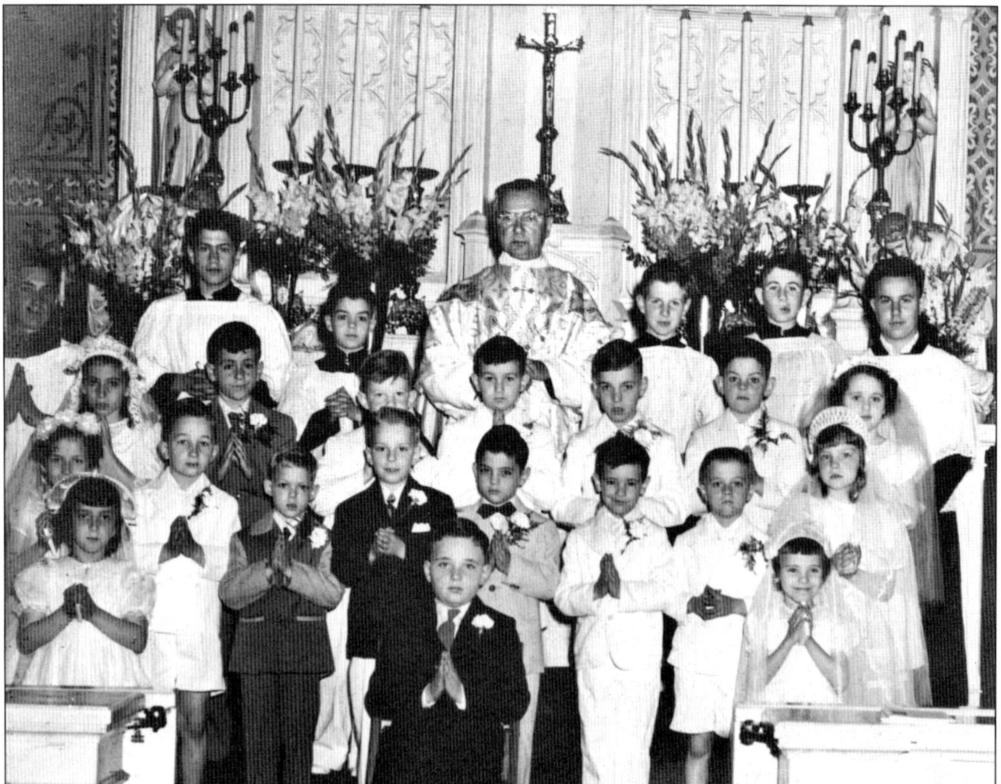

ST. CLARE'S CHURCH FIRST COMMUNION. In this c. 1956 image, a group of youngsters poses for First Communion with Fr. Michael Bacso. Standing in the front row and moving from front to back are, from left to right, (first row) Rosemary Frappolli, Bill Sweeney, and Judy Conselice; (second row) Jerry Clyde, Francis Legnaioli, John Berry, John Zolty, Lee Cicero, Bob Linda, Tim Mullen, and Connie Trader; (third row) Jean Rosconi, Sam Rinaldi, Henry Kelty, Joe McHugh, Nelson Daniels, Vince Carey, and Toni Joy; (fourth row) two unidentified, Jack Sweeney, Bacso, George Ingham, Louis Kiefer, and Paul Bertuccini. (Courtesy of the Joseph McHugh family.)

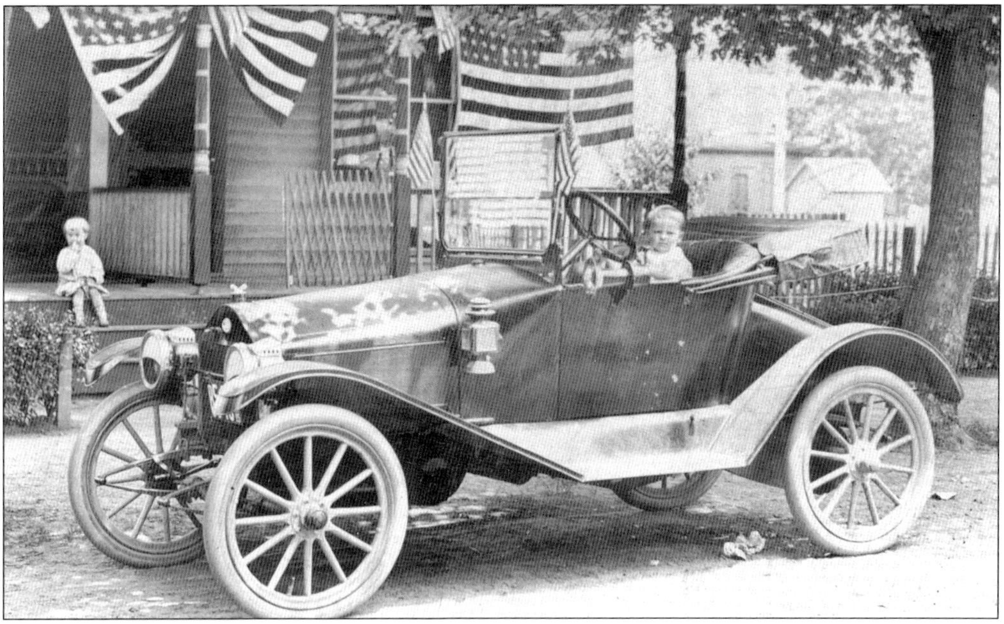

William F. Parker. This delightful picture shows William F. Parker, age two and a half, who was born in 1915. The early automobile appears to be part of a patriotic celebration around 1917 in front of his family's house on West Second Street. William later became the Burlington County sheriff. His grandfather, William F. Parker, was a dance trumpet player and conducted an orchestra that played at dances and other functions. (Courtesy of the Florence Historical Society.)

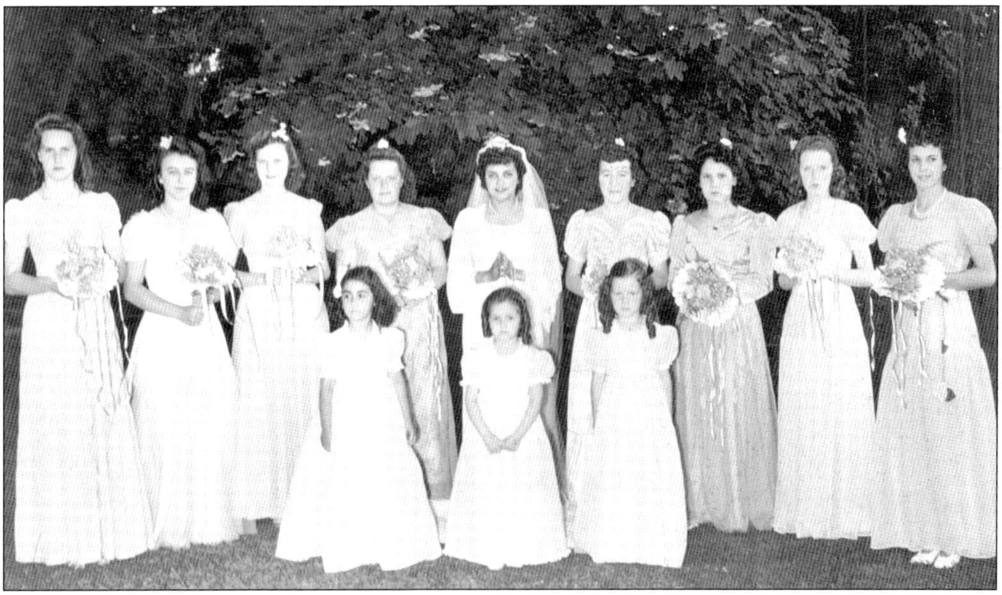

St. Clare's Church May Crowning. In the 1940s, St. Clare's Church had the May crowning of the Blessed Virgin Mary in the side yard on East Front Street. The young ladies who took part are (second row) Betty Boyle, Virginia Adair, Joan Keating, Jean Garwood, Dorothy Durham, Peggy Worthington, Regina Lubrano, Madeline Maloney, and Yolanda Capritti. The three little girls in the front are unidentified. This ceremony is an honor for those who participate, as they are chosen by their regular attendance at weekly religious instructions. (Courtesy of Dorothy McBride.)

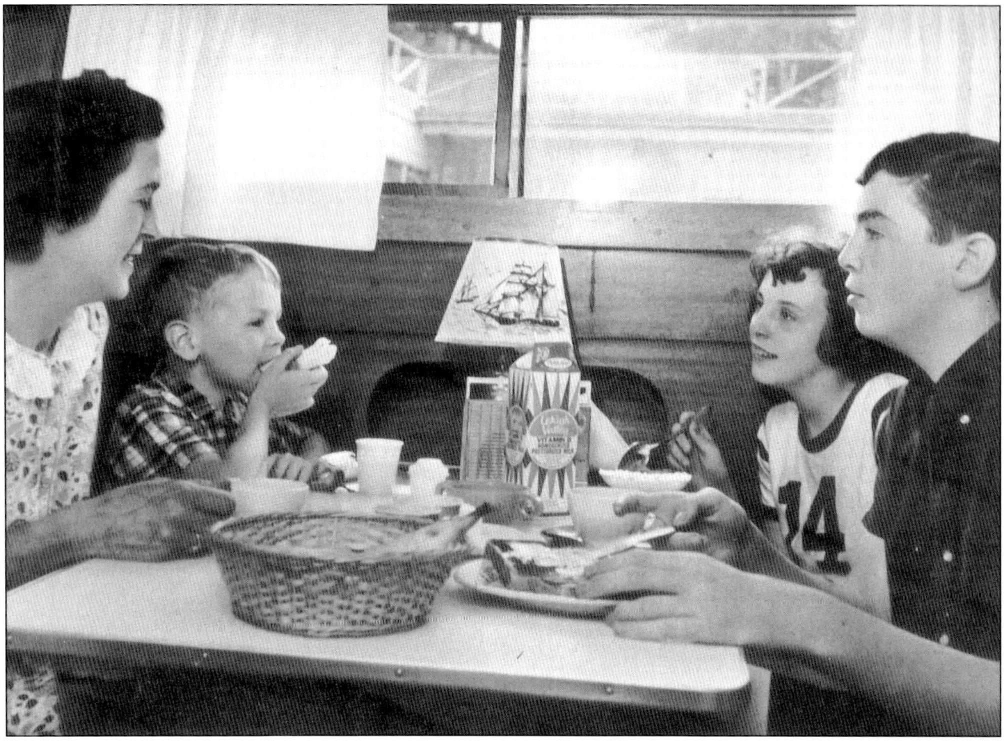

The Boyd Family. Sitting at the Bordentown Yacht Club overlooking the Delaware River, Constance Boyd enjoys lunch with her children in 1964. From left to right are Clinton, his sister Constance, and his brother L. Clark III. Clark later became a third-generation pharmacist at Boyd's Drug Store in Florence. (Courtesy of L. Clark Boyd III.)

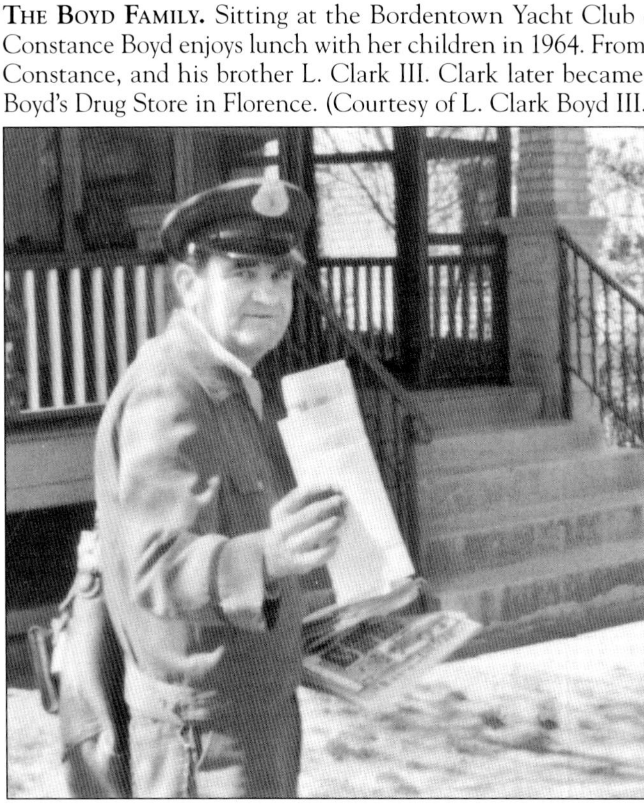

Samuel V. "Sam" Filippine Sr. A local postman for many years, Sam Filippine is pictured on duty delivering mail around town in about 1960. He was also a dedicated and loyal member of the Florence Fire Company No. 1, which he joined in 1951 and served until his death in 2010. It was also convenient that Filippine lived next to the firehouse on West Third Street for many years, enabling him to be an early responder to local fires. He was the fire company secretary for 45 years and the catalyst and main researcher for the book *History of Florence Fire Company No. 1*. (Courtesy of the Florence Historical Society.)

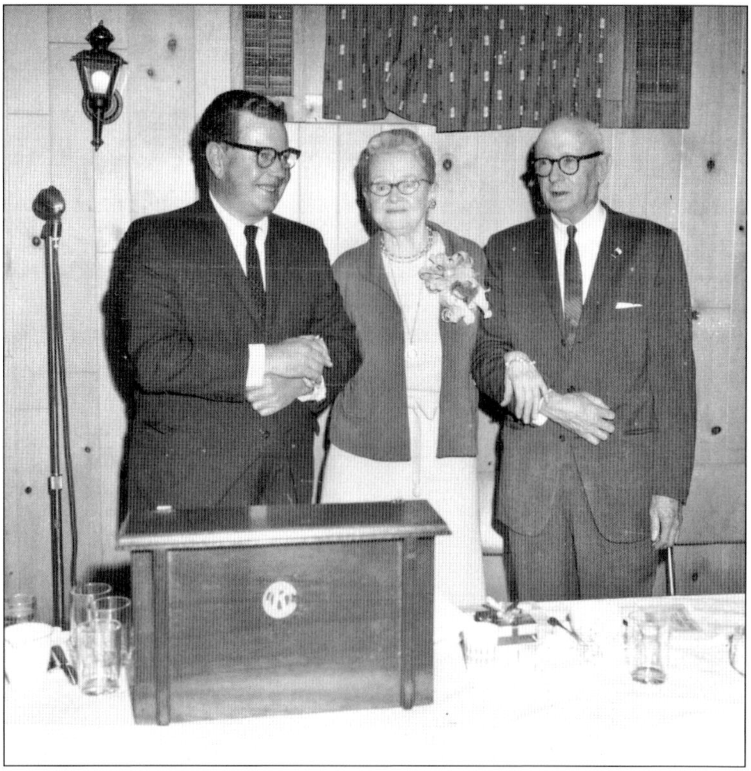

MARCELLA DUFFY. In 1966, Marcella Duffy was honored by Florence Township as Citizen of the Year. Making the presentation is Gov. Richard Hughes (left), an early Florence native. Marcella's twin brother, Francis Duffy (right), is also pictured. Governor Hughes was a very close friend of Marcella and Francis. Marcella was principal of Florence School No. 1 for many years, and the school was later named after her. (Courtesy of the Florence Historical Society.)

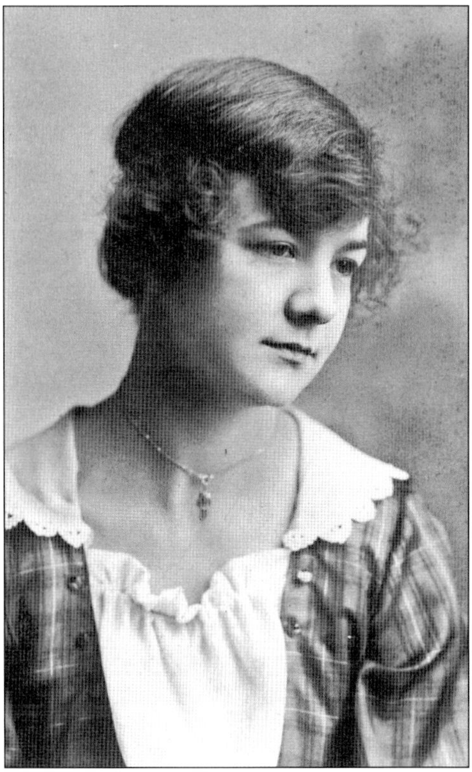

GRACE KIMBLE. In 1915, Grace Kimble poses for her portrait at the age of 18. She later married Frank Peacock, who ran a charter bus line in Florence for many years. They also ran the Crumpet Hut on Broad Street, after a contest was held to name the store. Grace's brother Charles Kimble conducted a popular band, the Midshipmen, in the 1930s and 1940s. (Courtesy of Thelma Tilghman.)

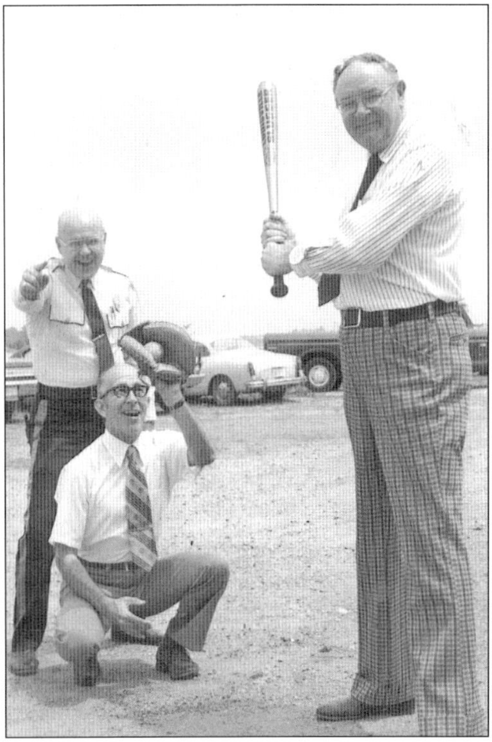

Mayor H. Kenneth Wilkie. Enjoying time away from normal duties in 1975, Mayor Wilkie stands at bat along with township administrator Charles Adams as catcher and police chief John Masiko as umpire. Mayor Wilkie's term of office ran from 1959 to 1979 consecutively. His son Craig Wilkie is presently mayor of Florence Township. (Courtesy of Charles Adams.)

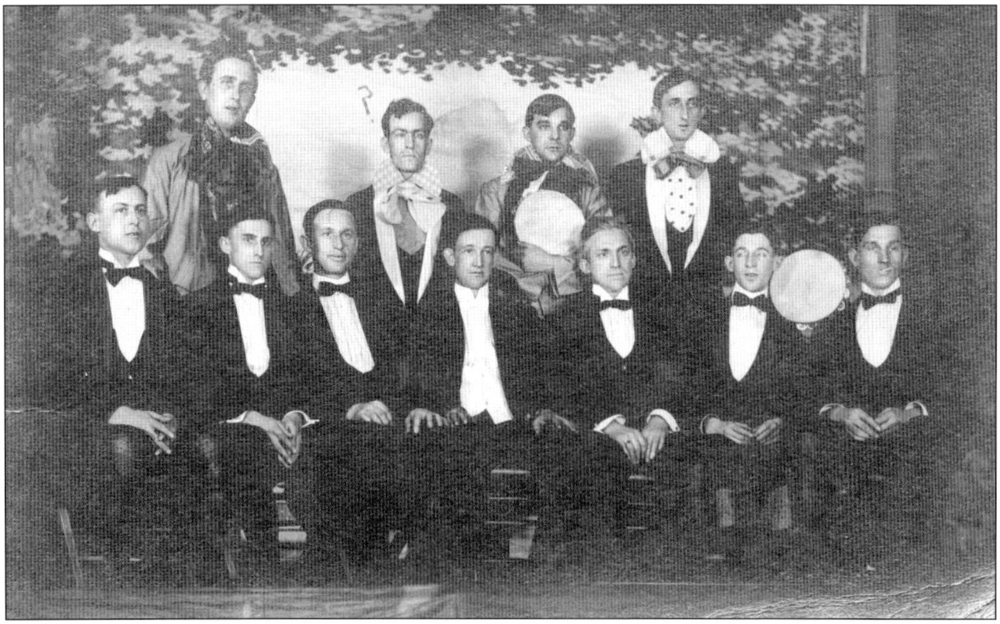

The Mohican Boat Club Minstrel Troupe. In 1913, the Mohican Boat Club Minstrel Troupe of Florence appeared in Pemberton at Grange Hall. This troupe was one of the finest amateur organizations of its kind in the county. Meetings were held in the Mohican Boat Club and Library Hall. Pictured are, in no particular order, Frank Absalom, Pete Absalom, John Coates, Albert Griffith, Albert Ireton, Bill "Gabe" McCune, Charles Peacock, Frank Pettit, Karl Weber, and two unidentified men. (Courtesy of Don Cooper.)

PADDY AND MAGGIE BROWN. Alfred "Paddy" Brown and his wife, Maggie, pose for their wedding picture around the late 1930s. Paddy joined the Florence Fire Company in 1923 and held many offices over the years. He was killed by a hit-and-run driver while directing traffic at the intersection of Old York and Florence-Columbus Roads while serving as a fire policeman on April 18, 1968. (Courtesy of the Florence Historical Society.)

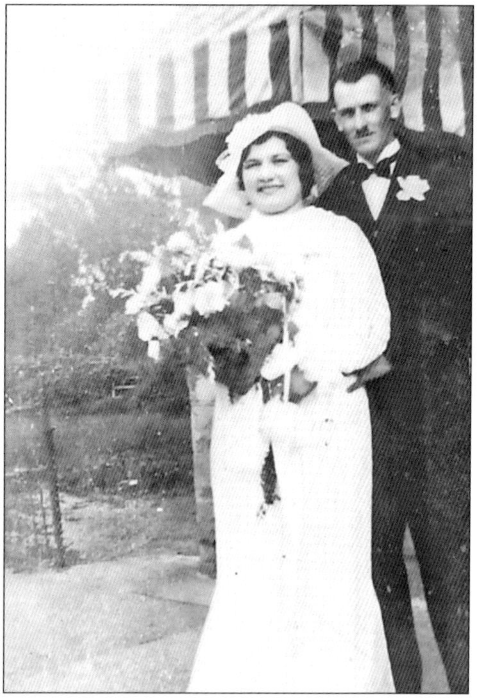

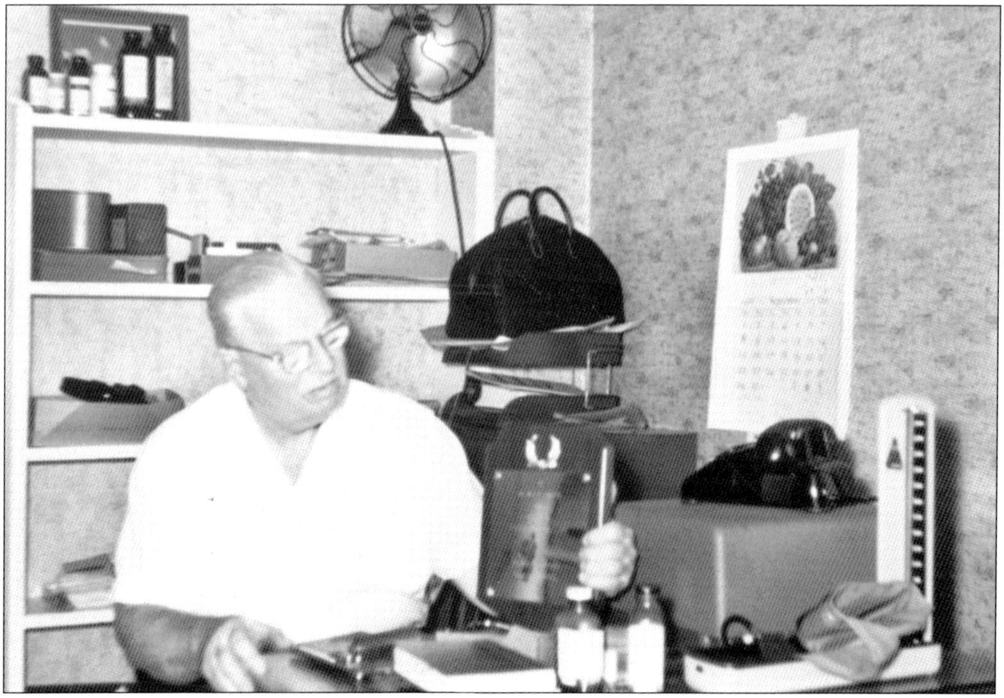

DR. MILTON M. SCHISLER. Dr. Schisler is seated in his office, where he also resided, on the northwest corner of West Second and Church Streets. He is remembered as the doctor who made house calls, no matter what hour of the day or night. Dr. Schisler came to Florence in the early 1930s. He was the attending physician for the Florence schools and all the sporting events in the town. (Courtesy of the Florence Historical Society.)

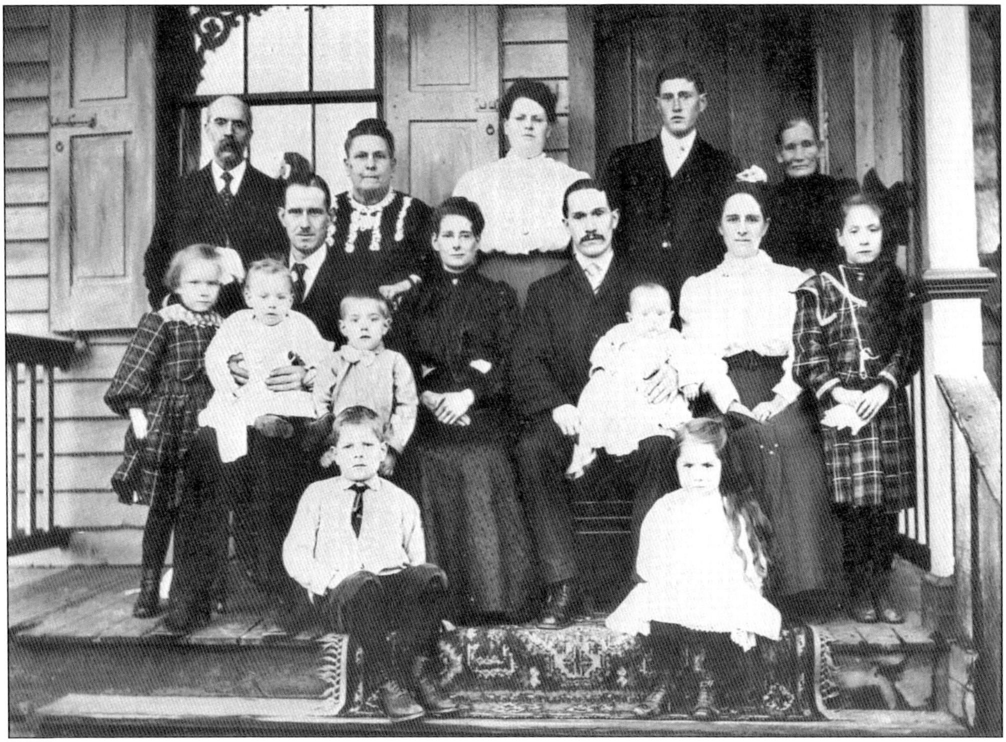

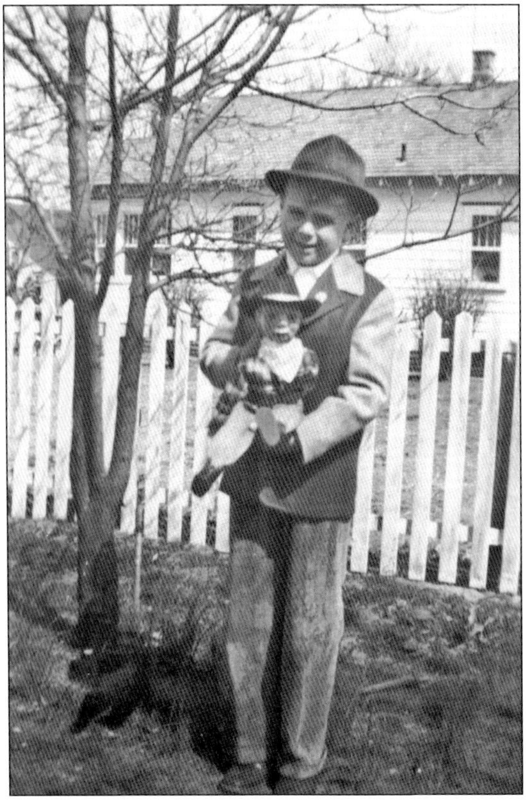

THE WILLITTS FAMILY. The Willitts family settled in Florence in the early 1900s. Minnie Willitts had 110 great-grandchildren when she died in 1967 at the age of 88. Pictured are (first row) Frank and Pearl Willitts; (second row) Gertie, Morris (holding Edgar), Irving Willitts, Minnie Etta, Haywood (holding Susie), his wife, Lizzie, and Roxy; (third row) Morris K., his wife, Maggie, Aunt Bertha, Uncle Elmer, and Aunty Huff (no relation). Morris worked at Florence Pipe Foundry and Machine Company. (Courtesy of Doris Jones.)

ALBERT L. KING. Standing with his Charlie McCarthy puppet, Albert King poses in the front yard of his home on West Fourth Street around 1949. His jacket was the popular style during this time period. He later became an outstanding machinist with US Steel and received several awards for his inventions. (Courtesy of Judith King.)

Seven

SCHOOLS

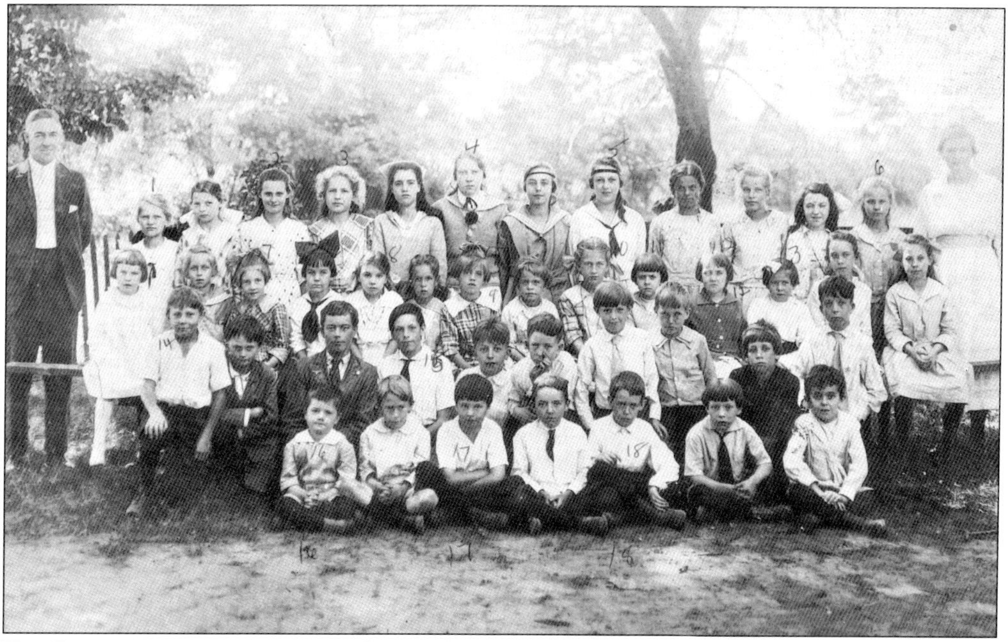

THE BUSTLETON SCHOOLHOUSE. The Bustleton schoolhouse was active in 1918, but it is now a private residence. Only Bustleton children attended, under Supt. Maja Mathis. The teacher in charge of one class was Rachel Harris. From left to right are (first row) Jim Carty, unidentified, Harry Carty, unidentified, Joe Tudor, and two unidentified; (second row) Stanley Wood, two unidentified, Biard Carty, and six unidentified; (third row) two unidentified, Edith Hathaway, unidentified, Nelly Carty, unidentified, Marie David, unidentified, Myra Hathaway, Florie Tudor, Doris Malseed, Edna Wood, and two unidentified; (fourth row) Margaret Malseed, unidentified, Isabel Bunting, Peg Abbott, unidentified, Adeline Malseed, unidentified, Marie Malseed, three unidentified, and May Handley. (Courtesy of Doris Malseed Krieger.)

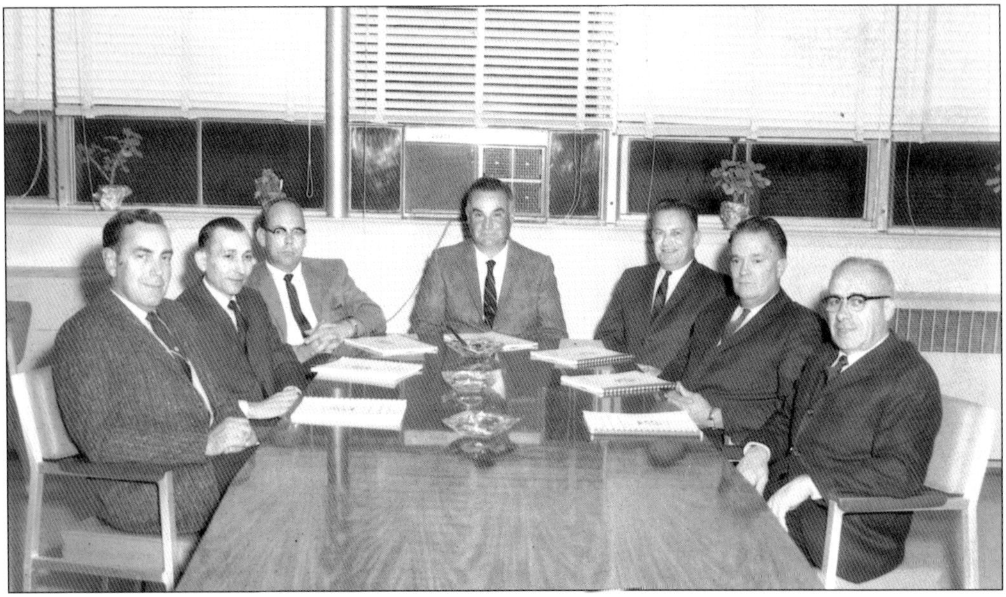

Florence Township Board of Education Members. Pictured in 1966 in the Florence Township Board of Education building are, from left to right, Lambert Rainier, Joseph Talpas, Clayton Mudge, John Oros, Robert Coates, Craig Bodine, and Samuel Cesaretti. Not shown is Nils Johnson. The building at 201 Cedar Street was known as "the Cottage" prior to 1964 and housed the home economics department of the high school. After an addition to the school, it became offices for the board of education. (Courtesy of Lynda Mudge Borgstrom.)

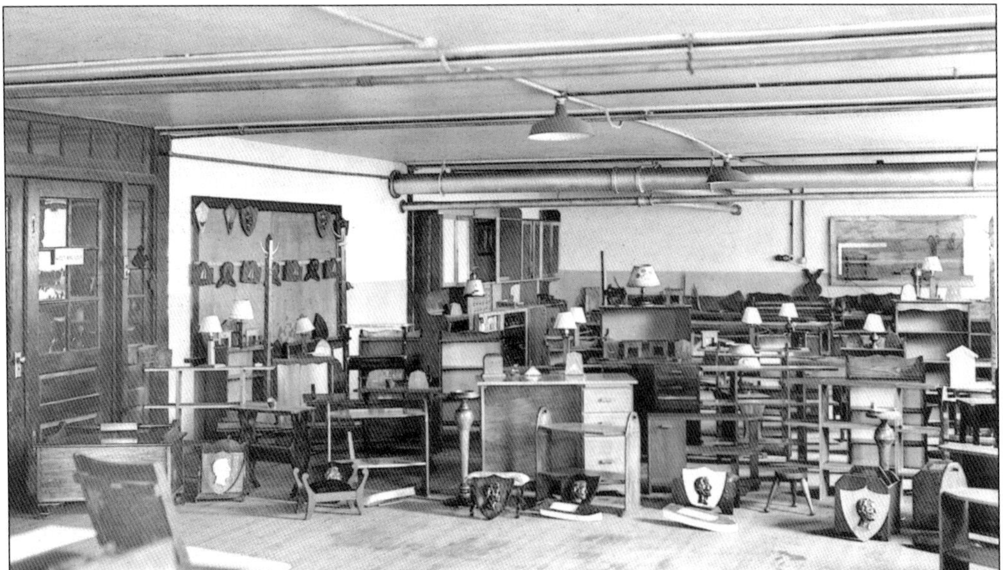

Industrial Arts. In the basement of Florence School No. 1, students learned industrial arts and created this large collection of items for home use. This late-1940s-era picture shows the large assortment of items the students chose to build. Some of the equipment used was originally from the H.B. Smith Machine Company in Smithville, which closed in the early 1900s. (Courtesy of Louis Borbi.)

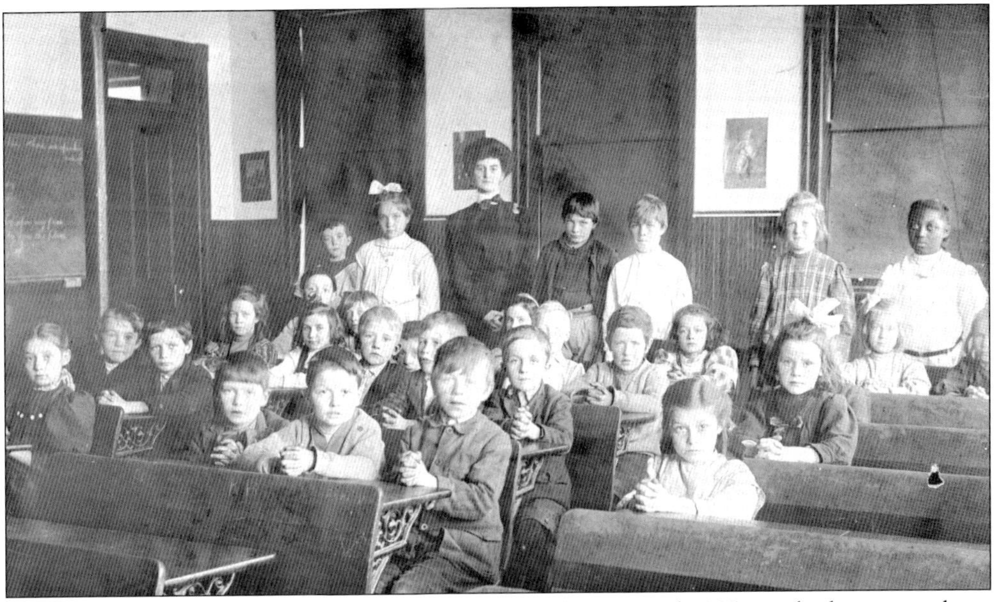

Cooking School. This delightful photograph was taken around 1905, at which time students from the Florence School were sent to Library Hall, located on West Front Street. There, cooking classes were held, the expense of which was covered by the Wood family, who operated the nearby foundry. One of the students is Lydia Brown, seated on the right in the second row and wearing a large bow in her hair. (Courtesy of Mary Bombelli Tapper.)

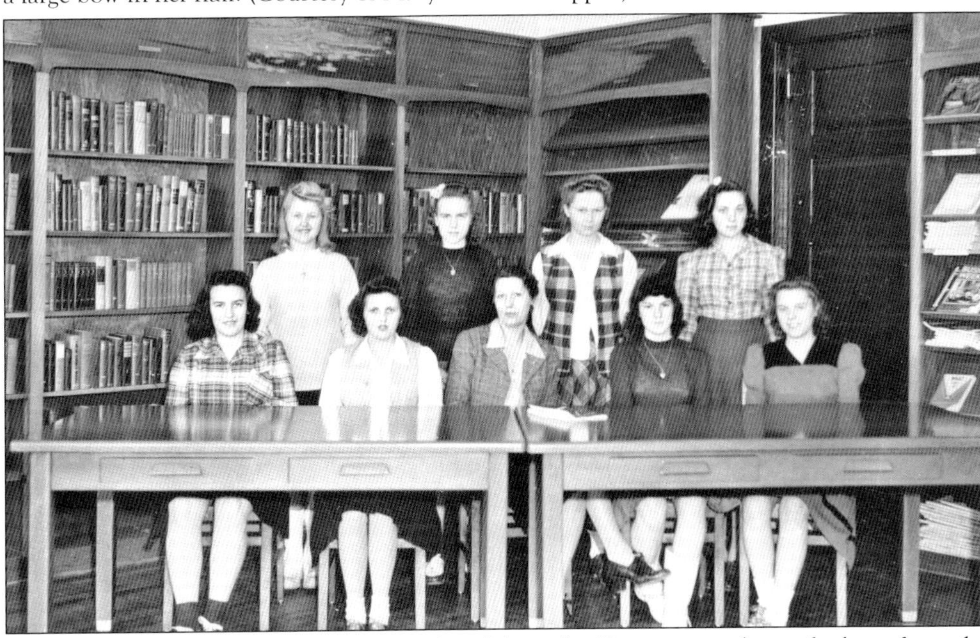

Junior Red Cross Club. The girls in this club made Christmas packages for boys from the high school who were in service in 1944. Here, they are pausing from making scrapbooks for the boys in an African hospital. From left to right are (first row) Barbara Trainor, Alma Thomas, Miss Strick (advisor), Agnes Cantwell, and Laura Jones; (second row) Claudine Quistberg, Doris Hamilton, Bernice Gorsky, and Dolores Wrabel. Absent is Gladys Henry. (Courtesy of the Florence Historical Society.)

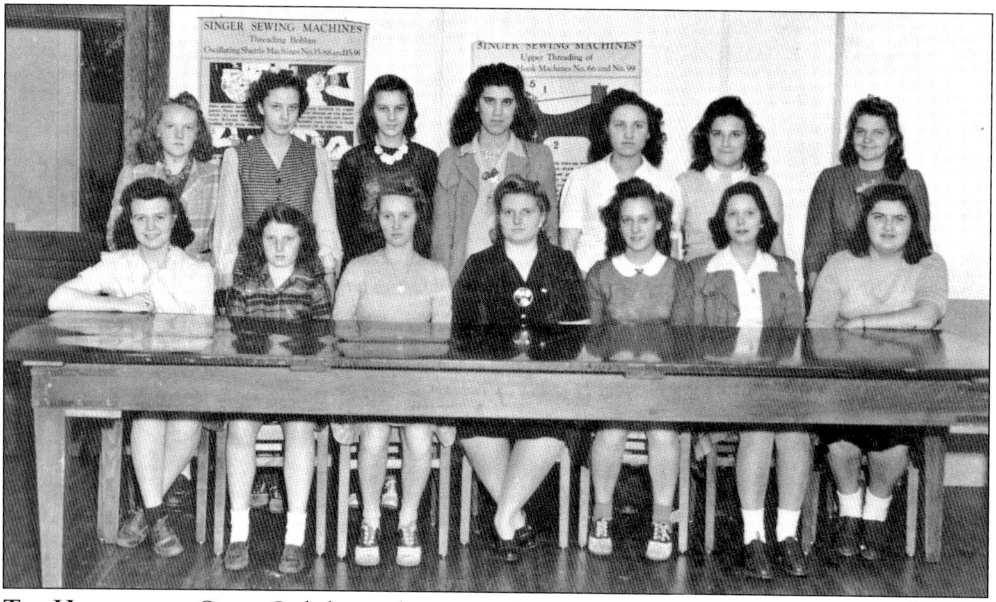

THE HANDICRAFT CLUB. Girls learned to sew, embroider, and crochet in this club, and in 1944, members aided the Red Cross Club in making Christmas packages for servicemen. Pictured are Helen Earley, Janet Hughes, Florence Adams, Miss Bragg (advisor), Doris Ullman, Margaret Csocsan and Dorothy Pustay; (second row) Alice Ekelburg, Vivian Andreason, Vivian Jones, Fannie Patriarca, Albina Lombardozzi, Catherine Bertuccini, and Arlene Shafer. (Courtesy of the Florence Historical Society.)

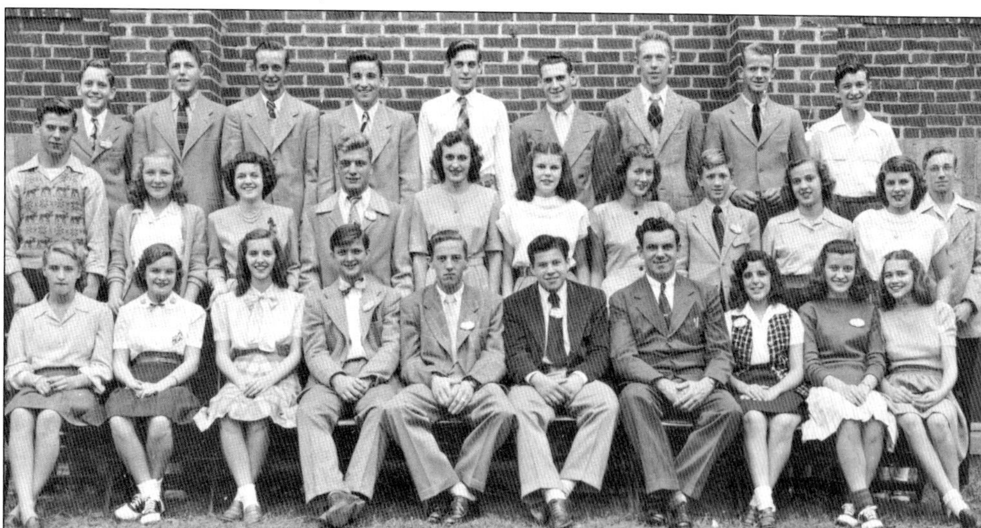

THE TRAFFIC COMMISSION. In 1948, the commission kept order and controlled traffic in the school building. Pictured are, from left to right, (first row) Shirley Watts, Nancy Lundin, Bettyjean Panaro, Lawrence Anderson, Alex Wargo, Robert Waterston, Mr. Krieger (advisor), Louise Fidati, Mary Szucs, and Yolanda Cepreghy; (second row) Thomas Phillips, Elaine Luyber, Jean Collum, Raymond Patriarca, Jean Adams, Claire Bonner, Betty Nell Gaskill, Mathias Kais, Janet Paykos, Kathleen McCabe, and Robert Miller; (third row) Robert Hughes, James Casey, Walter Giehl, Bruno Morichetti, Harold Roberts, Amerigo Mocini, Richard Hague, Walter Shafer, and Blair Craft. (Courtesy of the Florence Historical Society.)

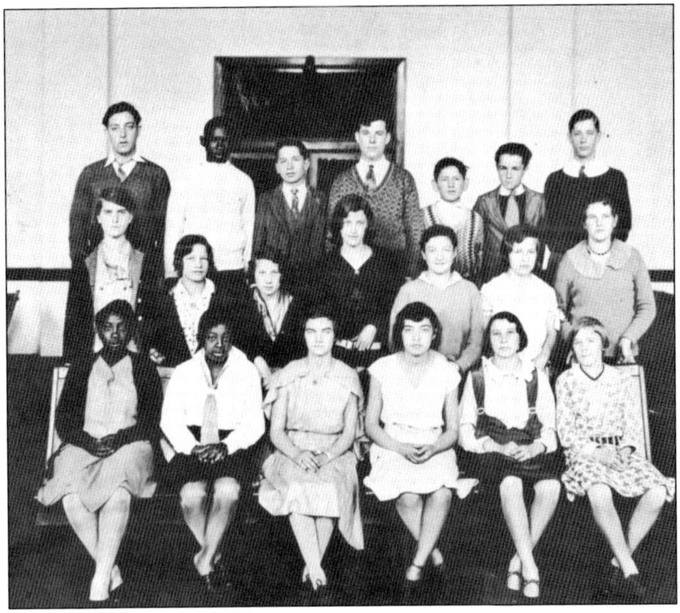

School No. 1. Around 1920, the following students posed for a formal picture. Pictured are (first row) Ann Yonnelle, M. ? Dobbins, Marge Garwood, Nellie Losito, "Sis" McHugh, and Mary Stackhouse; (second row) Katherine Conrey, Fannie Legnaioli, Linian Wilkie, Alice Meher, Viola Frappolli, Pauline Napoli, and Florence Runyon; (third row) Russell Woolston, Leroy Patterson, Tots Legnaioli, Olin Brinning, Benny Cardi, Elmer Hamilton, and Bob Patterson. (Courtesy of the Florence Historical Society.)

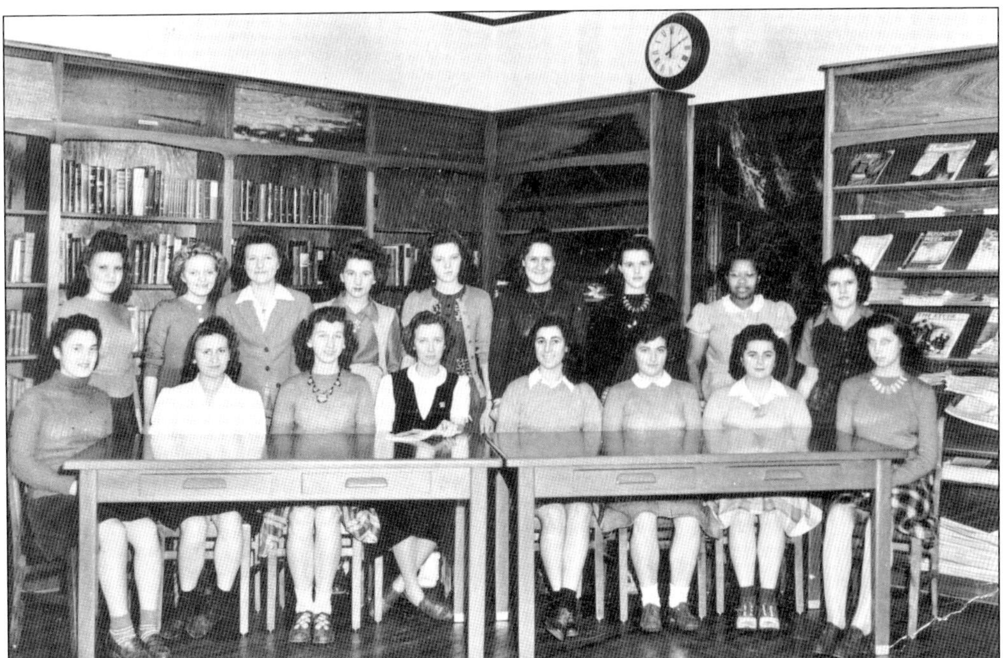

The Library Club. In 1944, the high school library club met as a committee to dust books, put books in order, and assist the librarians. Pictured are, from left to right, Catherine Carlani, Alice Conselice, Margaret Bojtos, Mrs. Zumeta (advisor), Lena Filipponi, Anna Gazsi, Loretta Kish, and Jean Cowan; (second row) Helen Zaniewski, Claire Gombos, Rose Barta, Margaret Bogdovich, Jean Pukenas, Irene Russ, Pauline Giehl, Ernestine Dobbins, and Matilda Dobos. (Courtesy of the Florence Historical Society.)

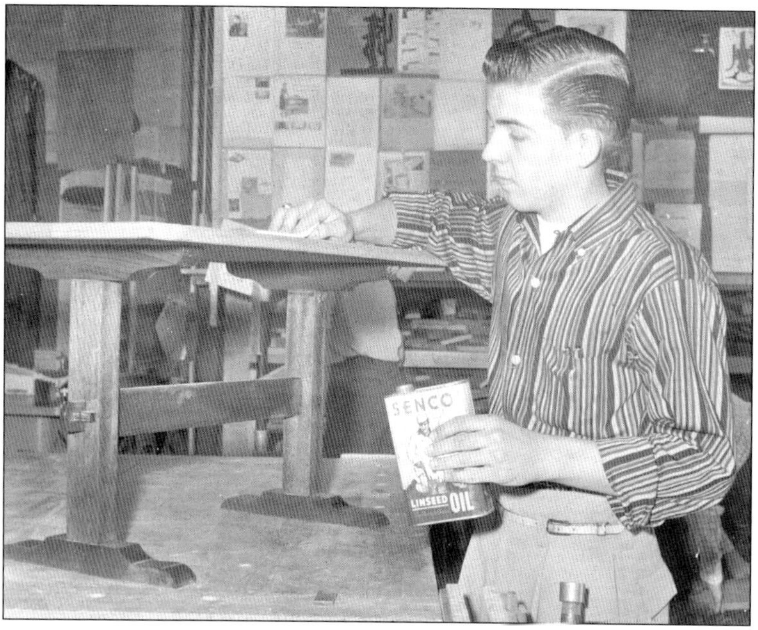

Paul Sisz Jr. At the sixth annual Mideast Industrial Arts Fair in the late 1950s, Paul Sisz Jr. applies linseed oil to the table he will enter for judging. He now owns the Sportsmen's Center in Bordentown, New Jersey. (Courtesy of the Florence Historical Society.)

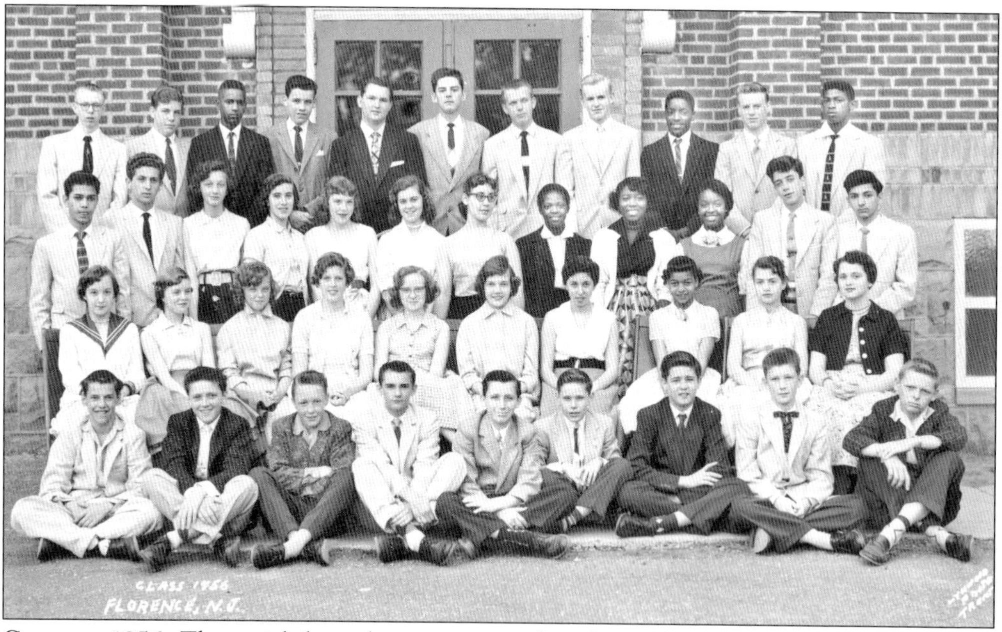

Class of 1956. These eighth graders are arranged in front of the Florence School No. 1 on West Second Street. From left to right are (first row) Frederick Knapp, Frank Sweeney, William Sweeney, James Mills, William Hulehan, unidentified, Earl Copper, Richard Coates, and Robert Sitzler; (second row) Joyce Woolston, Marsha Hughes, Catherine Mullen, Marie Smith, ? Dubell, Dorothy Lou Wright, Betty Farah, Helen Grice, Virginia Wieland, and Sharon Worth; (third row) Robert Lanzalotti, Jack Campbell, Shirley Chapman, Louvenia White, Inez Loftin, Evelyn Sayers, Loretta Black, Connie Trader, Jean Roscani, Barbara Wolfe, Wayne Savalli, and Dan Carnival; (fourth row) Richard Dennison, unidentified, Joel Burns, Steven Carr, John Doherty, Vincent Carey, Edward Schafle, David Ames, Robert Morton, Robert Campbell, and Gilbert West. (Courtesy of the Florence Historical Society.)

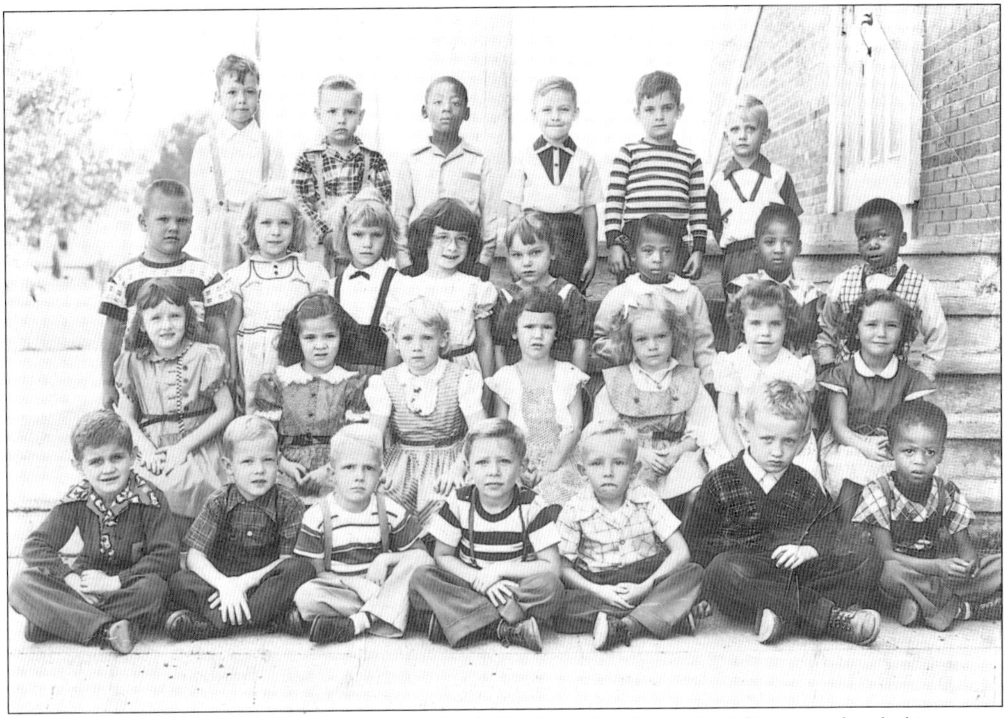

FOURTH STREET SCHOOL. Also known as Little Duffy School, this building was divided into two classrooms. Kindergarten students pictured in 1953, from left to right, are (first row) Billy Green, Bob Hammell, Dall Hammell, Larry Crammer, Bill Olevich, Michael Joy, and Victor Smith; (second row) Sharon Ford, Arlene Jones, Sharon Smith, Donna Stout, Marilyn Coates, Donna Boyle, and ? Lubrano; (third row) Ken Jobes, two unidentified, Linda Yannarella, Kathy Coates, two unidentified, and Tyrone Bond; (fourth row) Karl Birgl, three unidentified, Roger Brooks, and Claude Anderson. (Courtesy of Paul Anderson.)

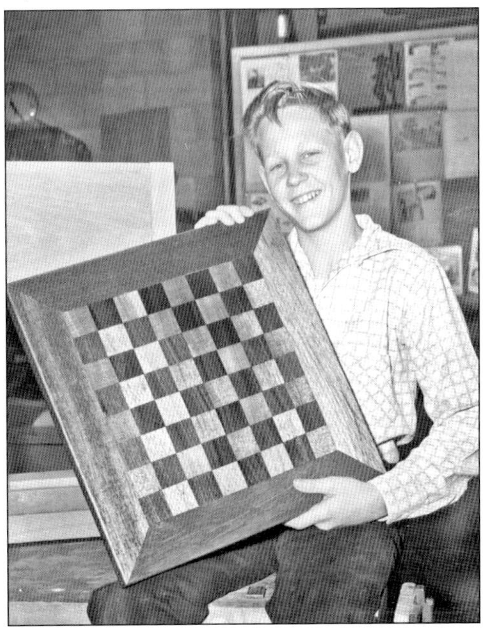

ROBERT CAMPBELL. At the sixth annual Mideast Industrial Arts Fair in the late 1950s, Robert Campbell proudly displays an inlaid checkerboard tabletop he will enter for judging. (Courtesy of the Florence Historical Society.)

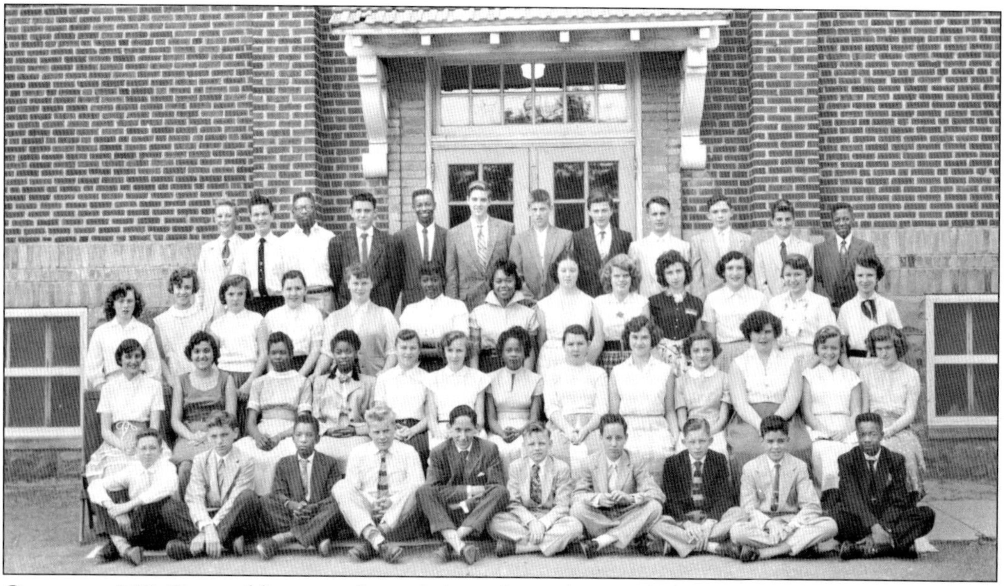

Class of 1955. Pictured here are the eighth-grade graduates of Florence School No. 1. From left to right are (first row) Francis Berry, Bruce Knapp, Clarence Johnson, James Jobes, Charles Farah, Paul Anderson, Terrence Hennessy, Woodrow Smith, Jack Sweeney, and Daniel Ellington; (second row) Dorothy Santoleri, Louise Cicero, Betty Cooper, Barbara Wilson, Doris DeCamp, Carole Jones, Rosaline Ellington, Carol Doherty, Jane Evans, Joan Durham, Georgeanna Smith, Shirley Johnson, and Hannah Elliott; (third row) Lorraine Lewis, Judith Molnar, Shirley Snyder, Judith Doherty, Marsha Hughes, Janice Tutt, Marcia Scott, Patricia Joy, Marie Bennett, Betty Lou Grovatt, Marie Baldarossi, Marianne Walk, and Janira Stowell; (fourth row) Joe Pasqualine, Joe Ingham, James West, Clark Carey, James Scott, Hilyard Simpkins, Joe Smith, Robert Trader, Robert Smith, Jack Fuls, Wilmer Bauer, and Markham Chapman. (Courtesy of the Florence Historical Society.

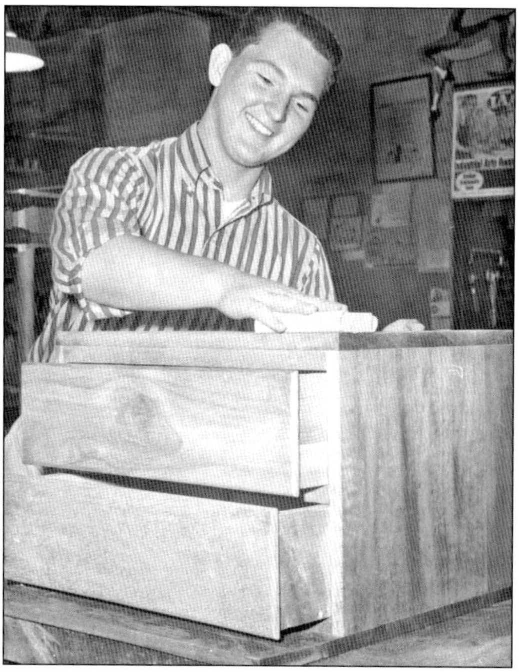

John Doherty. John Doherty begins the final sanding of a mahogany night table he will enter at the sixth annual Mideast Industrial Arts Fair in the late 1950s. (Courtesy of the Florence Historical Society.)

Eight

Social Organizations

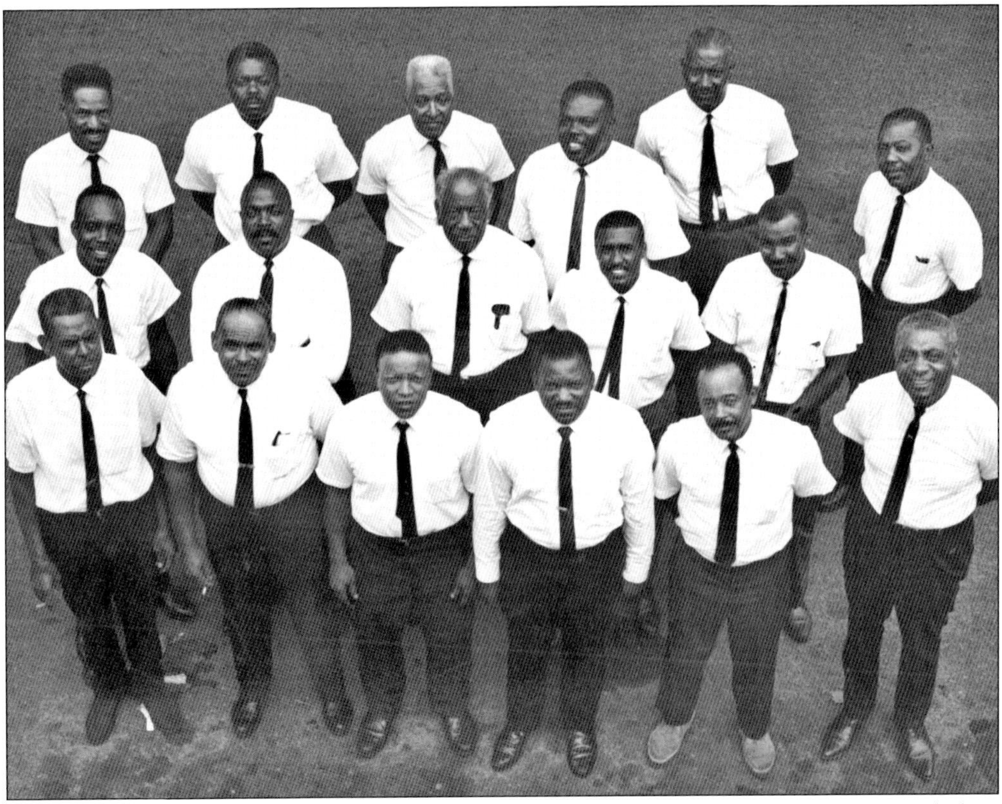

The Grand Dukes Club. Members of the Grand Dukes Club in downtown Florence, including some founding members, are shown in an undated picture. Located at the northwest corner of West Third and Iron Streets, the club is no longer in use. From left to right are (first row) Howard Furnell, Josh Tucker, Sylvester Morton, Ernest Curry, ? Nelson, and "Big Ed" Edmond Gorham; (second row) Richard Epps, Roscoe Cleveland, Alfred Shephard, Clifford Chapman, Elmont Henry, and Robert Hill; (third row) Herman Richardson, Horace Cleveland, "Old Man" Ulysses Morton, Mervin Johnson, and unidentified. Not in the picture is Ervin Scott, one of the originators. The Grand Dukes had a baseball team, and in 1958, seven members were on the Delaware Valley League All-Star Team. The club also had a crack drill team, with adults and children, who dazzled the spectators at local parades. (Courtesy of Thomas Sahol.)

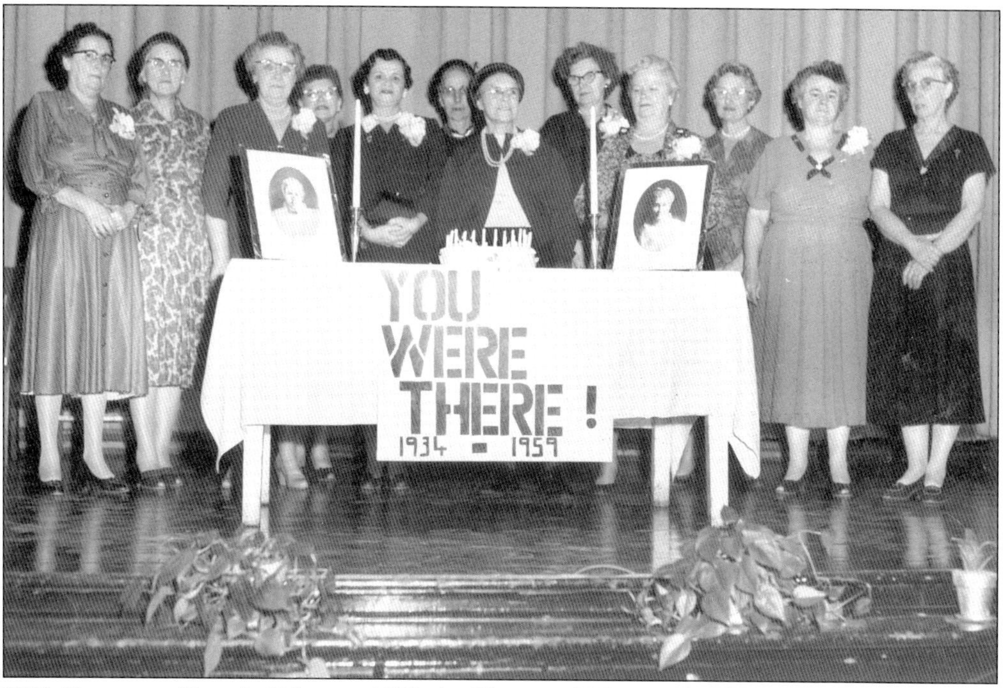

PTA Founders Day. In February 1959, the Florence PTA met for the presentation of pins to members. From left to right are Mrs. Arthur Foulks, Margaret Patrick, Mrs. Charles Peacock, Mrs. Charles Banks, Emma Trader, Alma Bozarth, Reba Troxell of Burlington (County PTA chairperson), Eleanor Donnelly, Irene Connors, Mary Quig, Nolah Sutphin, and Ada Hamilton. (Courtesy of the Florence Historical Society.)

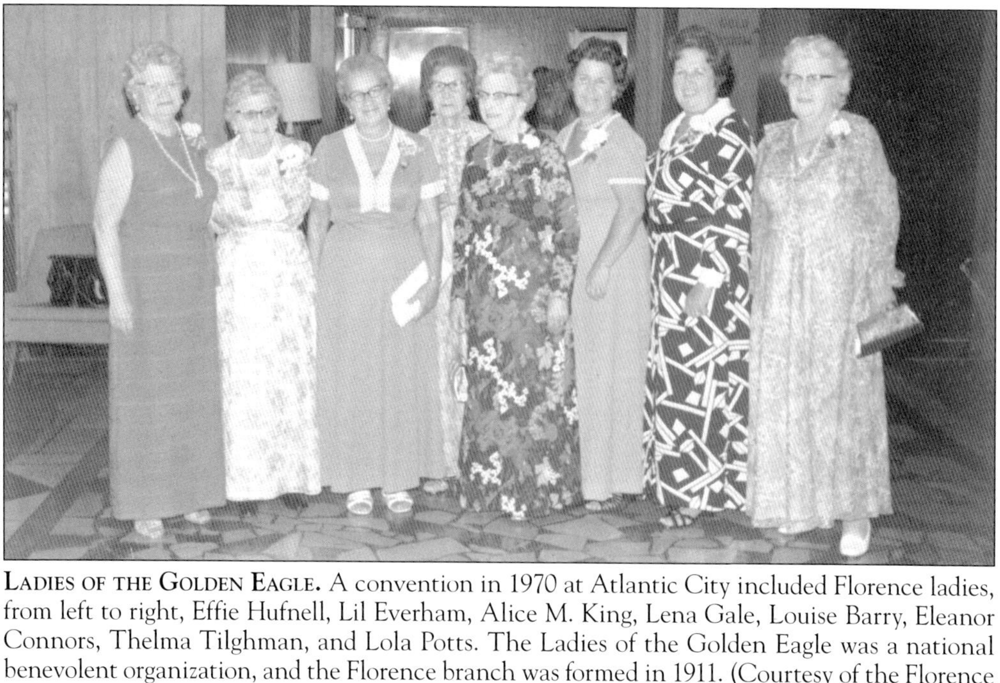

Ladies of the Golden Eagle. A convention in 1970 at Atlantic City included Florence ladies, from left to right, Effie Hufnell, Lil Everham, Alice M. King, Lena Gale, Louise Barry, Eleanor Connors, Thelma Tilghman, and Lola Potts. The Ladies of the Golden Eagle was a national benevolent organization, and the Florence branch was formed in 1911. (Courtesy of the Florence Historical Society.)

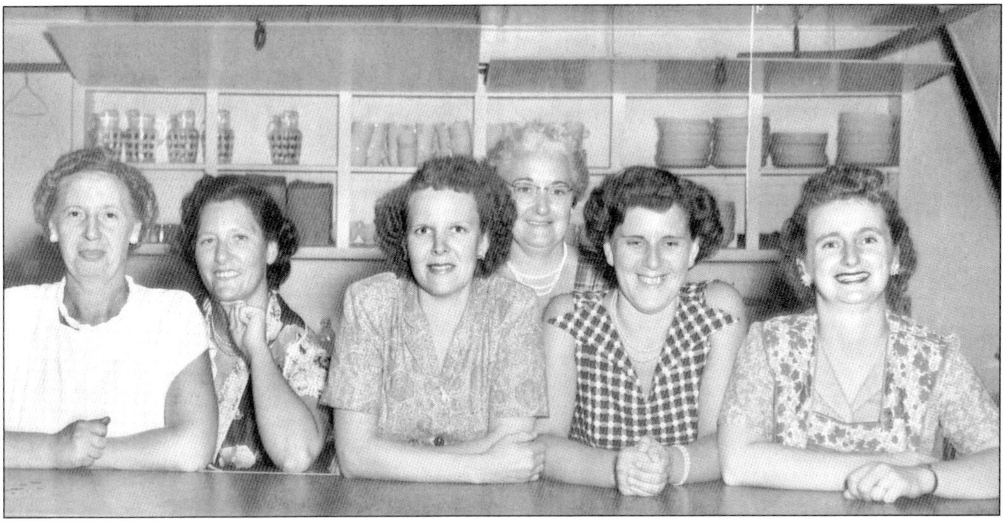

AMERICAN LEGION AUXILIARY. In July 1952, members of the Ladies Auxiliary of American Legion Post 194 pose at their building on West Second Street. In front, from left to right, are Jemima Sanderson, Catherine Kalwaitis, Edie Bryden, Mary Conrey, and Jean Hughes; in the back is Amanda Rue. Many wedding receptions and other social events were also held in this building. (Courtesy of the Florence Historical Society.)

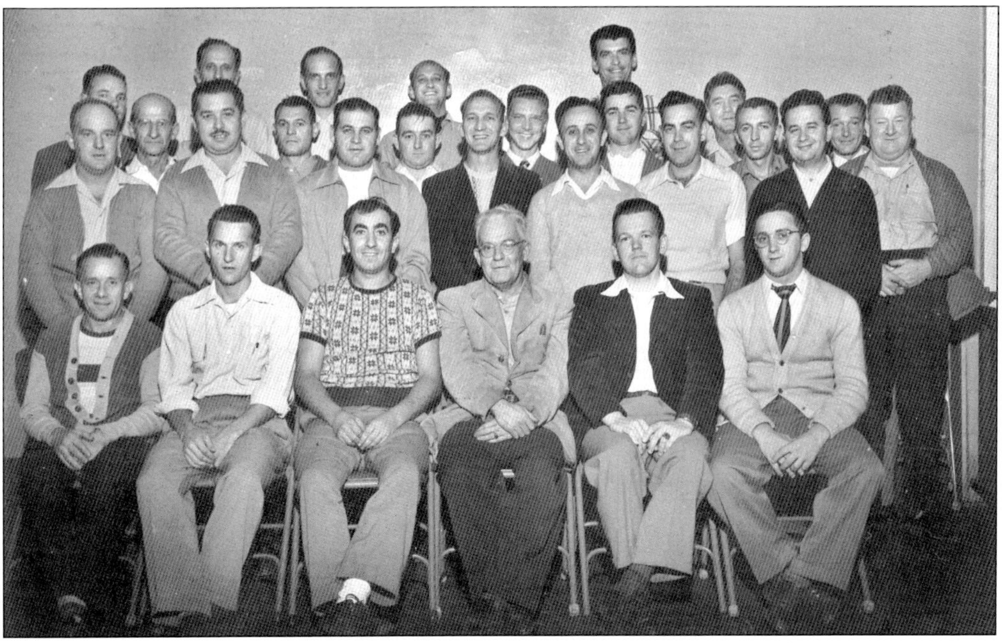

AMERICAN LEGION MEMBERS, 1947. This large group of men met for a formal portrait at Post 194. From left to right are (first row) Paul Hammell, Arthur "Corky" Warren, Robert "Crabapples" Filipponi, Arthur Green, Bill Spencer, and Mike Lubrano; (second row) "Reds" Miller, "Blimp" Cicero, Dave Lyons, Albert "Nudge" Hamilton, "Jingles" Carl Lubrano, Lambert Rainier, Tots Legnaioli, and Grady Walsh; (third row) "Big Nose" Dougherty, Marino "Sweaty" Agostinelli, Amerigo "Sacky" Stefanoni, Karl Sayers, Emmett Beckett, Al ?, and unidentified; (fourth row) two unidentified, Marvin Foulks, unidentified, and John Marinkos. (Courtesy of the Florence Historical Society.)

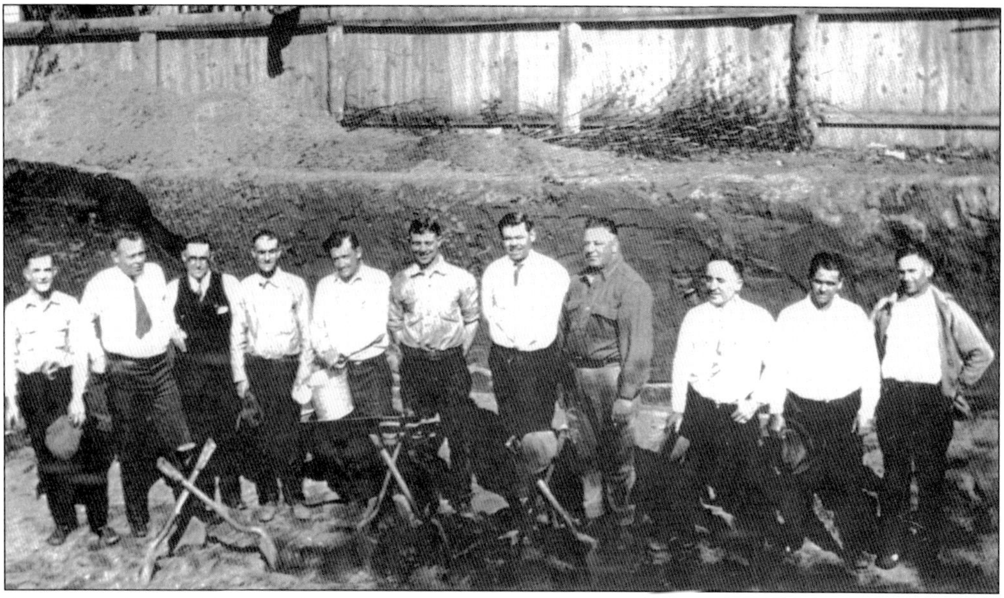

American Legion Ground Breaking. Ground breaking of the American Legion Post 194 took place around 1930 in the first block of West Second Street. Before that, the Legion met at the old hotel at the southwest corner of Front and Broad Streets. Standing are, from left to right, Ruby Gilbert, Clark Boyd, Frank Absalom, Raymond Thompson, Frank Peacock, Jim Cryan, Bud Pippit, "Skip" Griffith, Carlos ?, Tom Mullen, and Bill Roughton. This building is now a day care center. (Courtesy of the Florence Historical Society.)

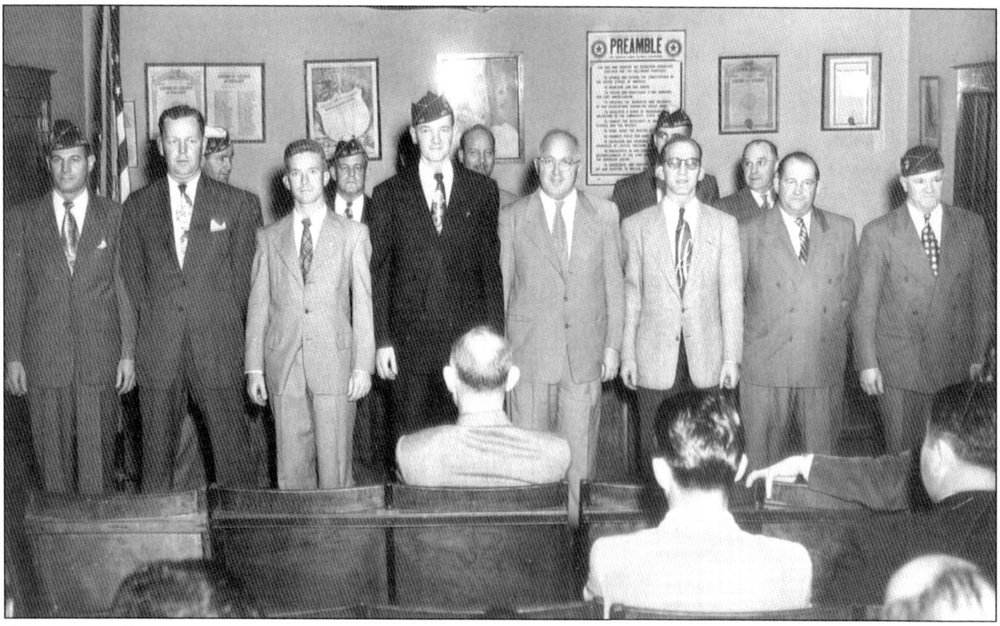

American Legion Installation, 1950. In October 1950, installation of members took place at the West Second Street building. From left to right are (first row) Hugh Lyon, Edward Shafle, Douglas Anderson, H. Kenneth Wilkie, Dick Cavanaugh, Albert "Nudge" Hamilton, Frank Peacock, and Joe Rue; (second row) unidentified, Nelson Tapper, Bill Parker, unidentified, and Frank Absalom. (Courtesy of the Florence Historical Society.)

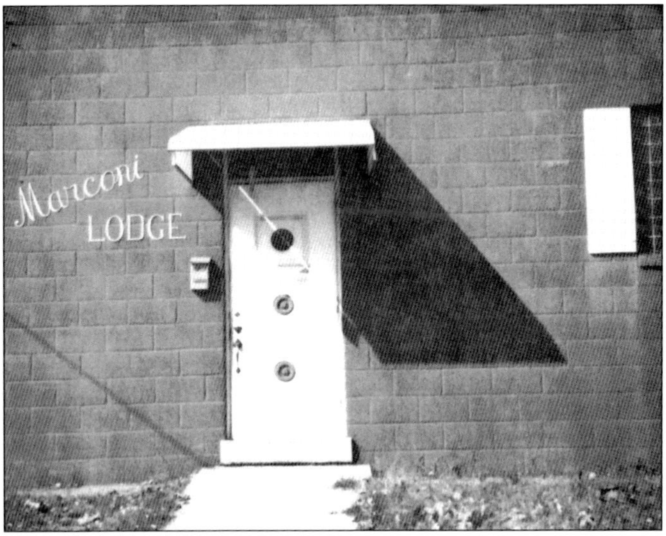

Marconi Lodge. Located at Foundry and West Third Streets, this organization was operating as far back as 1934 (and maybe even earlier). Its members made up the only undefeated team in the township softball circuit in 1947. Also known as Electra Marconi Lodge in 1963, it was a social organization of Italian people with activities such as weddings and dinners, and had a bocce ball court in the neighborhood. The building is no longer in use. (Courtesy of the Florence Historical Society.)

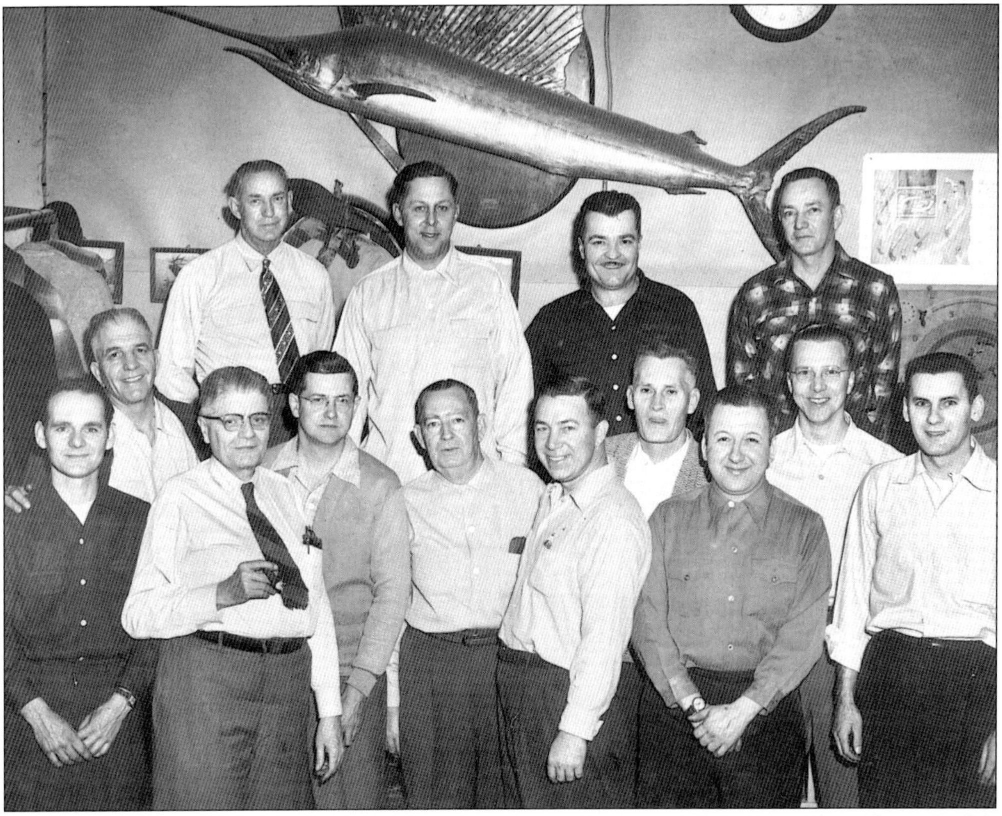

Florence Rifle and Pistol Club, 1955. In 1955, members of the Florence Rifle and Pistol Club again met for an informal photograph. This is thought to be their room at Library Hall where most meetings were held. Pictured are, from left to right, (first row) two unidentified, Arnold Sayers (standing sideways), and two unidentified; (second row) two unidentified, James Tapper Sr., Clair Daniel, and Karl Sayers; (third row) Bert Lutes, unidentified, Fred Linda, and Gus Nippins, (Courtesy of Norman Anderson.)

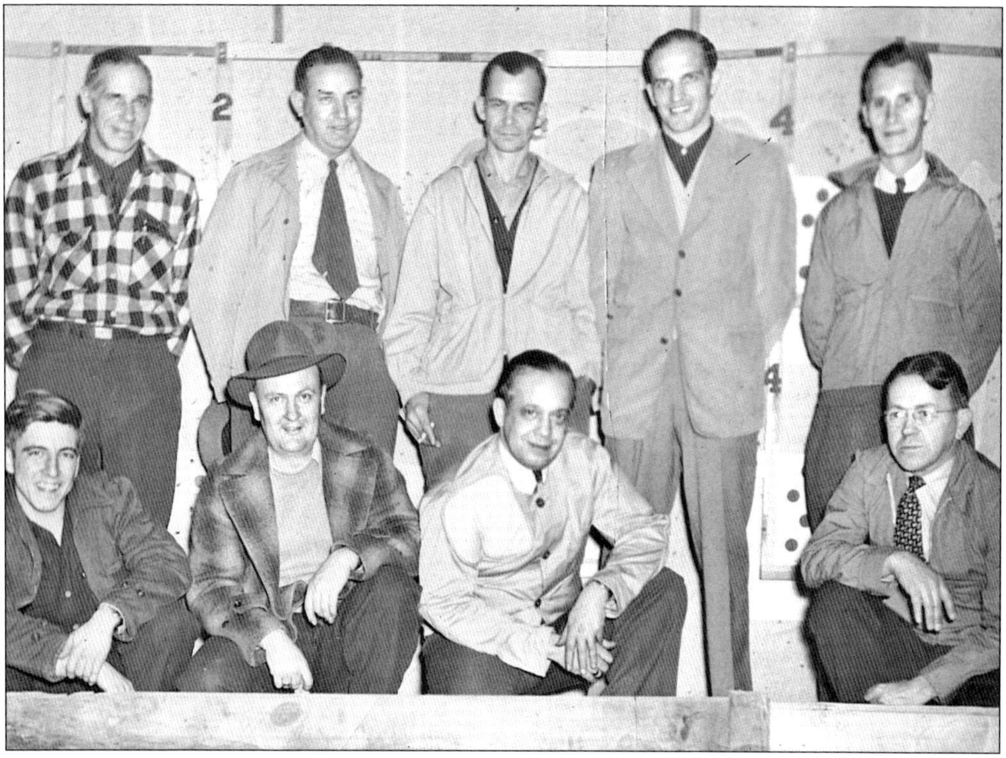

Florence Rifle and Pistol Club, 1940. Founded in 1937, the Florence Rifle and Pistol Club met at Library Hall, and meetings also involved target shooting in the basement. In this c. 1940s picture are, from left to right, (first row) unidentified, Raymond Joy of Florence, Frank DeGeorge of Mount Holly, and Wilber Bishop of Florence; (second row) Bill Fest of Mount Holly, "Bert" Lutes of Florence, Herb Miller of Roebling, Marvin Foulks of Florence, and Clair Daniel of Florence. (Courtesy of Norman Anderson.)

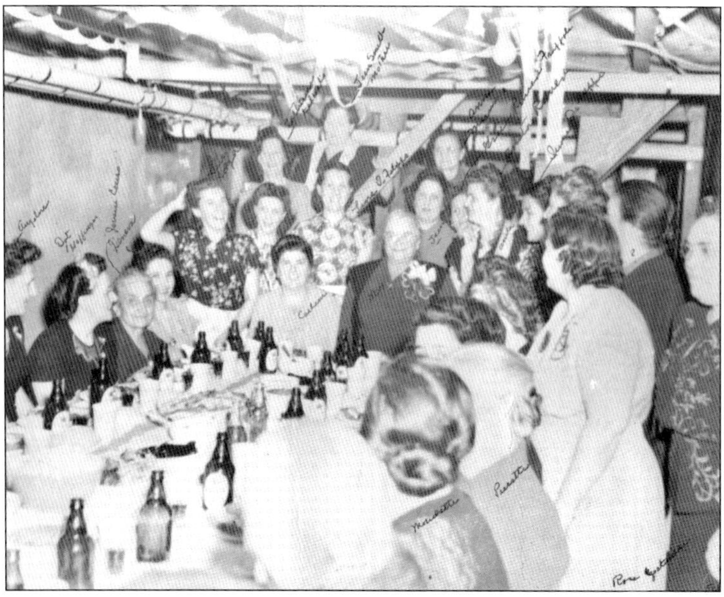

Marconi Lodge Ladies. This dinner celebrates the new president of the Italian Club Lodge, Aldemania Legnaioli (center with the corsage). Some of the other ladies pictured are Catherine Kalwaitis, Rose Agostinelli, Dot Hofflinger, a Mrs. Cicero, a Mrs. Carlani, a Mrs. Frappolli, Lena DiFilippo, a Mrs. Pieretti, a Mrs. Morichetti, Geneva ?, Jean Smith, and Sue Sozio. (Courtesy of Tots Legnaioli.)

Nine

SPORTS

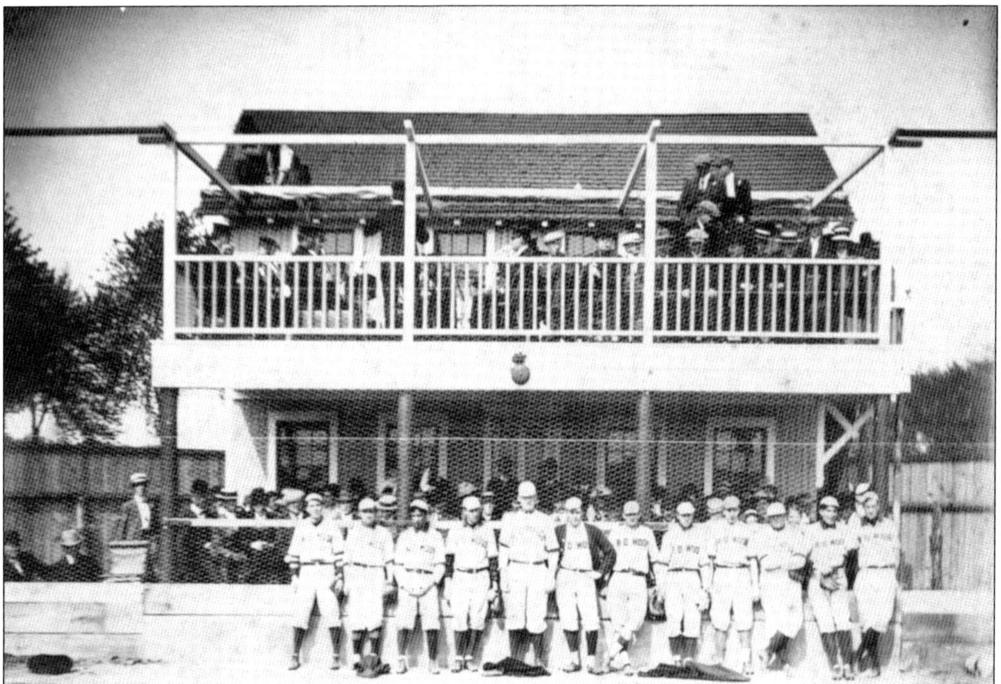

R.D. WOOD FIELD CLUBHOUSE. Designed from plans similar to Shibe Park in Philadelphia, this clubhouse on West Fifth Street hosted all local baseball games in Florence. This picture appears to be from the early 1900s, judging from the straw hats and other popular hats of the day. Twelve members of the R.D. Wood team ready themselves for another summer day of baseball. (Courtesy of Wayne Campbell.)

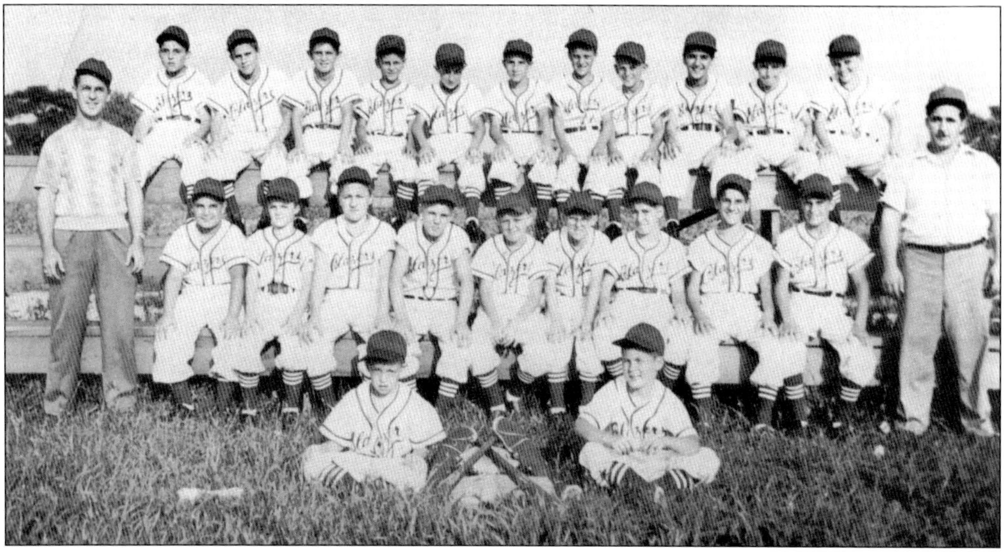

Florence Little League Baseball Team. In 1951, the Florence Little League baseball team had a large number of players. From left to right are (first row) batboys Bobby Sitzler and Edwin Bordoni; (second row) manager John Brining, Gino DiFilippo, Butch Bordoni, Bobby Buck, Dave Dennison, Lee Bassett, Warren Burmeister, Charlie Craft, Frank Santoleri, Tony Stefanoni, and manager Marrow Bordoni; (third row) Albert Morichetti, Bobby Pitman, Phil Cesaretti, Sam Rinaldi, Mike Fantozzi, Bobby Machion, Basil Santoleri, Richie Rinaldi, Bob Travia, Francis Baldorossi, and Les Sitzler. (Courtesy of Fran Legnaioli.)

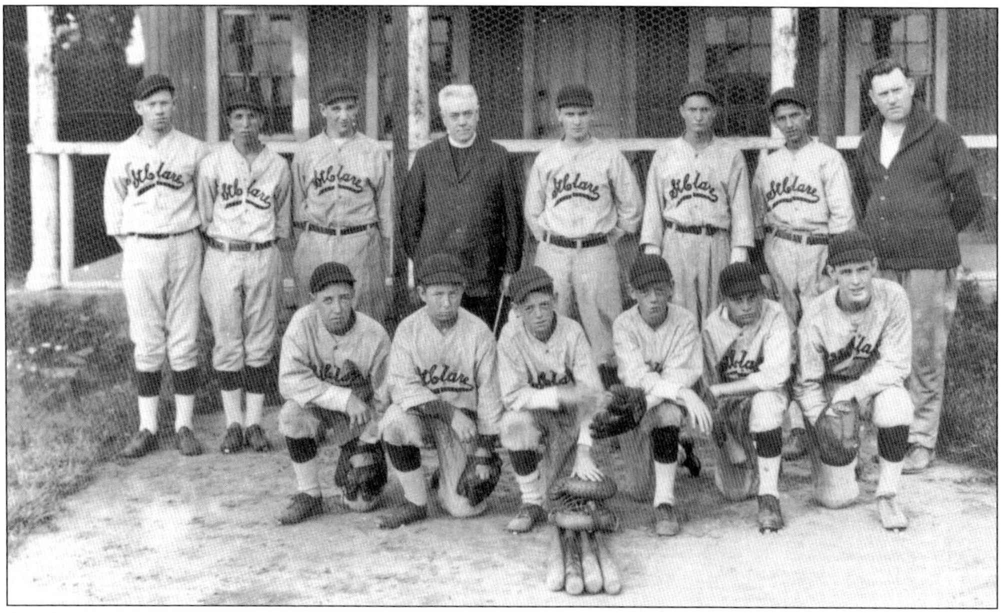

St. Clare Church Baseball Team. In the 1940s, St. Clare's Church also played baseball at the R.D. Wood Field on West Fifth Street. Pictured, from left to right, are (first row) Tom Watson, Leonard "Skeeter" Murphy, Jack Sweeney Jr., Frank Sweeney, Joe McHugh, and Joe Murphy; (second row) James "Toots" Downey, Joe Paglione, Cletus Cunningham, Fr. Edward Cahill (priest of St. Clare's), Ed Reed, Bill Woodington, Mike Drangula, and Jack Sweeney Sr. (manager). (Courtesy of the Florence Historical Society.)

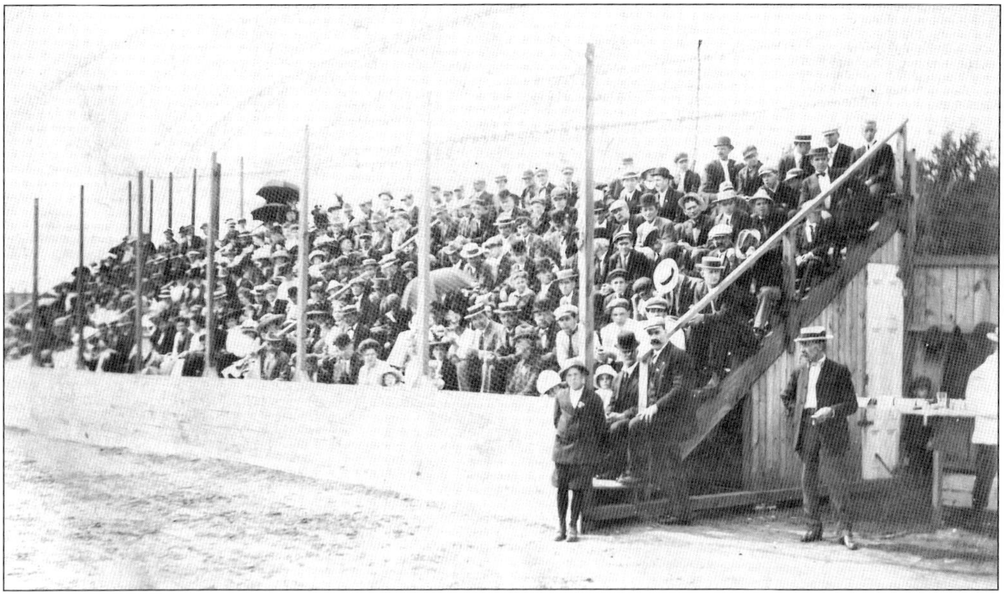

R.D. WOOD GRANDSTAND. Baseball was a popular sport in Florence beginning in the late 1800s. The Burlington County Baseball League formed in 1898, and Florence was admitted as a charter member. The Mayflowers were the first known baseball team for Florence, with the Rosebuds coming later. The national pastime of baseball has flourished in the county since 1846. This collection of spectators appears to date before 1920, judging from the men's straw hats and the upswept hair of the lady in the front row. (Courtesy of Wayne Campbell.)

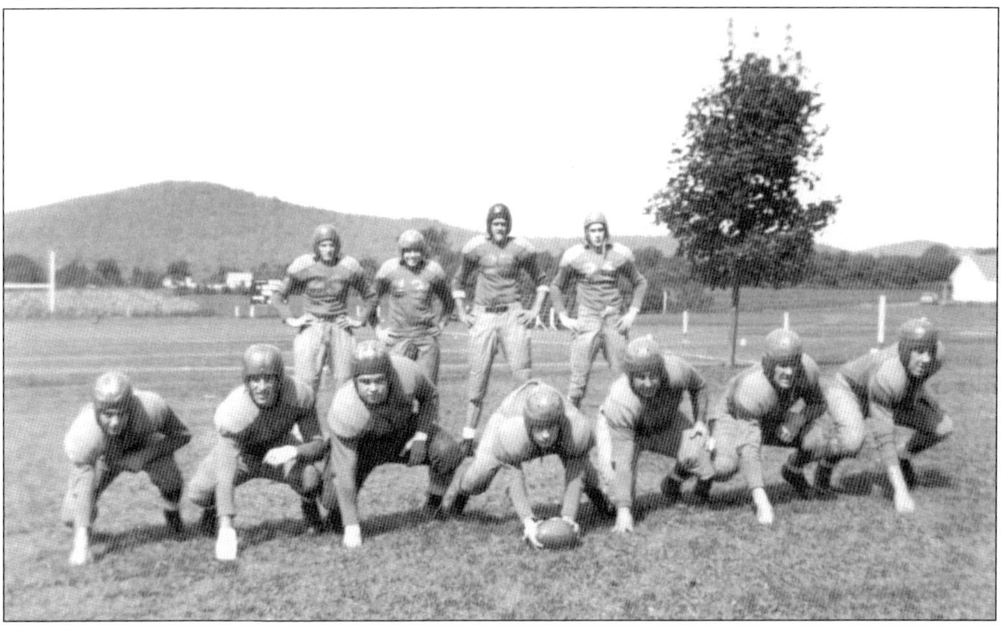

FLORENCE HIGH FOOTBALL, 1942. The first football team of the Florence High School played against Washington Township, New Jersey, in September 1942. Team members are, from left to right, (first row) John Mazur, John Livarchik, Ed Cronin, Al Joyce, John Malmos, Rodman Harris, and Thomas Maloney; (second row) William Elliott, Milton Hershberger, John Quig, and Robert Archibald. The Washington team won against Florence, 6-0. (Courtesy of Lou Borbi and Andrew Napolitan.)

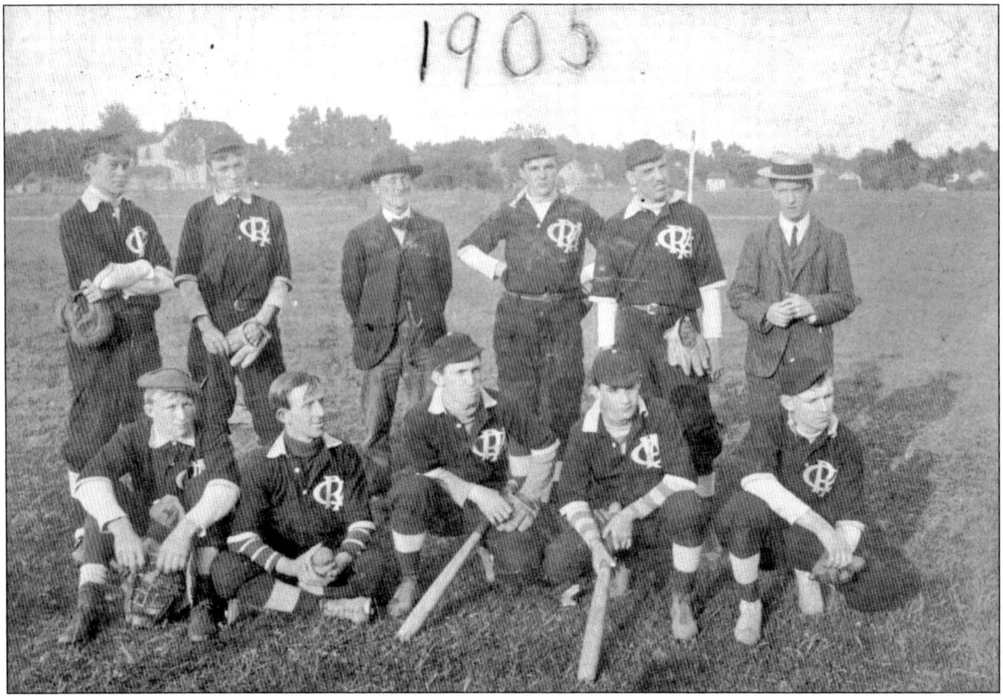

Baseball Team, 1905. This unidentified baseball team poses at R.D. Wood field in 1905. From left to right are (first row) are Bill Horn, Bill Foulks, Arthur Pettit, Bill Absalom, and Newt Gibbs; (second row) Fred Hamilton, John Roe, Bill Pettit, Frank Absalom, Carlton Parker, and Thomas Marr. (Courtesy of Edith Peacock.)

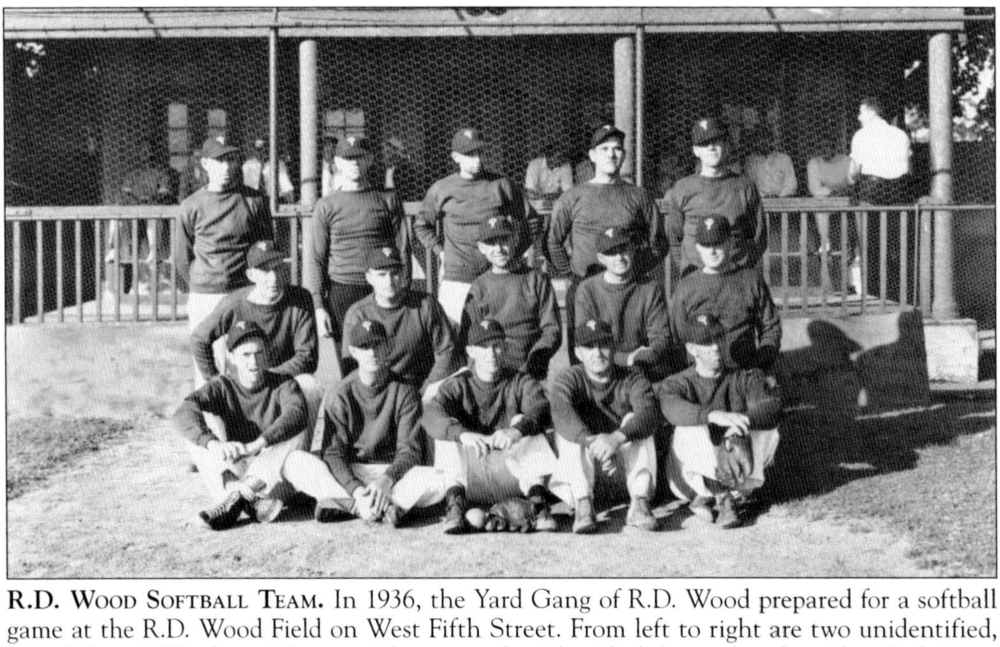

R.D. Wood Softball Team. In 1936, the Yard Gang of R.D. Wood prepared for a softball game at the R.D. Wood Field on West Fifth Street. From left to right are two unidentified, John "Nanny" Woolston, Norman Johnson, and unidentified; (second row) unidentified, Toots Downey, Bill Everham, and two unidentified. The entire third row is unidentified. (Courtesy of Sam Filippine.)

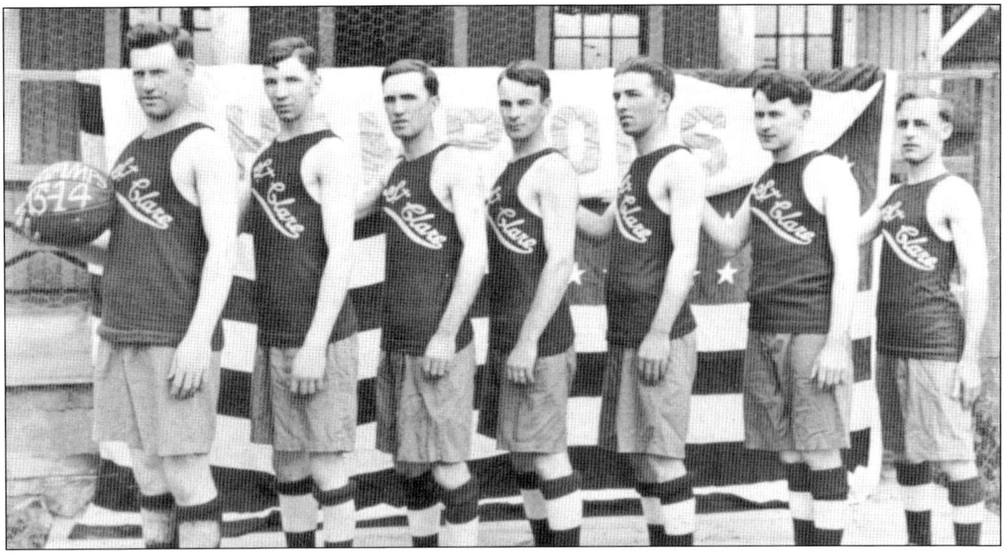

St. Clare's Basketball Team. This c. 1925 photograph shows the St. Clare's Church basketball team preparing for another competition in Florence. Most basketball games were held in the St. Stephen's Church Parish Hall on Broad Street on the first floor. The ball was thrown over the crossbeams of the building into the basket at the far end. From left to right are Jack Sweeney, Emmett Beckett, Philip McGrath, Tom Keely, Martin McGrath, Frank Fitzpatrick, and Bill McGrath. (Courtesy of John Williams.)

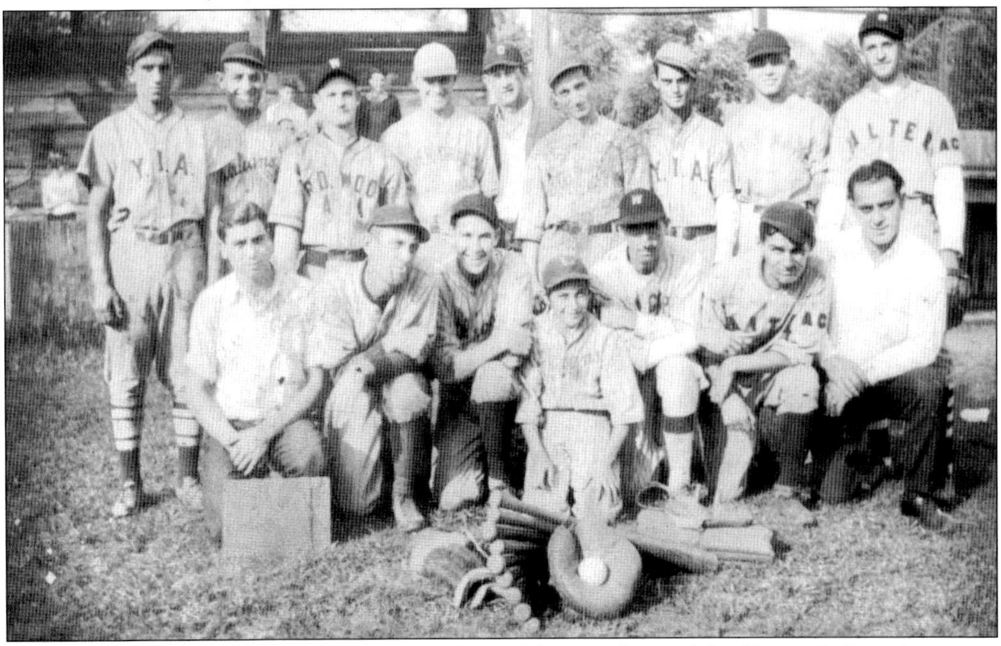

YIA All Stars Baseball Team, 1935. Most of the members of the Young Italian American club lived downtown. From left to right are (first row) Renaldo Rinaldi, Jesse Foulks, Joe McHugh, Marino Agostinelli (batboy), Cletus Cunningham, Jack Rhoda, and Tony Moscati; (second row) "Cow" Cicero, Sam Rinaldi, "Reds" Frappolli, "Mimi" Wallace, Charlie Peacock, "Bardy" Frappolli, Bill Woodington, "Buck" Beaudry, and Mike Buccigrossi. (Courtesy of the Florence Historical Society.)

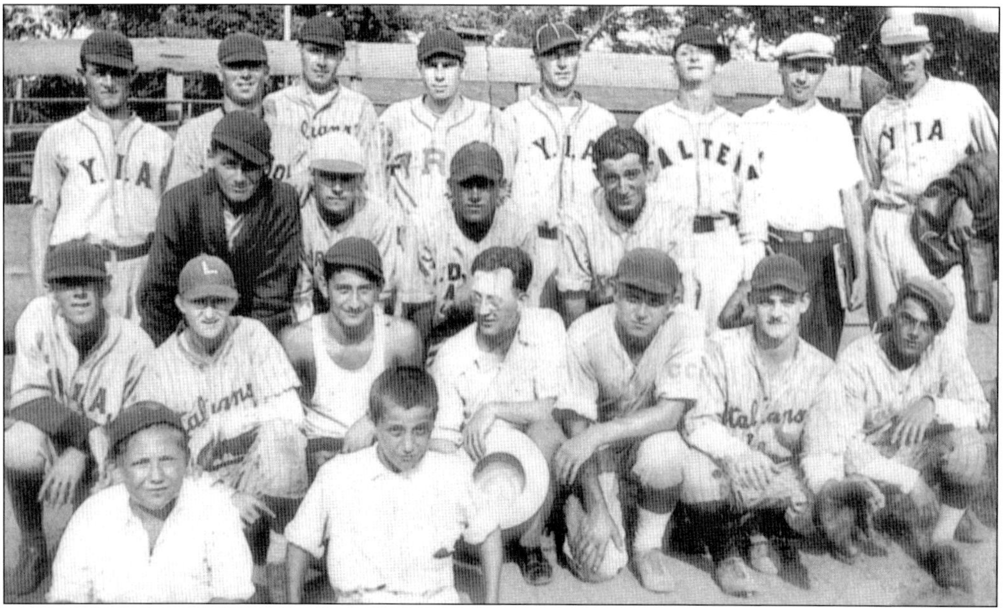

The 1940 YIA All Stars Baseball Team. This c. 1940 photograph shows a large number of team members on a summer day in Florence. From left to right are (first row) batboys "Beans" Agostinelli and Marino Agostinelli; (second row) ? Foulks, Fritz DeFlece, Mike Buccigrossi, Jimmy Dinucci, unidentified, Reds Frappolli, and Bill Woodington; (third row) unidentified umpire, Mimi Wallace, Jack Rhoda, and Bardy Frappolli; (fourth row) Sam Rinaldi, Merski Cardi, Joe McHugh, two unidentified, Renaldo Rinaldi, and two unidentified. (Courtesy of the Florence Historical Society.)

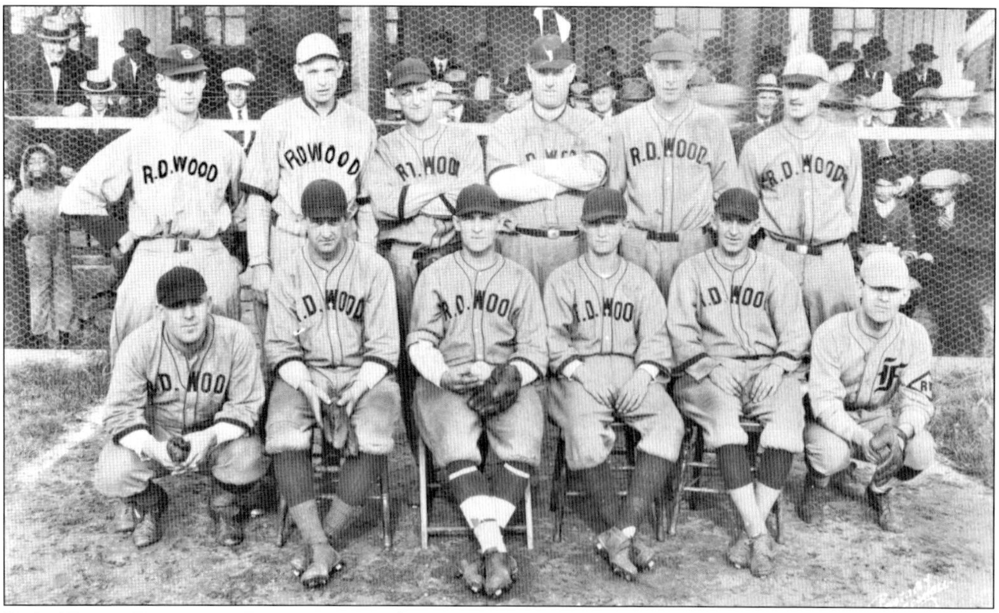

R.D. Wood Baseball Team, 1924. Champions of the Burlington County League again in 1924, the R.D. Wood baseball team is pictured at the R.D. Wood Field in Florence. From left to right are (first row) Buck Beaudry, Charlie Peacock, Nanny Woolston, Nick Frappolli, Ruby Gilbert, and ? Hafey; (second row) Lou Kite, Bill Everham, John Rhoda, Jack Sweeney, Jess Foulks, and ? Algie. The R.D. Wood team defeated Mount Holly, 4-2. (Courtesy of Wayne Campbell.)

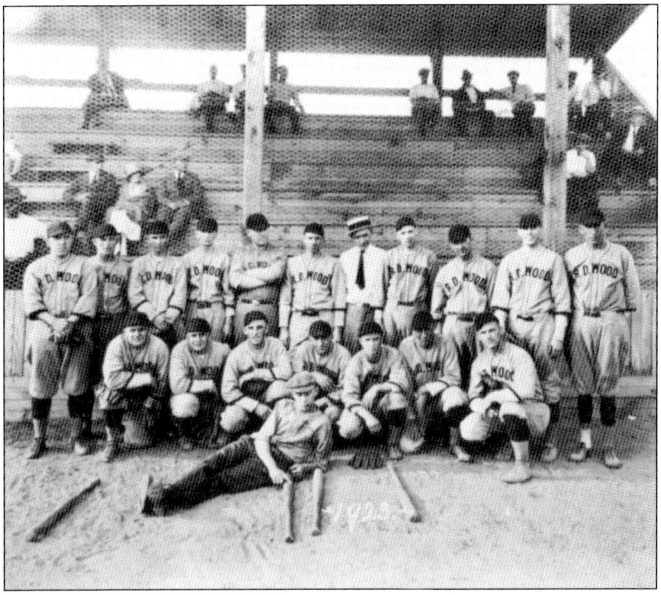

R.D. WOOD BASEBALL TEAM, 1923. Champions of the Burlington County League are shown, along with spectators, at the R.D. Wood grandstand on West Fifth Street in 1923. The score was 4-0 against the Roebling team. The R.D. Wood team copped the title 10 times in the next 15 years; more than 3,000 fans were present for this victory. Among the players are, in no particular order, Ruby Gilbert, ? Fox, Charlie Peacock, Darby Foulks, John Rhoda, Bill Everham, Marty McGrath, Nick Frappolli, and Luke Doyle. (Courtesy of John Williams.)

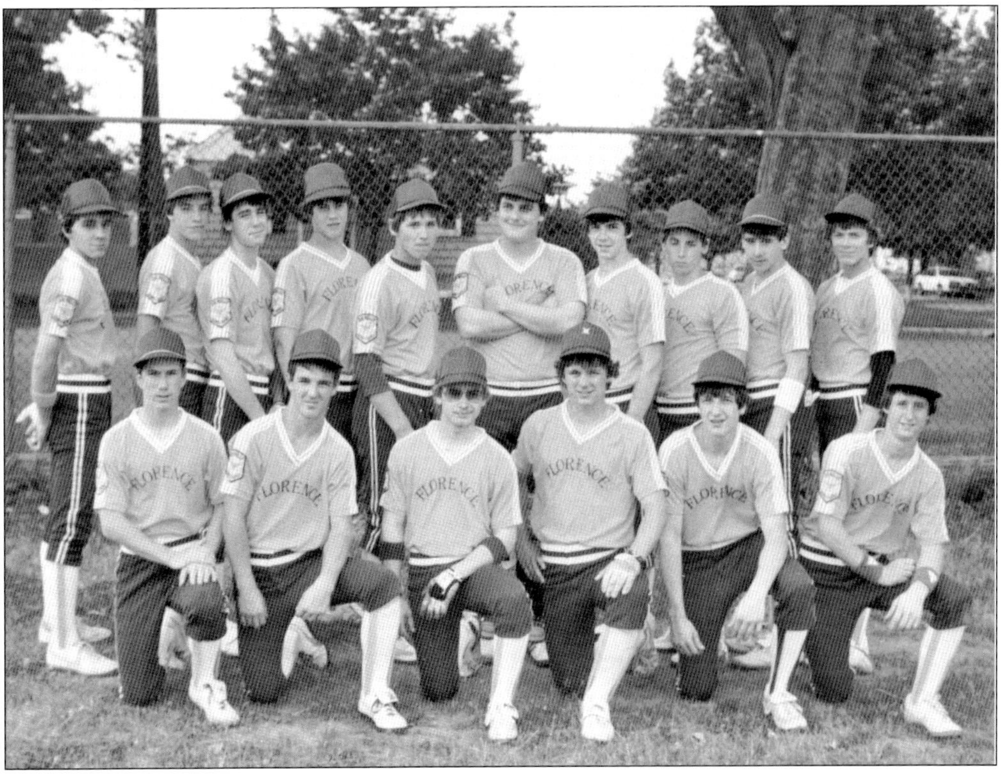

SENIOR BABE RUTH BASEBALL, 1984. Florence also encouraged younger players to join the Babe Ruth team, and they proudly wore the Florence colors of blue and gold. From left to right are (first row) Mike Reed, Bruce Campbell, Don Machovoe, Dave Horton, Ken Baldorossi, and Steven Hovart; (second row) Steve Prokolyshen, Darrin Kotch, Mike Dengler, Raymond Ferranto, Mark Kremper, Steve Fazekas, Kevin Ingham, Jeff Kremper, Brian Stinglen, and Howard Furth. (Courtesy of Gene Olaff.)

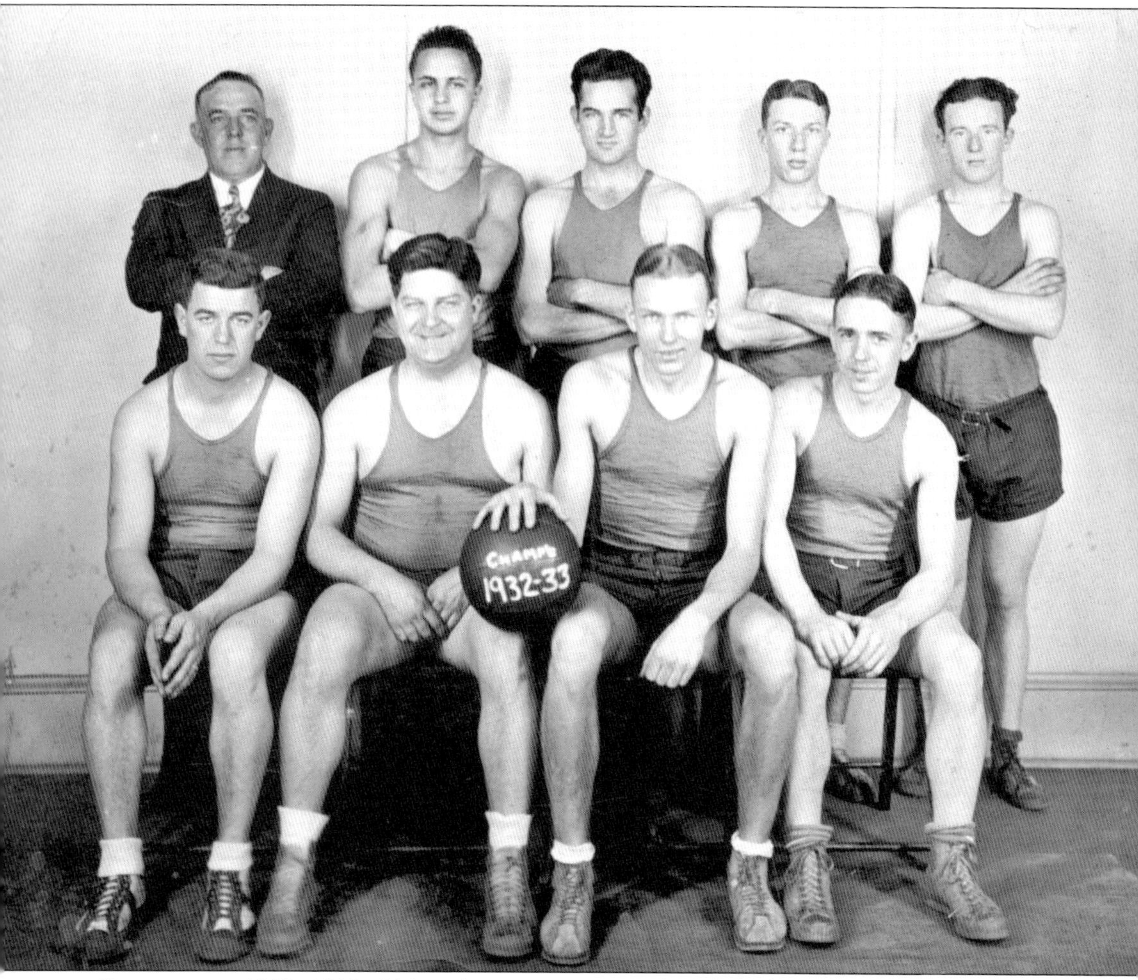

Basketball, 1932–1933. Although its name is not identified, the team is made up of Florence boys who won the championship in 1932–1933. Florence participated in the Burlington County Basketball League in 1908 and later in 1926. Included in this photograph are, in no particular order, Buck Beaudry, Albert Lynch, George Miller, Reds Miller, Jimmy Kelly, and Vaughn Donnelly. (Courtesy of the Nichols-Lynch family.)

Ten

It's Been a Long Time

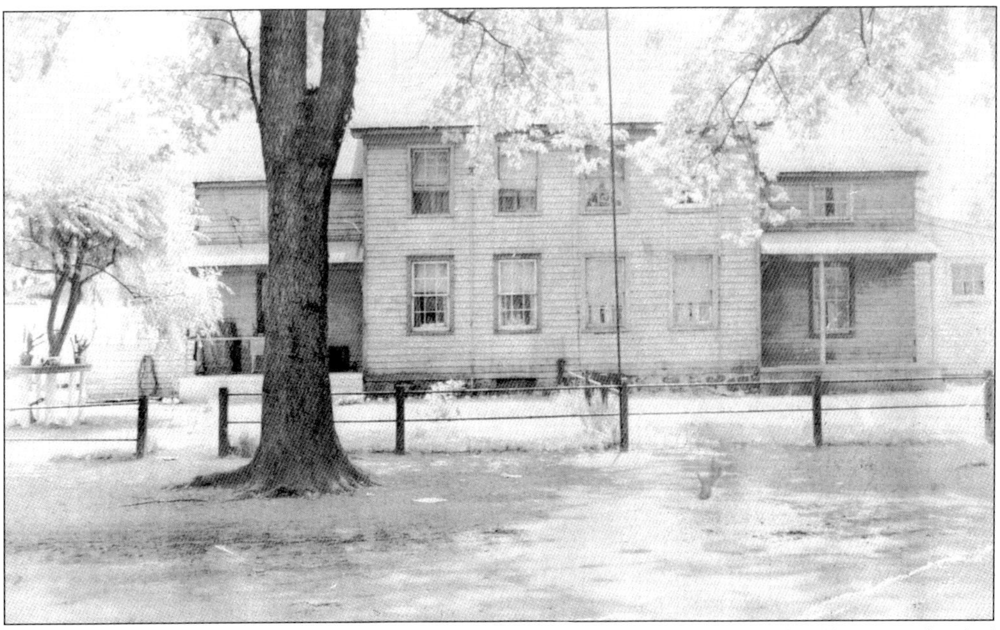

Skunktown. One of six quad homes is pictured at West Third Street. Each building was divided into four units, with a large water pump in the middle for all families. These were also called "bouquet houses." They were demolished in the early 1950s to make way for a HUD housing project, which still stands today. John Williams's relatives the McGrath family lived in one unit and then rented two units as the family grew. (Courtesy of John Williams.)

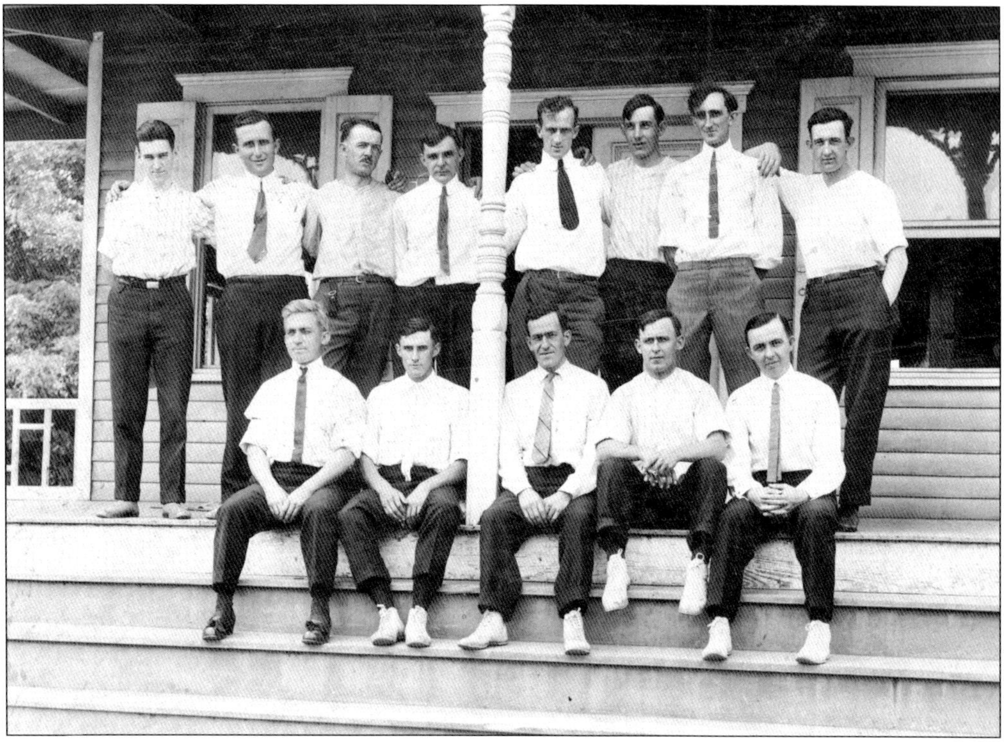

Mohican Boat Club, c. 1920. Located on Riverview Avenue, this building hosted a meeting of the boat club. From left to right are (first row) members Arthur Pettit, J. Milton "Pete" Absalom, Frank Pettit, Albert Ireton and William L. Hamilton; (second row) Alfonza Adams, Bill McCune, Jim Hamilton, Frank Absalom, Dr. Francis Weber, Albert Griffith, Carl Weber, and Charles Peacock. The boat club also hosted dinners, dances, and minstrels for many years. (Courtesy of the Florence Historical Society.)

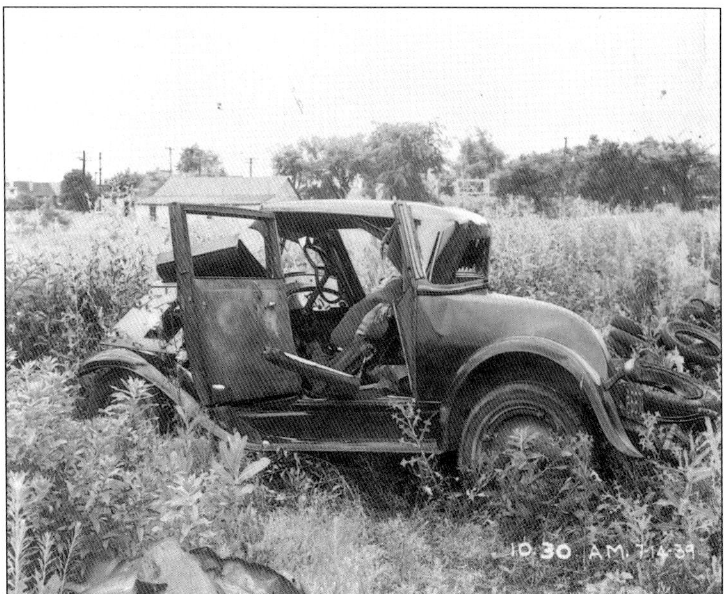

The Anderson Car. In July 1939, Claude Anderson was involved in an automobile accident with his Ford Model A. Struck by an automobile, his car was then thrown into another car on Route 25 near Burlington. With Anderson suffering a skull fracture, his car ended up downtown awaiting repairs. In 1961, he had another Model A with a rumble seat that was often seen around town in nice weather. (Courtesy of Marjorie and Paul Anderson.)

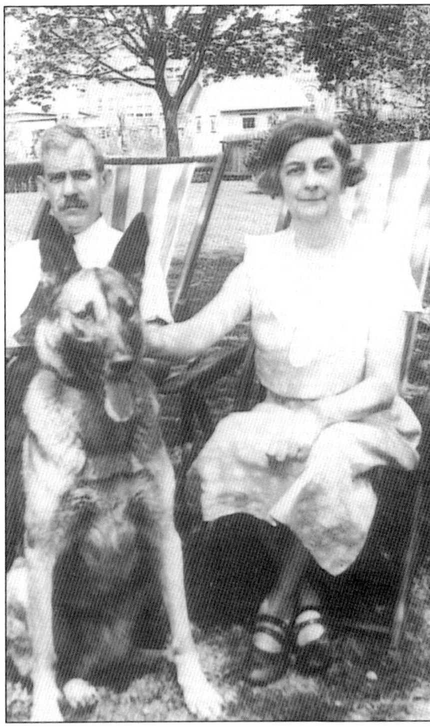

The Reed Family. Oliver and Lila Reed pose with their dog in their side yard at the intersection of West Third Street and Summer Street in 1942. Their large yard was near the Florence Greenhouse on Summer Street. Behind them is the Second Street School. Lila, Oliver, and Harold Reed are listed as their children in the 1930 census. (Courtesy of Helen Henderson.)

The Buccigrossi-Rinaldi Wedding. In January 1955, a wedding took place in Florence at St. Clare's Roman Catholic Church. From left to right are Mary Buccigrossi, maid of honor; Michael Buccigrossi, father of the bride; Ellen Buccigrossi, bride; Herman Rinaldi, groom; and James "Spady" Sozio, best man. Mary has since married, and her last name is now Butcher. (Courtesy of Mary Butcher.)

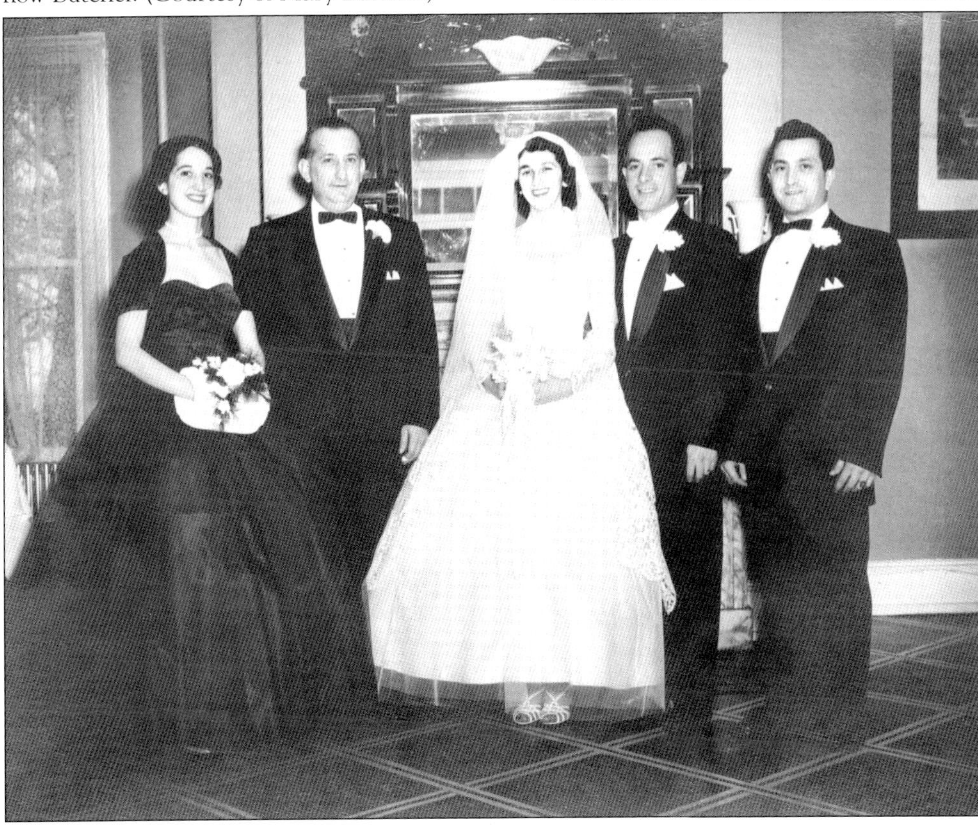

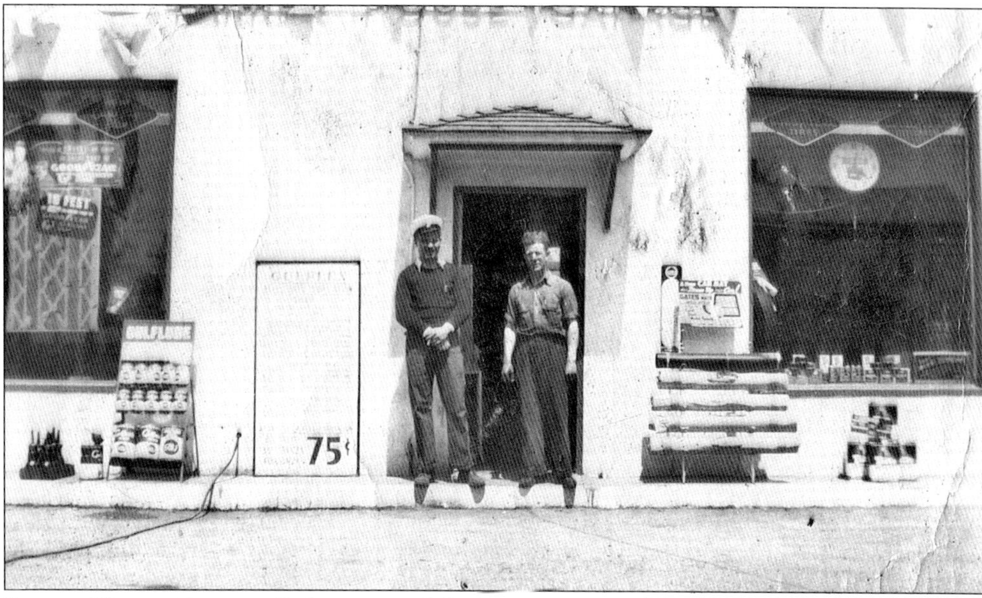

Parker House Garage. Before automobiles were in town, this garage was in business in the 1920s. In the 1940s, it was run by Bill Dale, and in the 1960s, by Richard and Russell Woolston. Gulf gasoline was sold at the pumps. The garage was razed for an apartment complex in the 1980s. (Courtesy of the Florence Historical Society.)

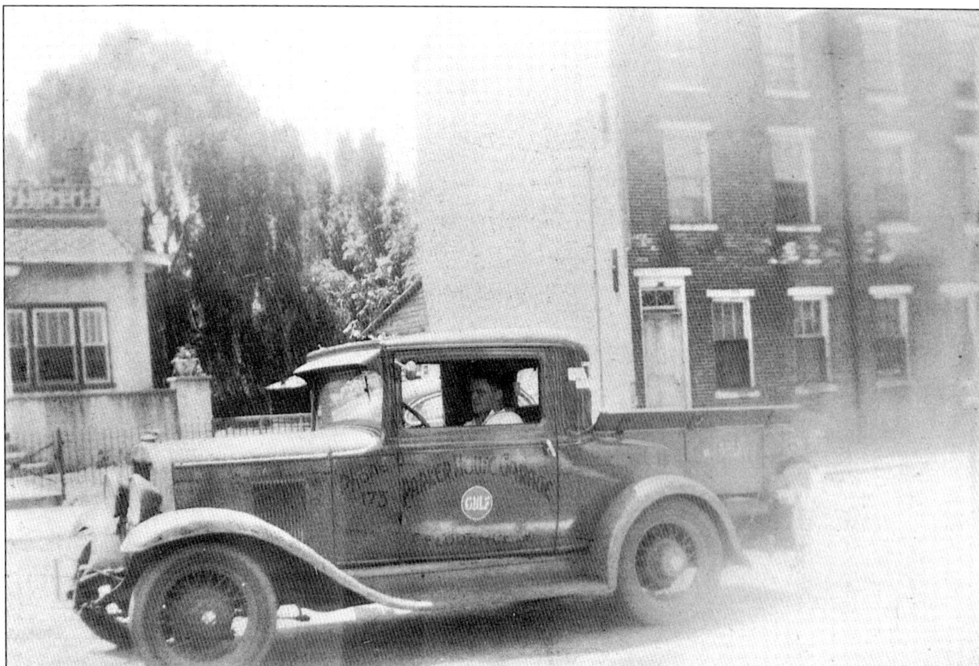

The Parker House Truck. Parked across from Parker House Garage, its service truck shows that the garage sold Gulf gasoline. This c. 1929 view includes the American Legion building on the left and a double Richard Jones house—two row house–style brick homes built by Florence Foundry owner Jones in the 1850s. The garage was located in the first block of West Second Street. (Courtesy of the Florence Historical Society.)

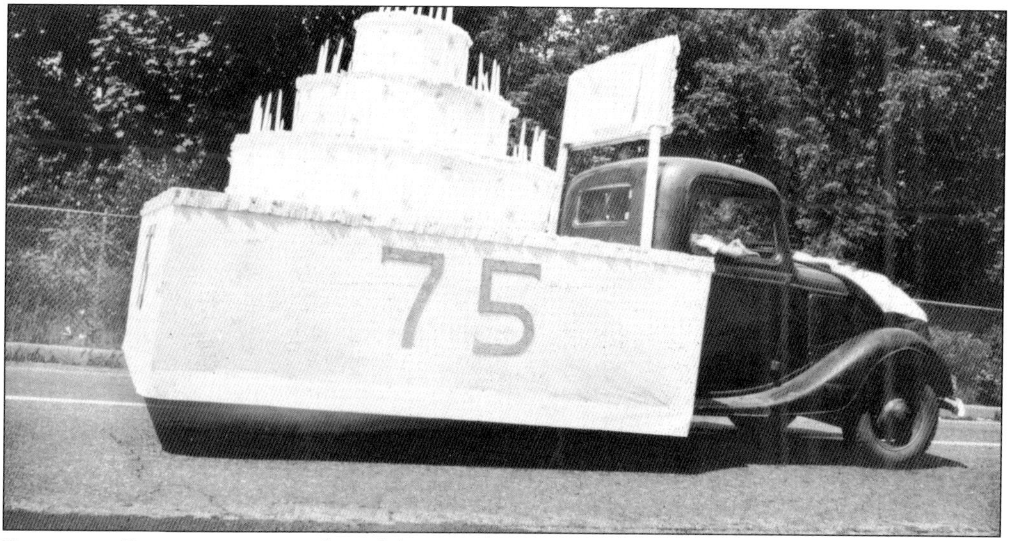

Parade in Florence, 1947. The celebration in 1947 marked the 75th anniversary of Florence's incorporation and the Fourth of July holiday. This event also included a soapbox derby, fireworks, and a memorial gathering, as well as other events throughout the day. This mid-1930s truck with a very large birthday cake was one of the parade entrants. (Courtesy of the Florence Historical Society.)

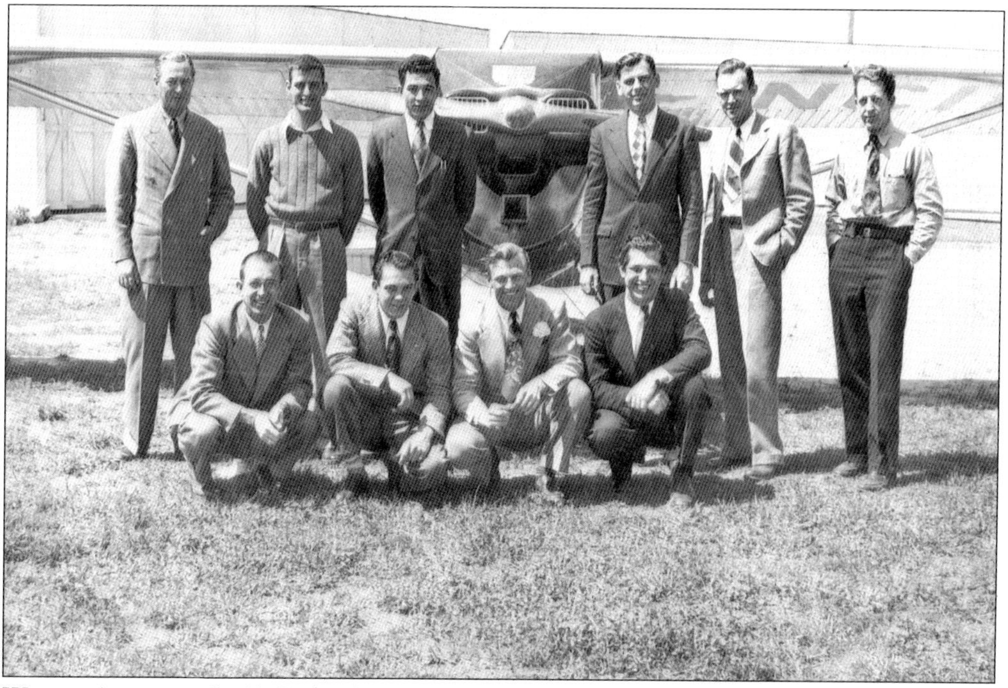

Worth Aviation. In 1947, the first graduating class poses at the Worth Airport in Florence Heights. From left to right are (first row) Charles Adams, ? Thompson, John Mako, and Joe Ordog; (second row) owner Ray Worth, North Brooks, Silvio Capritti, Bud Reed, Elsworth Jones, and instructor Jack Founds. This company offered flying lessons to returning servicemen in the township. A petition was filed by Florence Heights residents to cease operation of the airport because of low-flying airplanes. (Courtesy of Charles "Scoots" Adams.)

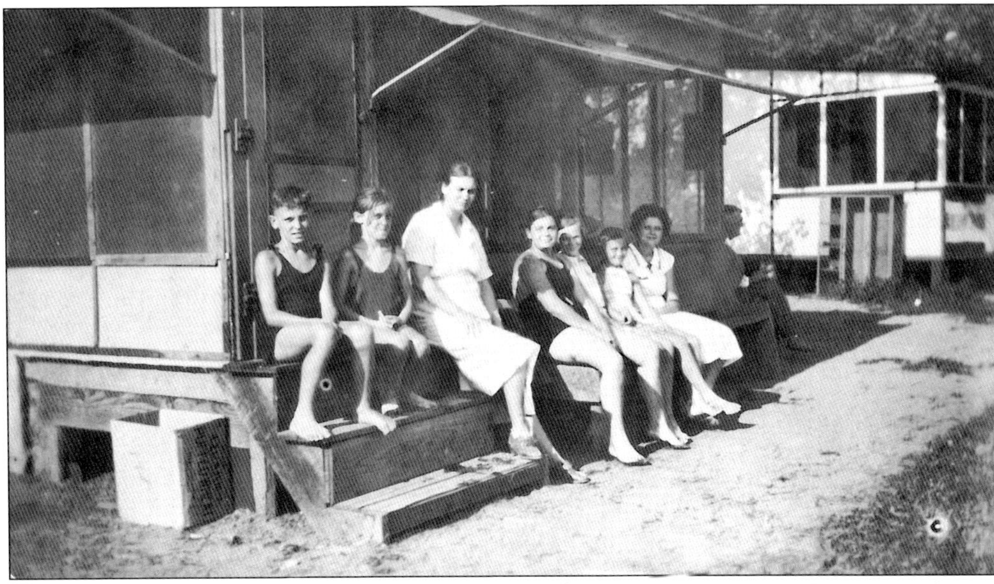

Money Island. Money Island was located in the Delaware River north of Florence, and was a popular vacation spot for many local families. They could rent a cottage, and Billy Moore would row them to the island and to the mainland for groceries and mail during the summer months. Pictured are, from left to right, Walter McDermott, Shirley McDermott, Sara Austin (Moore), Alma Austin, Betty Austin, Dolores "Topsy" McDermott, Dorothea "Dot" Paul McDermott, and Joe Glass. (Courtesy of John Wojcik.)

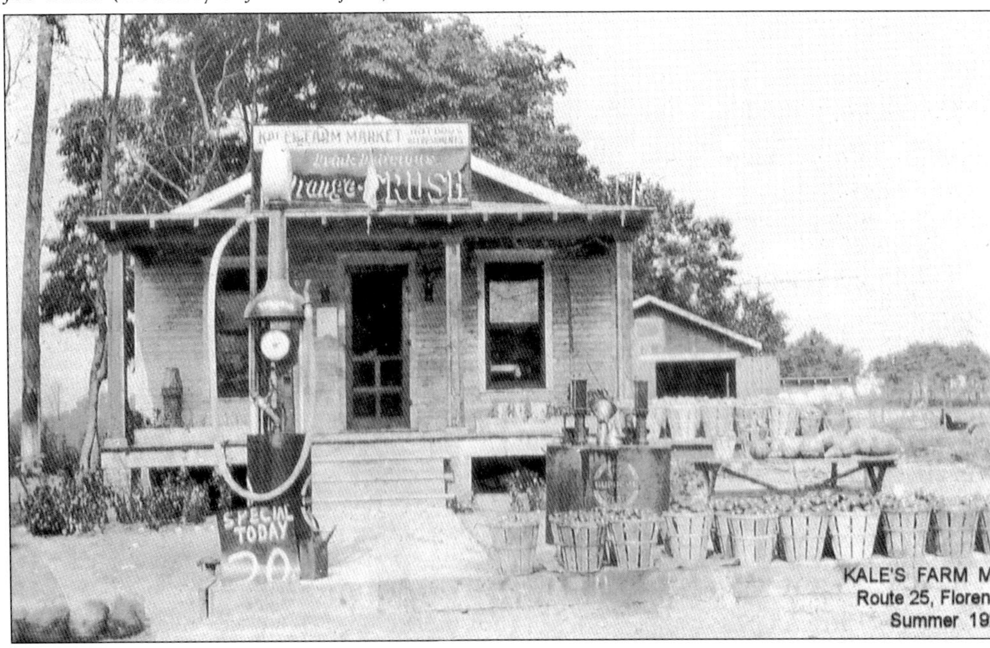

Kale's Farm Market. As it appeared in the summer of 1926, this stand was located on Route 25 south of Florence. (Route 25 became Route 130 in the 1950s.) Baskets of fruit and vegetables surround the building. According to the sign, refreshments, including Orange Crush, could also be purchased. Note the gasoline pump in front of the stand with a 20¢-per-gallon special. (Courtesy of Ken Brown.)

The Home at 45 West Third Street. This home is located on the same block as the Florence Volunteer Fire Company No. 1. Even though the Kale family settled in the area in the late 1700s, there are few, if any, citizens remaining of that name. Pictured from left to right are Edna Leggett Kale, Billy R. Brown, Anna Beitl Leggett, Edna Kale Brown, and Betty Rae Brown in front of their home in 1955. (Courtesy of Ken Brown.)

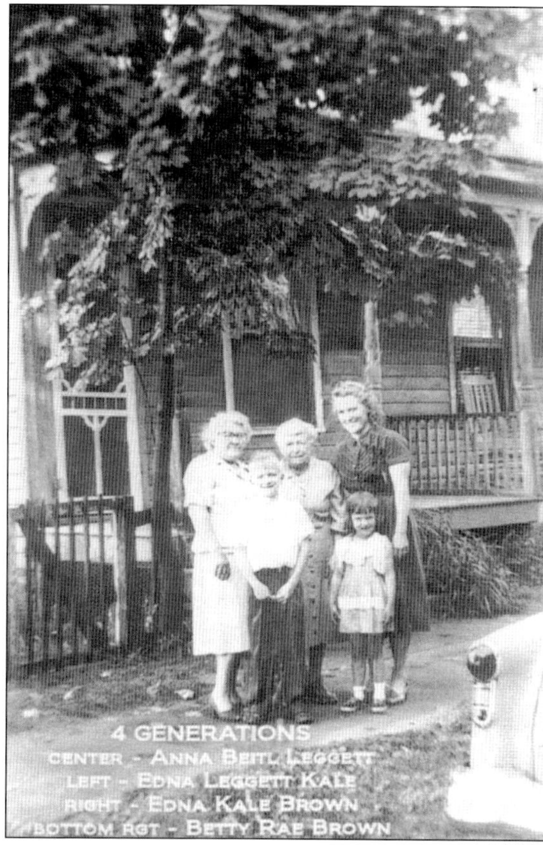

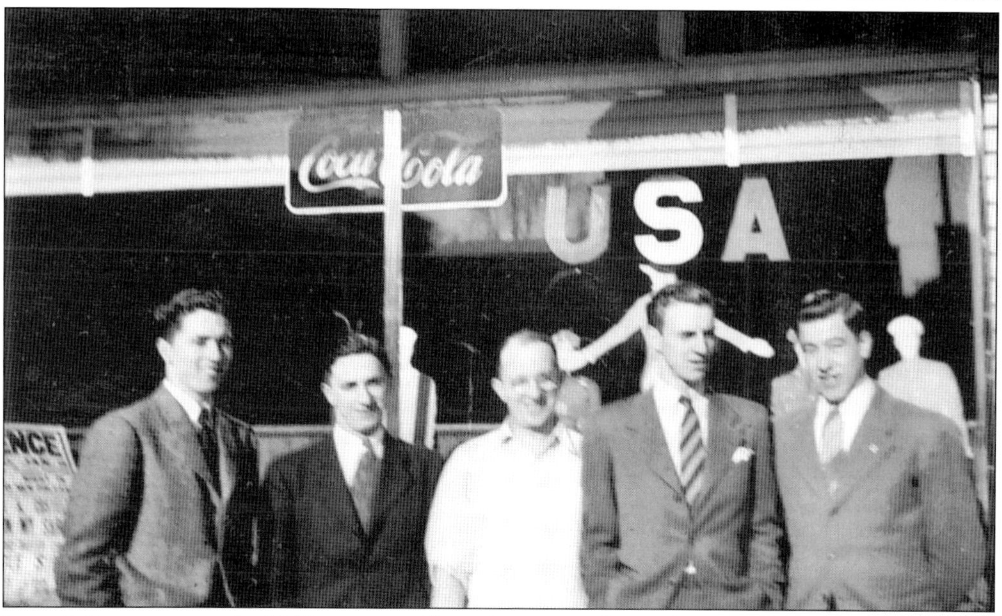

Jimmy's Restaurant. In 1943, a group of friends poses in front of Jimmy's Restaurant downtown on West Second Street. From left to right are Tom Roe, Mike Lubrano, Jimmy Dinucci, Dick Sweeney, and Nick DiLullo. (Courtesy of Jack Ulmer.)

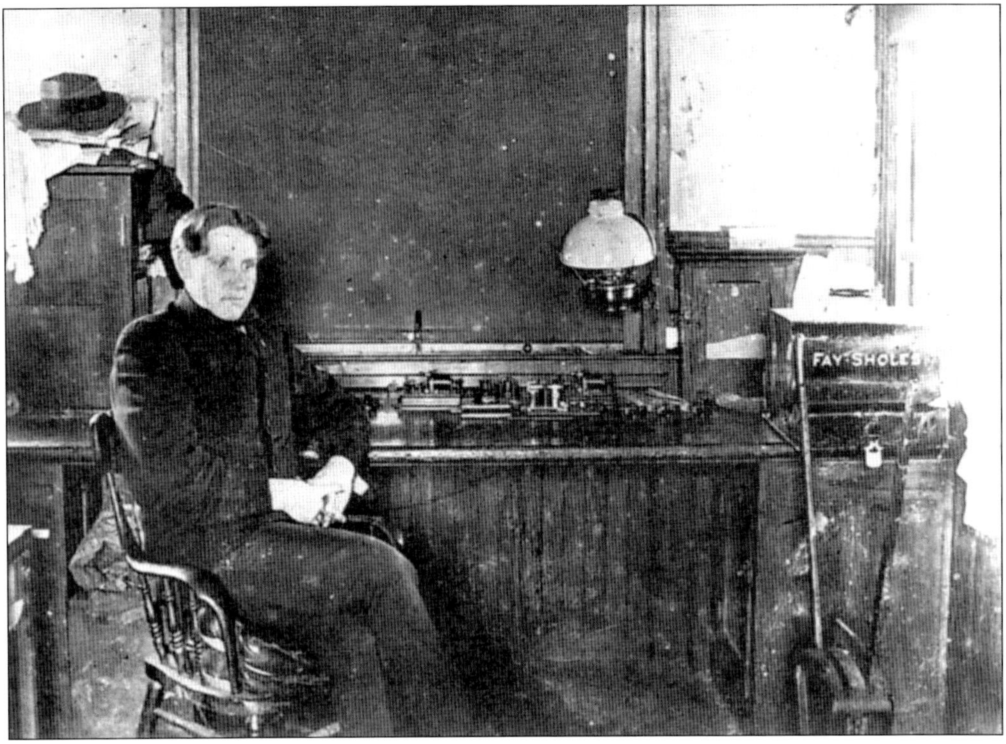

WILLIAM C. WORRELL. William C. Worrell is shown at his desk at the Florence passenger station around the turn of the 20th century. On May 7, 1904, an accident could have resulted with very serious consequences. A car was on the wrong track, and the Nellie Bly express train was almost due. Worrell set the danger signal, and the last train pulled up just in time to avoid a crash. His telegraph keying instrument on the desk is now housed in the Florence Historical Society museum. (Courtesy of Tom Worrell.)

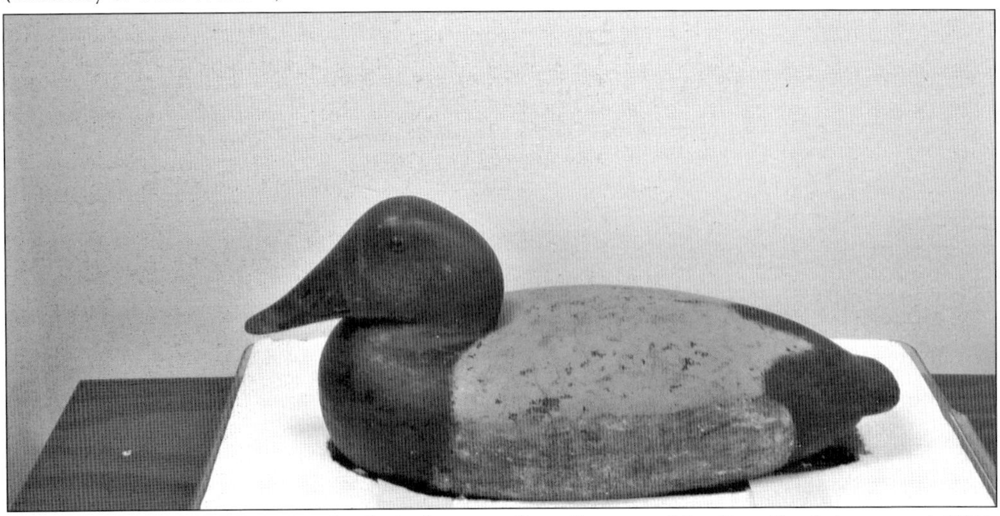

A DRAKE DECOY. This canvasback drake was allegedly carved by Dan English around 1930. Dan is from the noted Delaware River family of John English; the English family was made up of carvers who produced many fine and early working decoys that command large sums of money at decoy auctions throughout the country. (Courtesy of Judy King.)

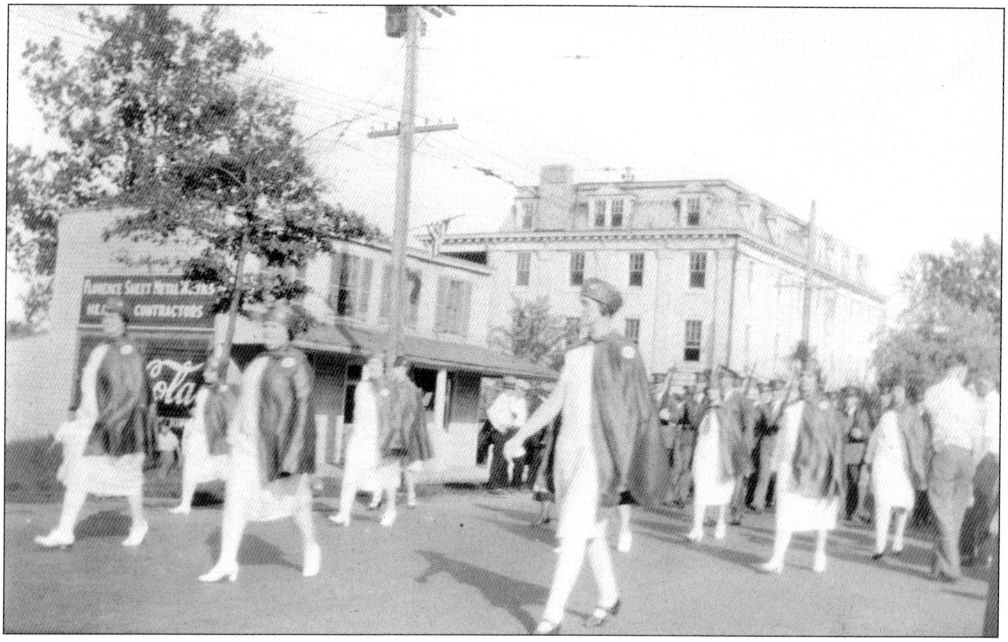

A Florence Parade. Florence is fond of parades, and seen here is either a Memorial Day or Fourth of July parade in the late 1920s. In the left background is what used to be a stagecoach stop and later the Acme Market. To the right of it is the old Florence Hotel before the top floor was removed by McElven Fuel. The ladies appear to be with the American Legion, and a military group marches behind them. (Courtesy of Janet Griffith.)

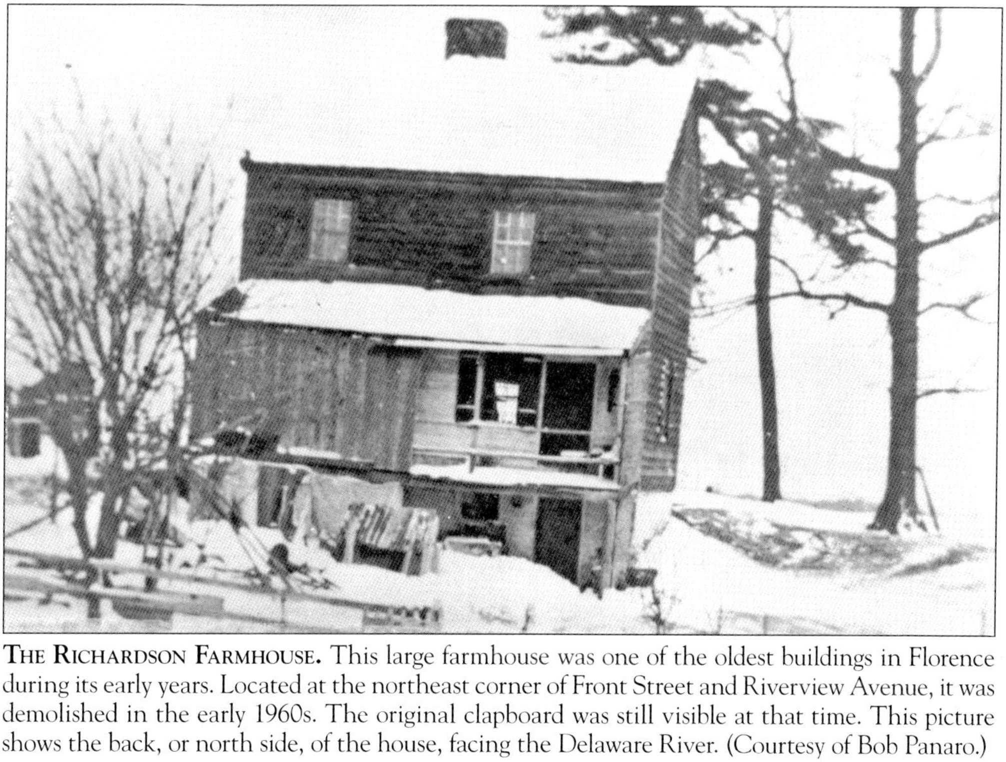

The Richardson Farmhouse. This large farmhouse was one of the oldest buildings in Florence during its early years. Located at the northeast corner of Front Street and Riverview Avenue, it was demolished in the early 1960s. The original clapboard was still visible at that time. This picture shows the back, or north side, of the house, facing the Delaware River. (Courtesy of Bob Panaro.)

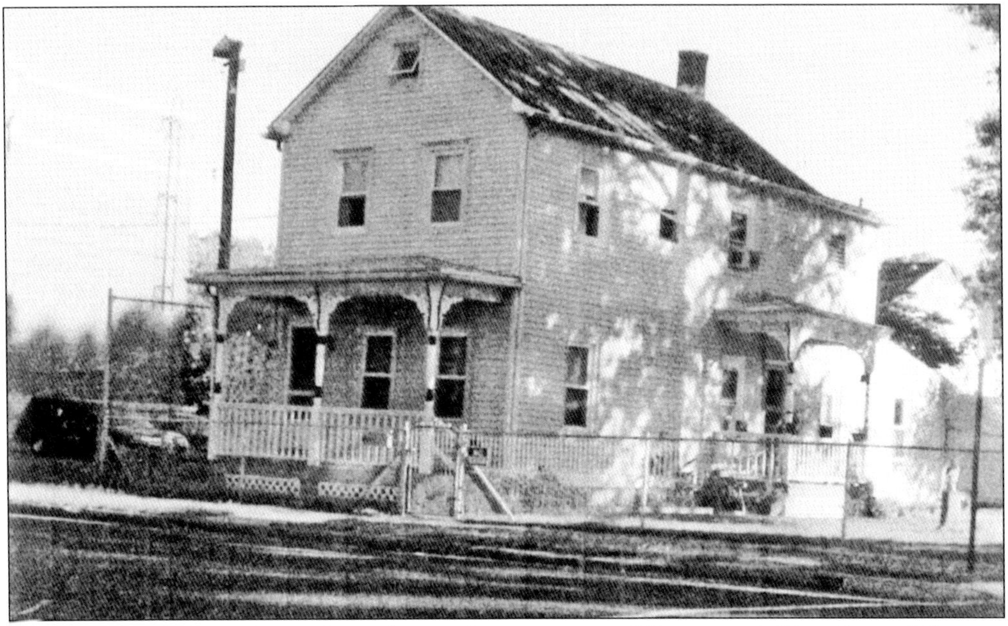

The Pierson House. Located on the northwest corner of Spring and West Second Streets, this house was razed in 2014 as part of the Duffy School Apartments renovation. The Piersons had a brass nameplate dating the home to the late 1800s installed in the front sidewalk. After renovations, the contractor reset this marker in keeping with the property's history. (Courtesy of Judy King.)

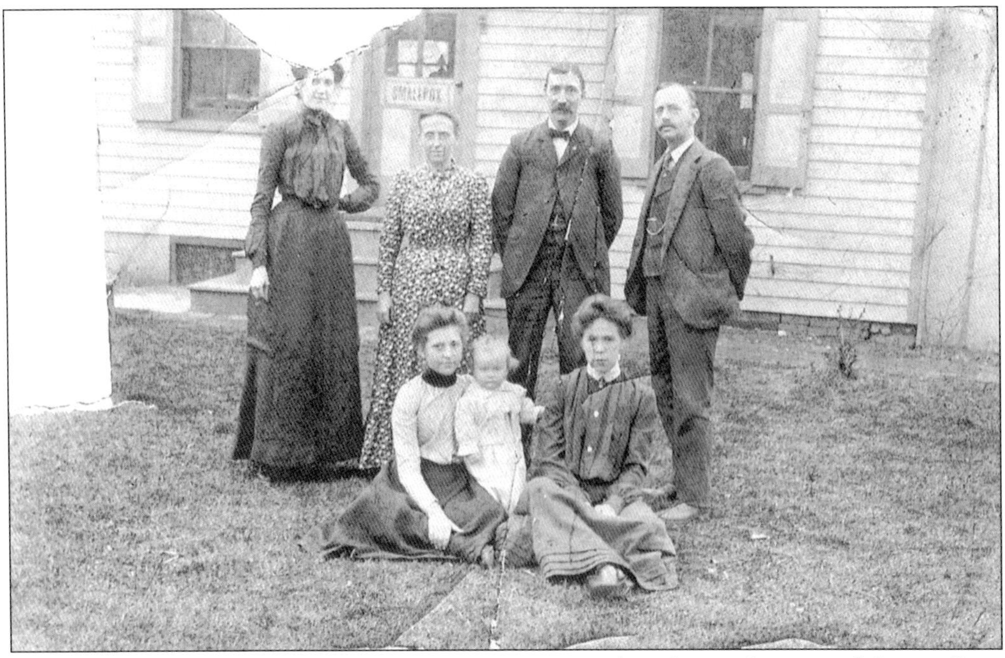

The Pierson-Wilcox House. This c. 1899 picture was taken during the time of the smallpox outbreak. The children in first row may be, from left to right, Harrison Pierson, John Pierson and Lena Pierson. Standing from left to right are unidentified (but believed to be a boarder), Mrs. Joseph Pierson, and Joseph Pierson. (Courtesy of Emily F. Pierson Wilcox.)

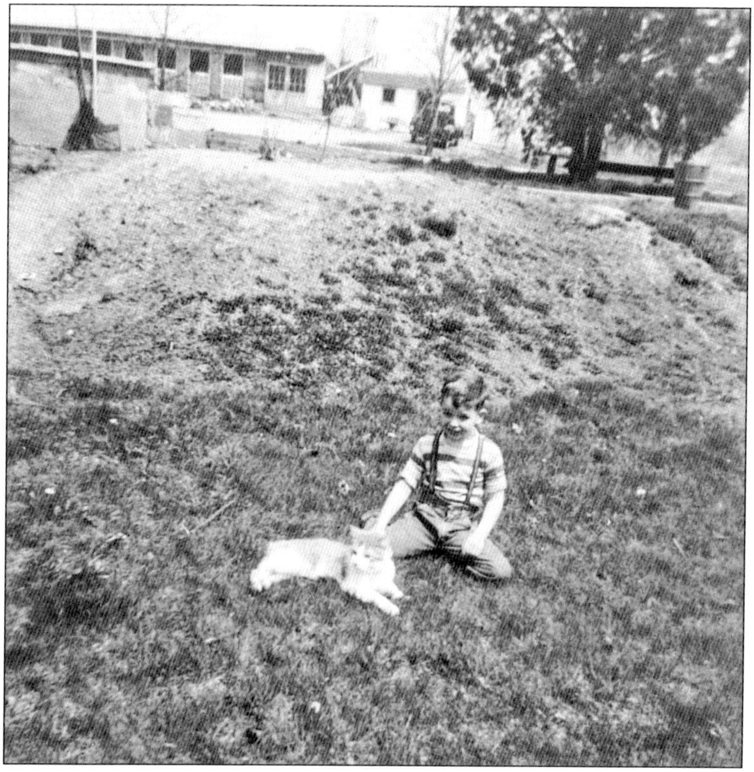

Little Creek Poultry Farm. In business from the 1950s to the early 1970s, Little Creek Poultry Farm housed up to 3,000 chickens at a time. The building is pictured at top left. All doors and windows were salvaged from the old Clara Barton School in Bordentown when it was demolished in the 1950s. In the foreground is Brian Mudge, age 4, grandson of the owner, Clayton Mudge, with his cat Sandy. (Courtesy of Lynda Mudge Borgstrom.)

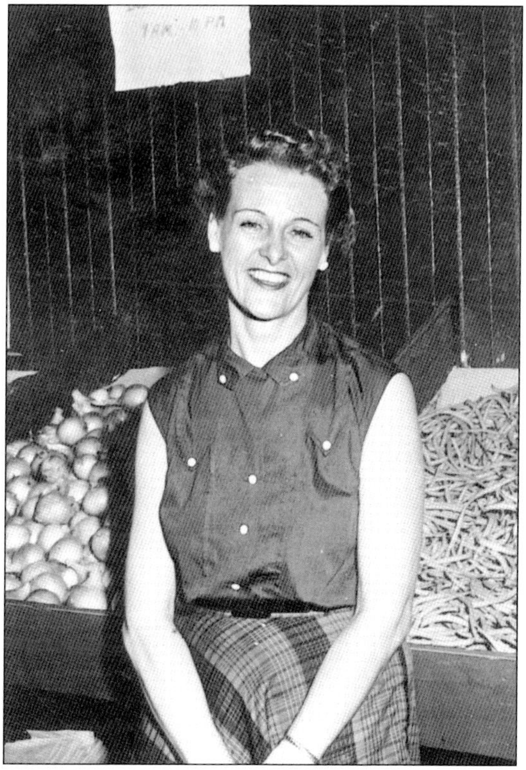

Natalie Simpkins. Natalie Simpkins was overseer of the roadside market at the southwest corner of Route 130 and Cedar Lane. This operation also included her husband, Hilyard Simpkins, and their three sons. Fresh produce was sold for many years from their 560-acre farm. Located across the road from Hunt Brothers Circus winter quarters, the Simpkins boys were often recruited to round up ostriches and other animals that invaded their cornfields, wreaking havoc on the crops. (Courtesy of the Florence Historical Society.)

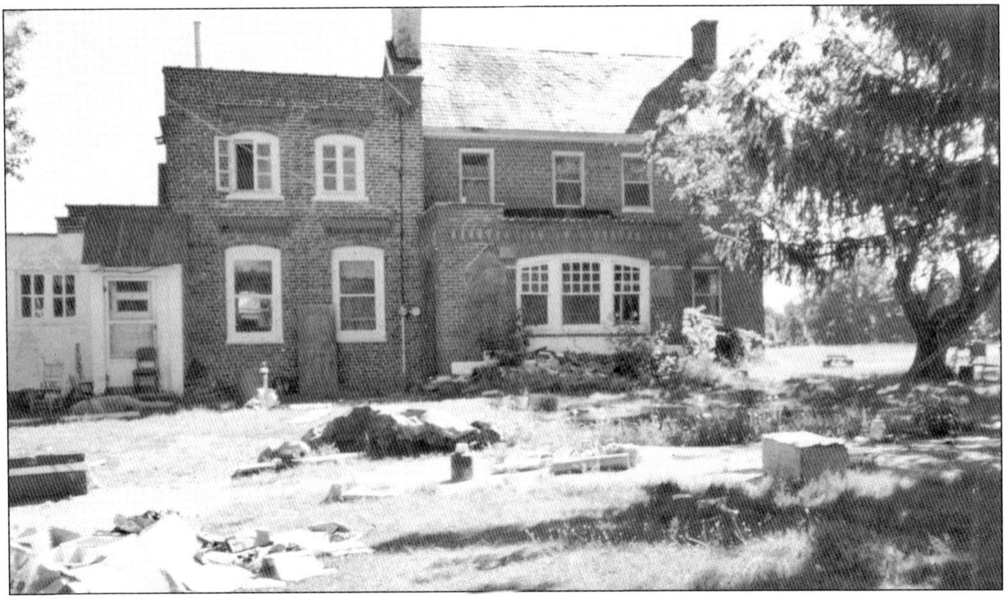

The Ivins House. Carroll Carty Ivins's house was on the east side of Potts Mill Road. Possibly built in the 18th century, this brick house has been much altered as seen here. It was demolished in 1997. The large picture window on the right was supposedly from the Fox Movie Theater in Burlington, after that building was demolished. Carroll Carty Ivins owned a tavern in Florence Station, in addition to approximately 100 acres of land in Florence Township. (Courtesy of the Florence Historical Society.)

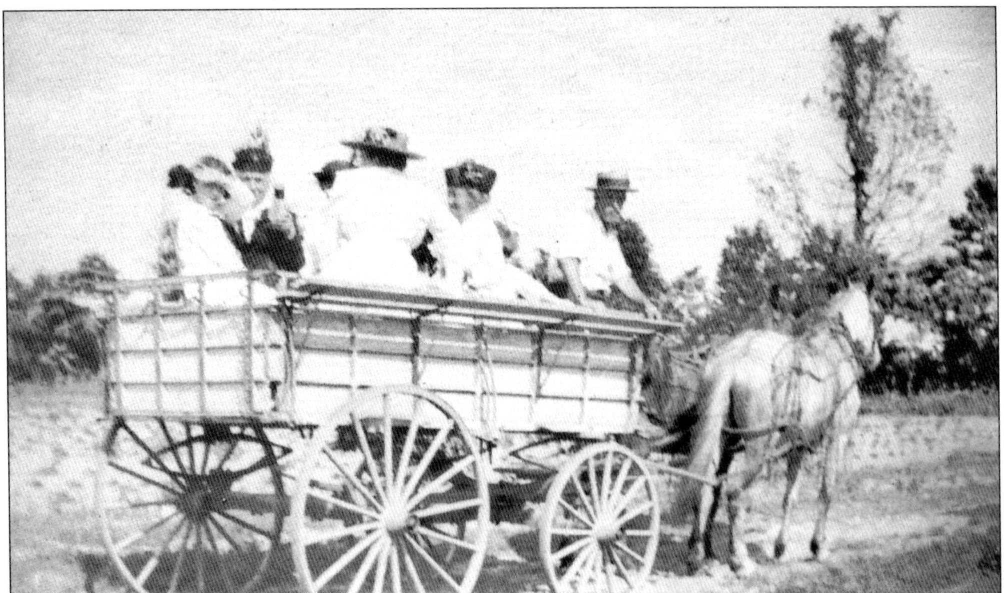

The John Kale Family. Going to church in 1918, John Kale and his family use a wagon and horses, as automobiles were only owned by the wealthier people in the area. John was a descendant of Henry Kale, who settled in what is now Florence Township in the late 1700s. At that time, he owned 240 acres of land along what became the Amboy Division of the Pennsylvania Railroad and is now the River Line. (Courtesy of Ken Brown.)

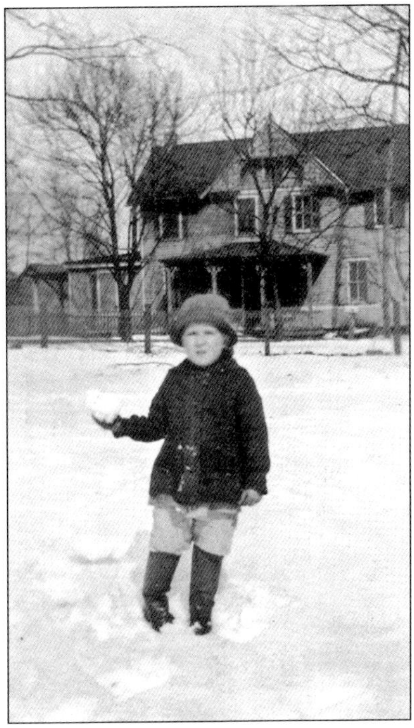

The Ivins Hotel. The Ivins Hotel stands on the southwest corner of Delaware and Railroad Avenues in Florence Station. Located across the street from what is now Bob's Corner Deli, this building dates back to the 1860s, as shown in an early photograph, and was a stagecoach stop near the railroad station. Young Jack Quig, armed with a snowball, is ready for action in February 1920. Only the center section of the hotel remains today, due to a fire after this time period. The train tracks are to the left of the building, across what is now Railroad Avenue. (Courtesy of Jack Quig.)

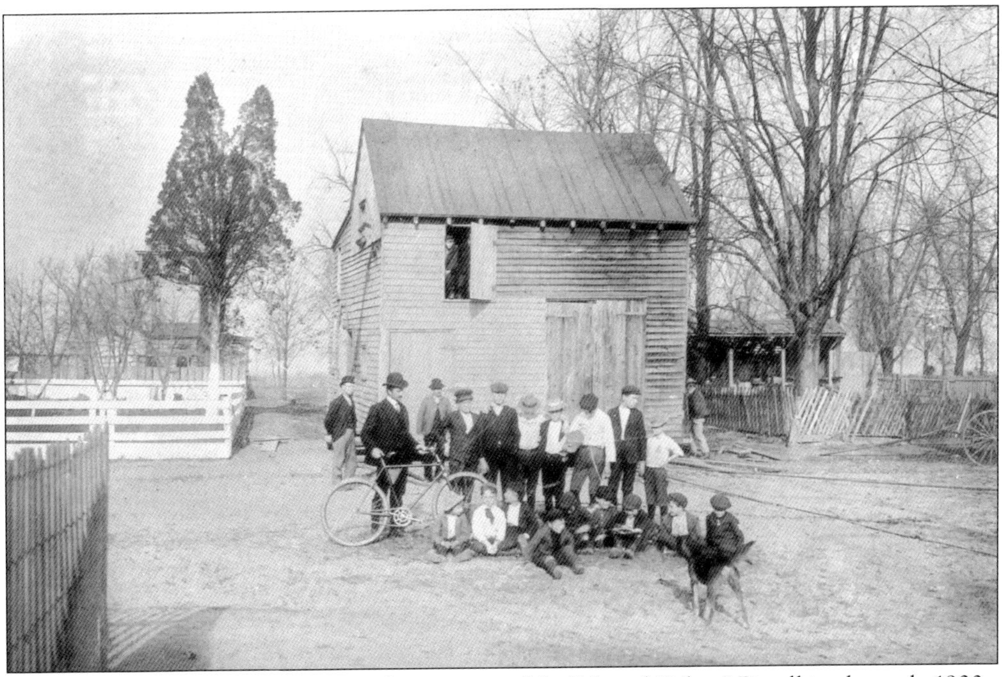

Edward "Jakey" Durell. Moving day is pictured for Edward "Jakey" Durell in the early 1900s. He was a renowned carpenter and worked on the new schoolhouse. In 1902, he converted his barn into a dwelling, and there was no trace of its pedigree when finished. He owned trotting and race horses, one of whom was called Florence Boy. During a hunting expedition, he shot what appeared to be a railbird, and it gave four loud quacks before giving up the ghost. (Courtesy of Ed Noval.)

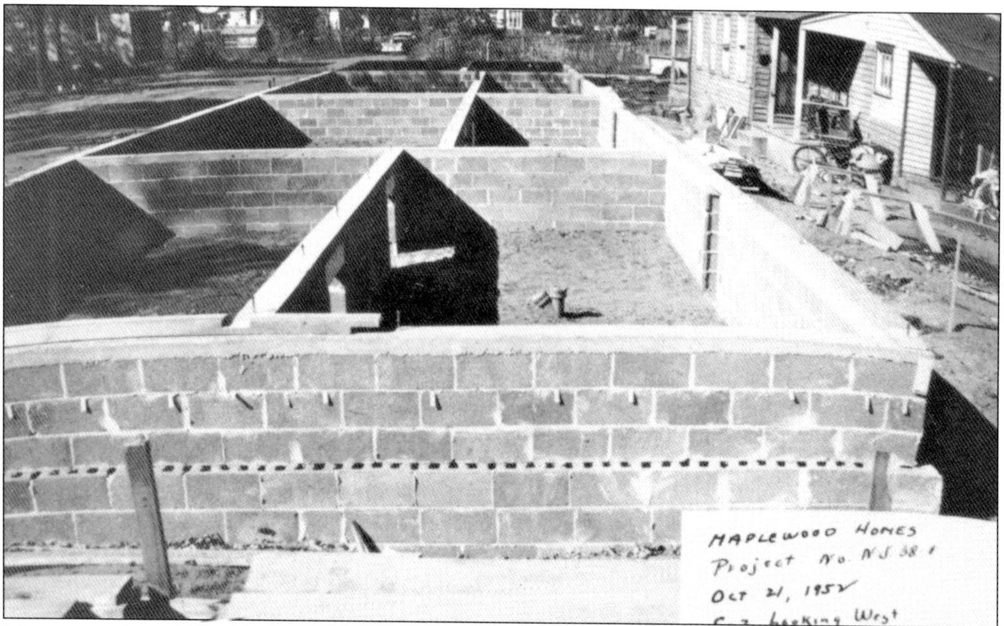

MAPLEWOOD HOMES. Thirty-six houses were demolished during the month of October 1952 to make way for the Maplewood Homes HUD housing project. The architect was Henry Petty, a former Florence native. On November 5, 1953, the public was invited to the dedication of the homes. The ceremonies were held at the Administration Building, an official US Department of Housing and Urban Development office, on West Third Street between Eyre and Iron Streets. (Courtesy of Wayne Campbell.)

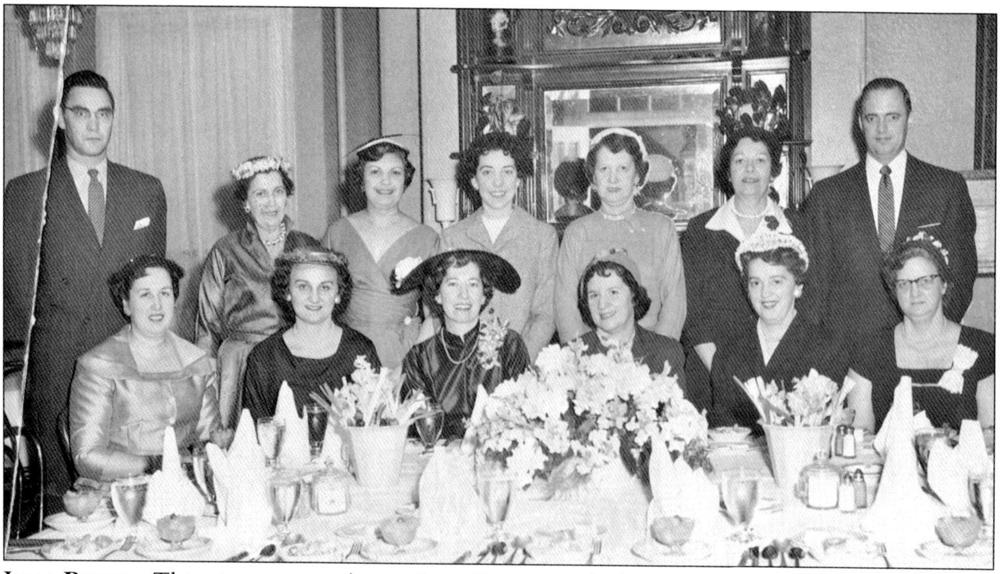

IRMA BROWN. This picture was taken as Irma Brown, a telephone operator, celebrates 25 years of service in 1956. A banquet was held at the Mansion House in Fieldsboro to honor this milestone. Pictured from left to right are (first row) Edith Peacock, Bert Ryan, Brown, Laura Collum, Rose Zdanciewicz, and Edna Hamilton; (second row) Josephine ?, Ceola "Toots" Sweeney, Joan Fenimore, Mary Daniel, and Gladys Cooper. The gentlemen are Marvin H. Kierstead (left) and John O. Stone. (Courtesy of Mary Buccigrossi Butcher.)

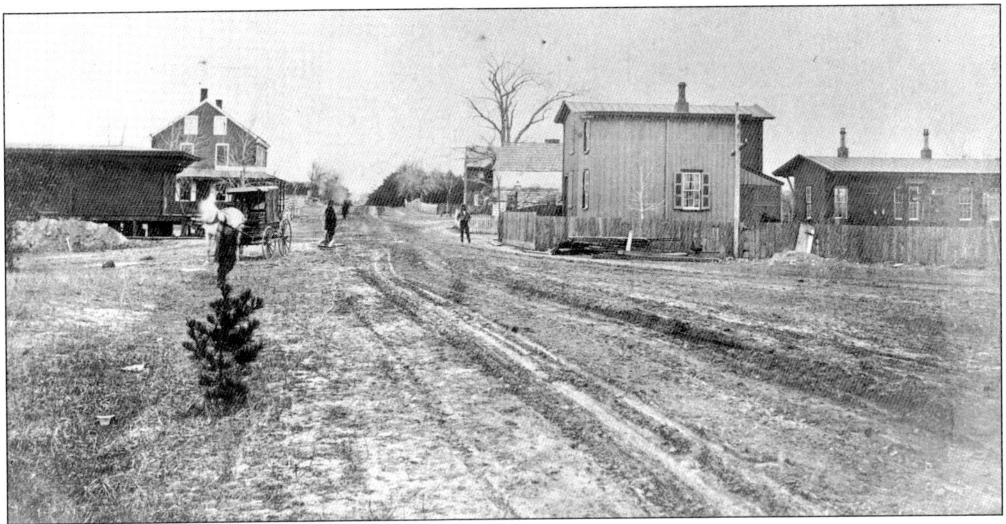

Florence Station, c. 1860. This view of what is now Delaware Avenue looks toward the Delaware River and the city of Florence. On the left side of the road is the freight station. Beyond that is the three-story Ivins Hotel, which catered to rail and stagecoach passengers. The railroad passenger station is the low building at the far right side. The dirt road that became Station Road is also visible. (Courtesy of Thomas Worrell.)

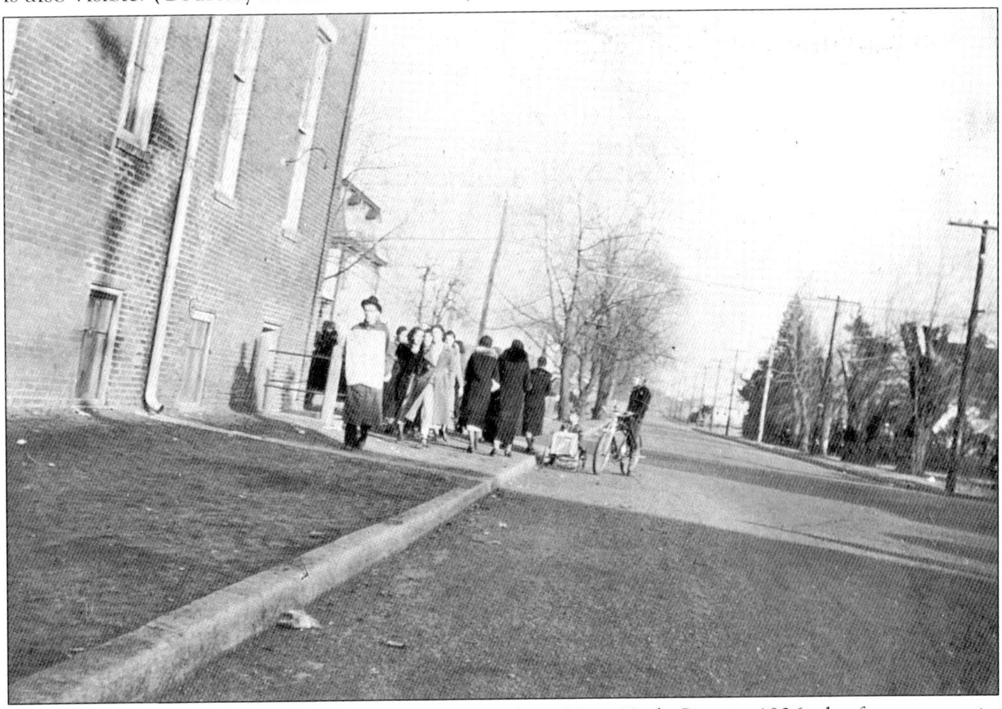

Gem Dress Factory. Established by a company from New York City in 1936, the factory was in this building, formerly Redmens Hall. In 1937, a near riot took place as over a hundred girls, all dissatisfied employees, surrounded the manager's home on Chestnut Street. One of the many complaints was overdue wages. Finally, Louis Misselman, the manager, agreed to unionize the factory. He was also cited for not contributing social security funds to the federal government. This happened only after the girls went on strike. (Courtesy of the Florence Historical Society.)

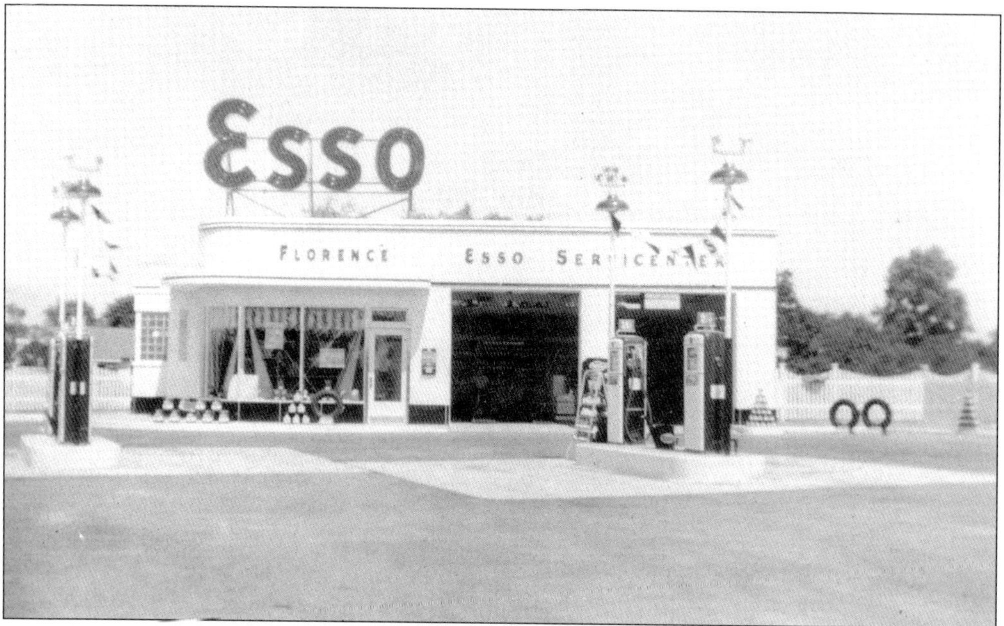

ESSO STATION. This service station still stands on the north side of Route 130 near the Burlington Township line. The price on the pumps is 25¢ per gallon, offering an approximate date of 1961. The station, run by Ben Saia, was kept spotless at all times. These were the Esso days, when an attendant would wash the car windshield and check the oil without being asked. The station now sells Valero gasoline and is somewhat altered. (Courtesy of Dominick Cucinotta.)

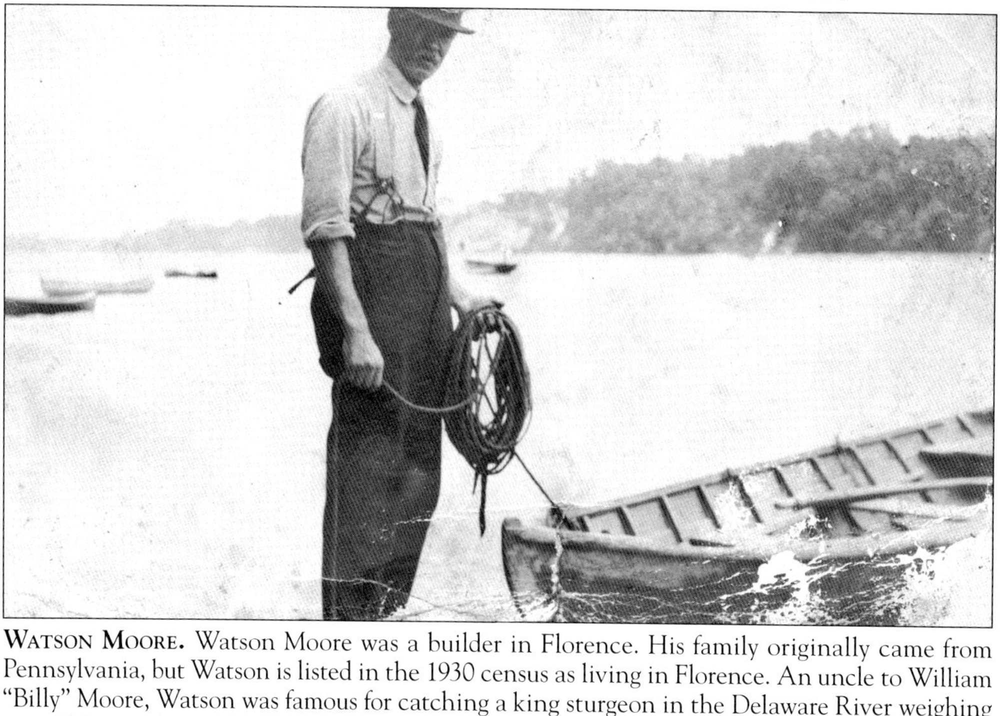

WATSON MOORE. Watson Moore was a builder in Florence. His family originally came from Pennsylvania, but Watson is listed in the 1930 census as living in Florence. An uncle to William "Billy" Moore, Watson was famous for catching a king sturgeon in the Delaware River weighing over 200 pounds in 1910. A retired railroad engineer, he never married and died in 1931. He was buried in Yardley, Pennsylvania. (Courtesy of the Florence Historical Society.)

William "Billy" Moore. Billy Moore plies his rowboat on the Delaware River near Florence around 1930. His father, Warren Moore, had a contract with Delaware River Sand Dredging Company to maintain Money Island and its cabins and trees in the 1930s. Billy took over these duties for many years. He died in 1962 at the age of 59 and is buried in Cedar Hill Cemetery, Florence. (Courtesy of the Florence Historical Society.)

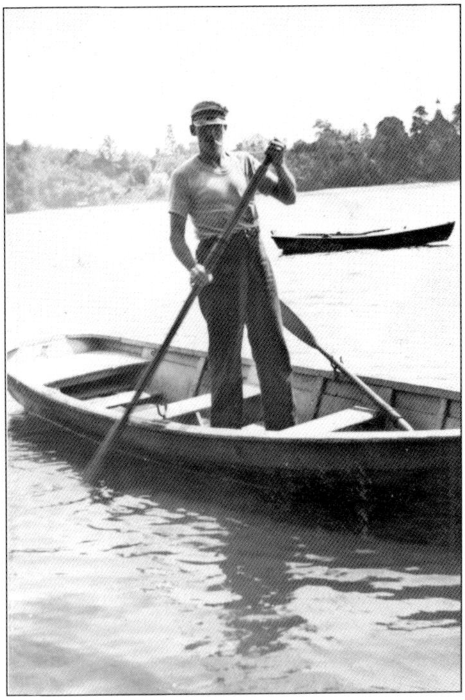

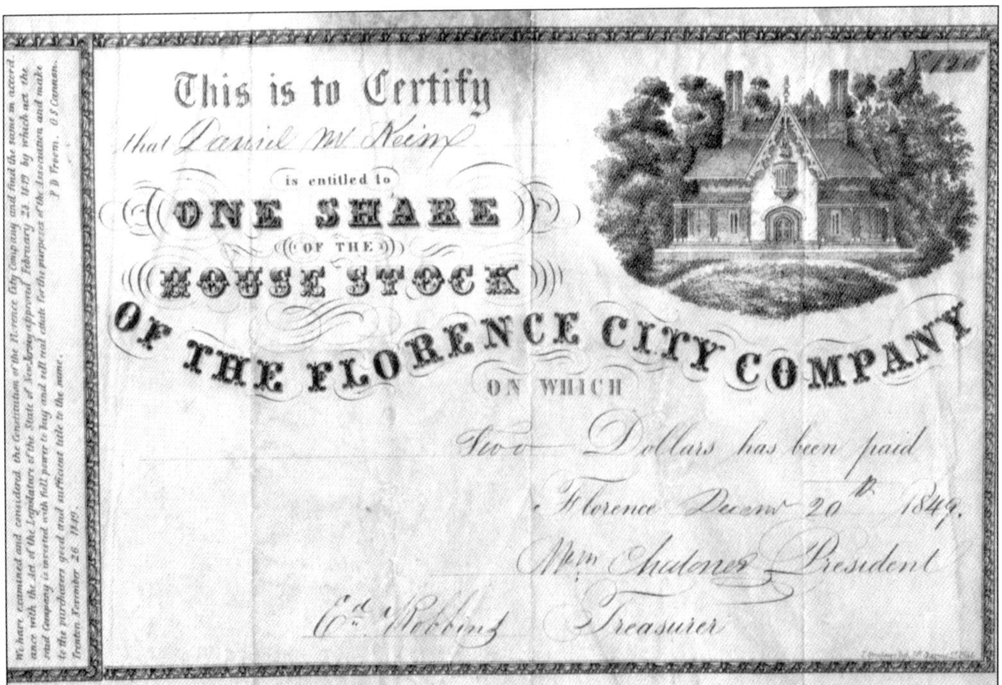

We have examined and considered the Constitution of the Florence City Company and find the same in accordance with the Act of the Legislature of the State of New Jersey approved February 23, 1849 by which act the said Company is invested with full power to buy and sell real estate for the purposes of the Association and make to the purchasers good and sufficient title to the same.
Trenton November 26, 1849.
P D Vroom. G S Cannon.

This is to Certify
that Daniel M. Keim
is entitled to
ONE SHARE
OF THE
HOUSE STOCK
OF THE FLORENCE CITY COMPANY
ON WHICH
Two Dollars has been paid
Florence Decem 20th 1849.
President
Treasurer

Stock Certificate. The Florence City Company formed the town of Florence in 1850. A share of the house stock is shown, dated 1849. The original certificate is housed at the Florence Historical Society's museum in Florence, and this is the only existing certificate known to be in existence. The Florence Historical Society acknowledges with grateful appreciation this donation by Shewell "Bud" DeBenneville Keim. (Courtesy of the Florence Historical Society.)

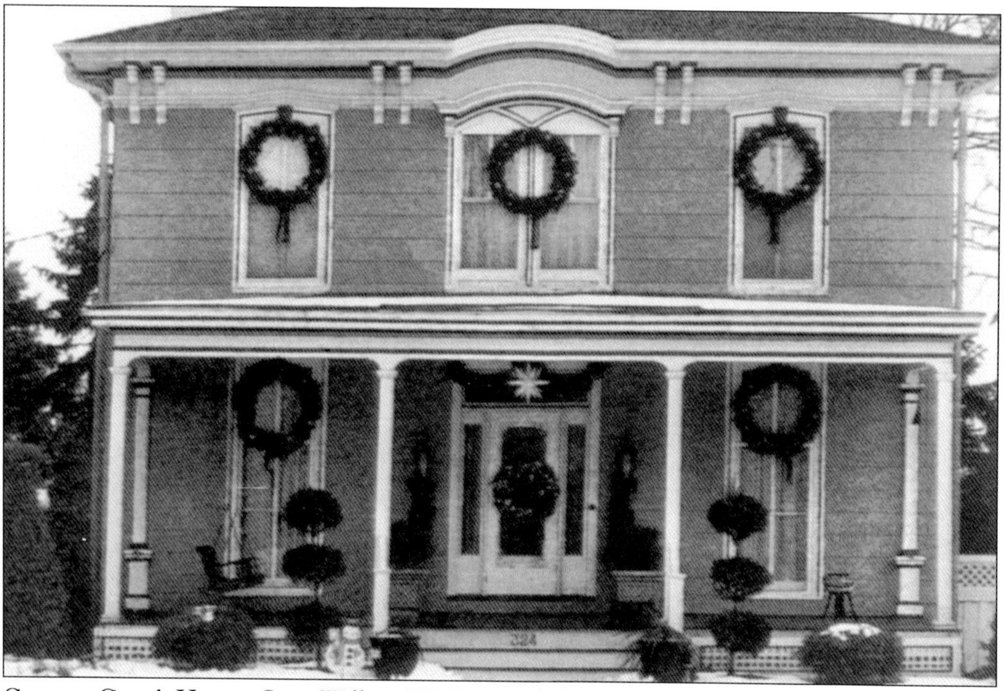

CAPTAIN GRAY'S HOUSE. Capt. William W. Gray, with the Florence boys, joined the 1st New Jersey Cavalry, Company C, 1st Regiment during the Civil War and fought at Gettysburg. His beautiful Italianate house on East Front Street is largely unchanged since then. When this photograph was taken, the house was gray, which seemed appropriate, given its previous ownership. During a boardinghouse fire on New Year's Eve in 1879, Captain Gray adjourned the guests to his house for the evening festivities. (Courtesy of Mark and Cindy Hollern.)

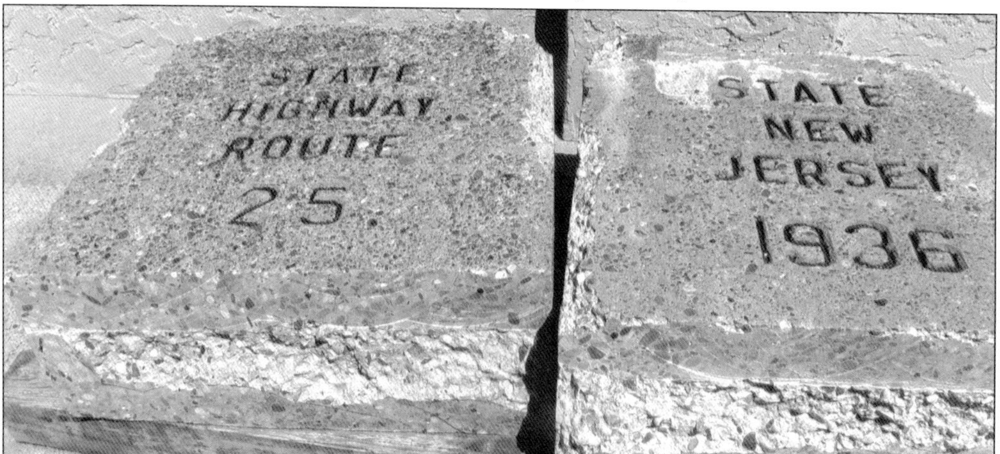

HIGHWAY MARKERS. Shown at their new location at the Florence Firehouse No. 1 on West Third Street, these were part of a bridge which was demolished in August 2012. This section of the highway is located on the north side of what is now Route 130 near Roebling, Florence Township. Formerly Route 25, this was a major state highway in New Jersey prior to renumbering in 1953. When these markers were scheduled for the demolition pile, Florence Township authorities, residents, and the Florence Historical Society took action to have them relocated. (Courtesy of the Florence Historical Society.)

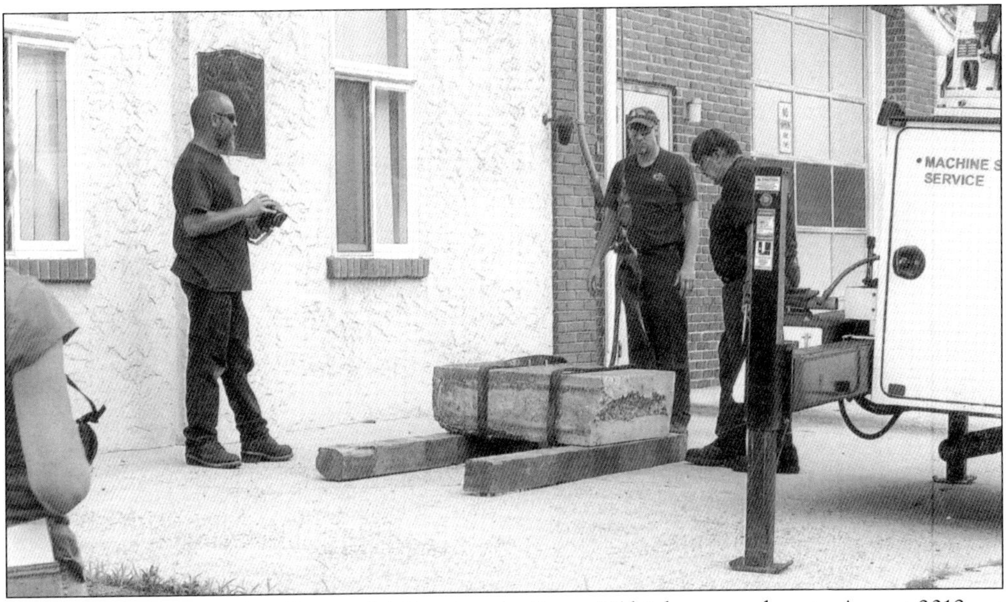

Shafts and Sleeves, Inc. Pictured delivering the Route 25 highway markers in August 2012 are employees of Shafts and Sleeves, Inc. From left to right are Bill Cross, welder; Scott Bell, owner; and Dave Monti, machinist—all of whom volunteered to place the markers at the Florence Firehouse. Their large crane truck, shown on the right, was needed to lift the markers, weighing approximately 800 pounds each. Shafts and Sleeves is located adjacent to the bridge project on Route 130. (Courtesy of the Florence Historical Society.)

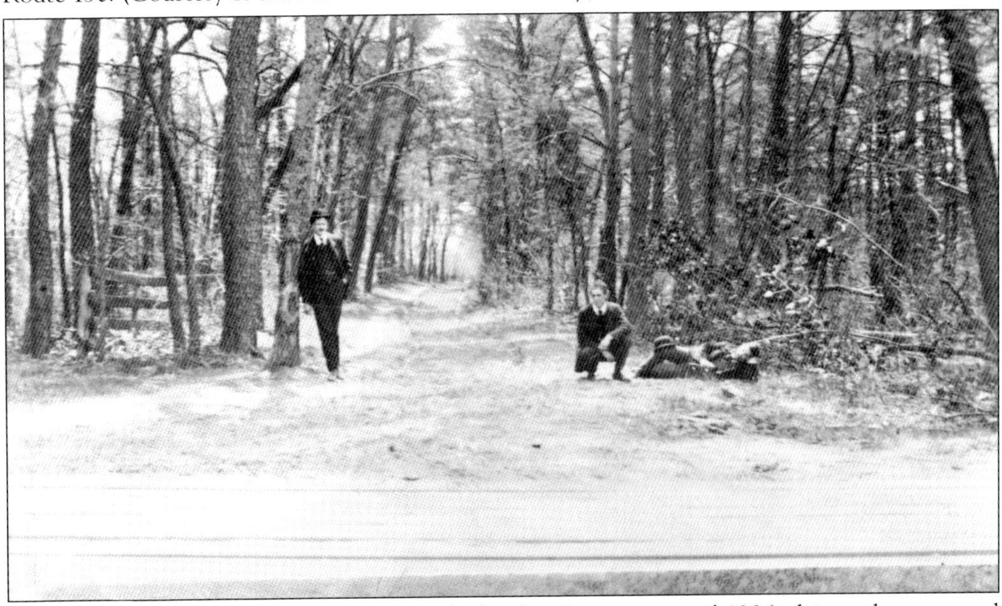

Kinsman Road. Shown intersecting Knickerbocker Avenue around 1906, this road was named after Henry Kinsman, who lived there and operated a silk factory. An old photograph shows a large four-story building where silk thread was made. The trolley tracks are visible at the bottom of the picture, which ran from Florence into Roebling and on to Trenton. In 1874, Kinsman shot his only son, who was 13 years old at the time, after mistaking him for a thief who had been stealing feed from his barn. His son did not recover. (Courtesy of Bob Panaro.)

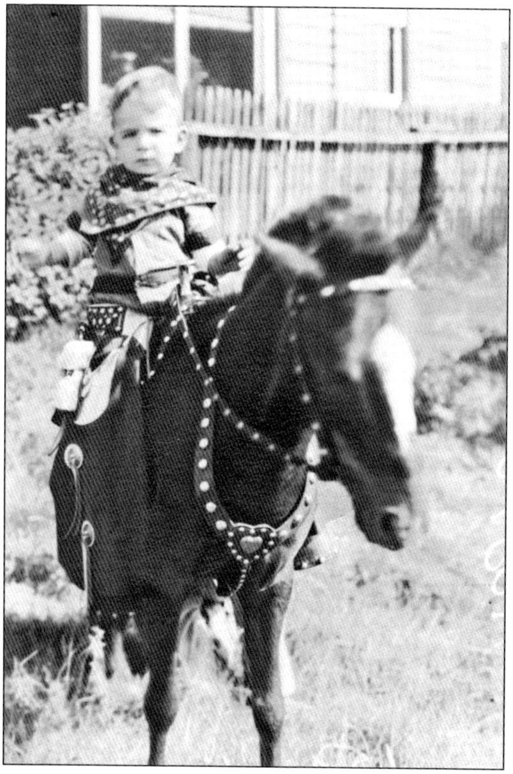

HAROLD BLAKESLEE. Harold Blakeslee sits proudly for this c. 1939 picture at his family's home on East Front Street near Broad Street. The large double house is now gone and has been replaced by a four-unit apartment house. Harold's mother was Evelyn Ireland, who married John Blakeslee, and their family also included Harold's brother, Edward Blakeslee. He later became a mailman and is now retired from the US Postal Service. (Courtesy of Joan Shafer.)

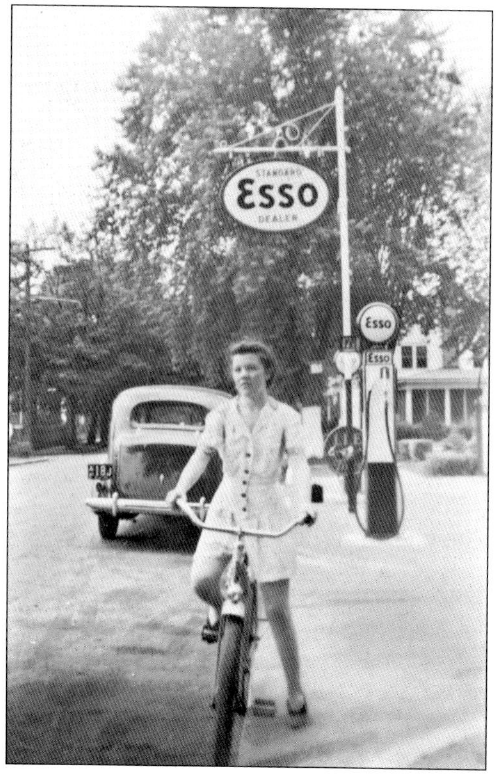

CARLANI'S GARAGE. Located on West Second Street near the Boulevard, this garage was run by the Carlani brothers, Joseph and Tony, for many years. The young lady on the bicycle has not been identified, but the picture is dated 1942. In this view looking west toward the Boulevard, Dr. Shisler's house is seen on the right. (Courtesy of the Florence Historical Society.)

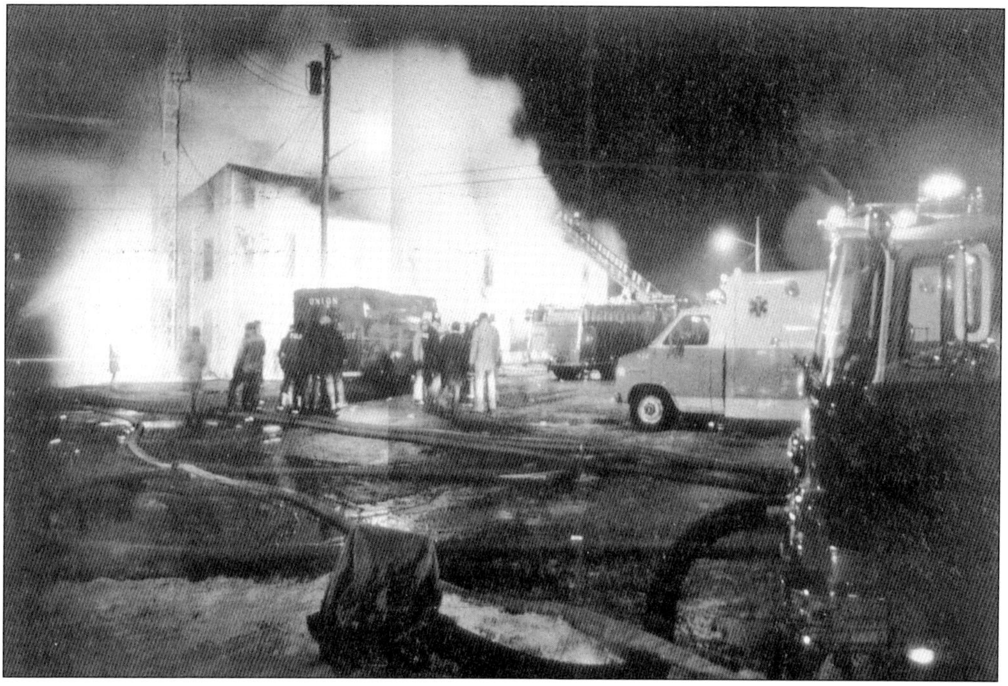

MUNICIPAL BUILDING FIRE. On February 20, 1979, at 6:05 p.m., a fire was reported at the more than 100-year-old, two-story municipal building on East Front Street along the Delaware River. The building housed the municipal offices, the police station, and municipal courtroom. Several explosions were heard, believed to be caused by the police ammunition stored inside. Officials did manage to save some of the records. (Courtesy of John Williams.)

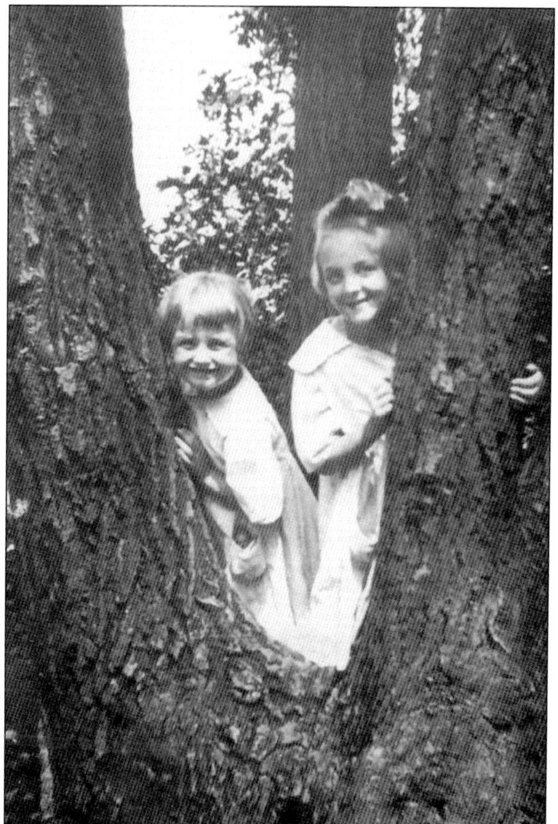

LUCAS GIRLS. Sisters Ella Lucas and Elizabeth (or "E.") Vivien Lucas are shown playing in Florence Heights. Their home was on Third Street in the 1920s, and the girls' mother was Sarah Lucas. At the time of the photograph, Ella was eight years old, while E. Vivien was five and a half years old. (Courtesy of Barbara Durham.)

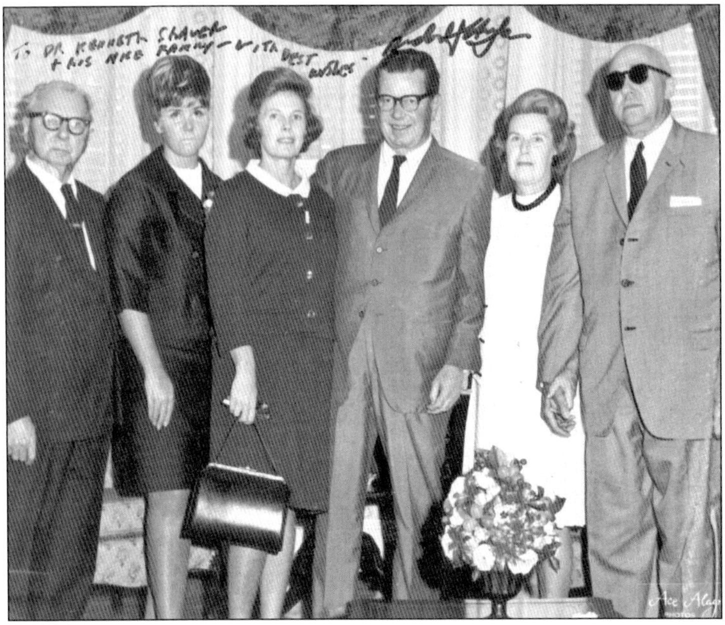

GOVERNOR HUGHES AND DR. SHAVER. Around 1960, Gov. Richard J. Hughes and his wife pose with the Shaver family. The Shaver family now live at the Hughes homestead on East Front Street. From left to right are unidentified, Ginger Shaver, Betty Hughes, Governor Hughes, Virginia Shaver, and Dr. Kenneth Shaver. Dr. Shaver is wearing sunglasses as he is recovering from an eye infection. (Courtesy of Mrs. Shaver.)

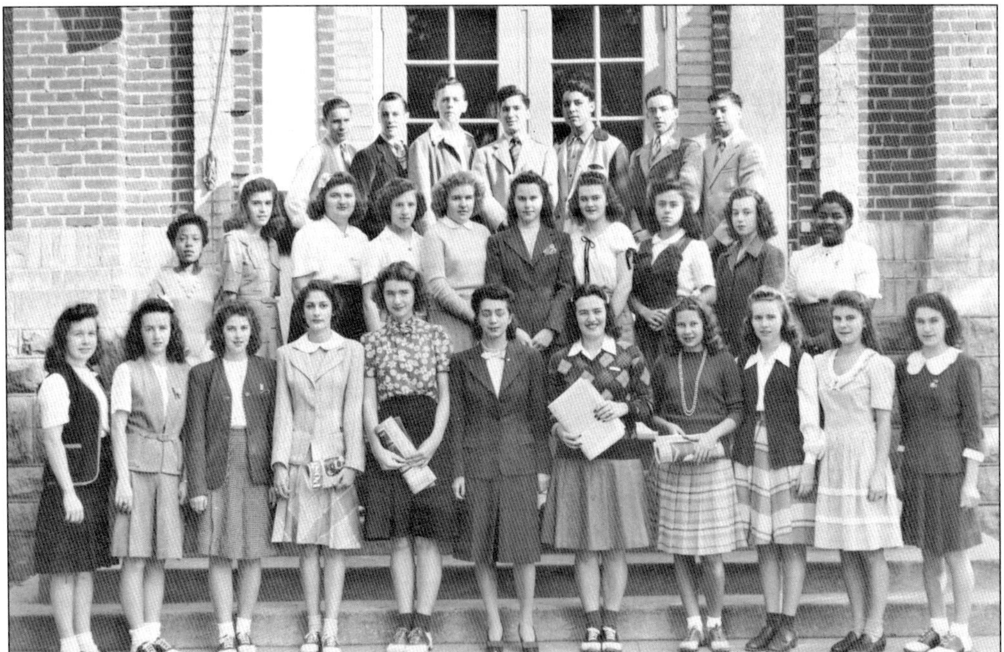

EIGHTH-GRADE CLASS, 1942. In 1942, Florence High School was housed in part of Florence School No. 2. Pictured are, from left to right, (first row) Helen Dragos, Irma Spotts, Betty Wilson, Laura Ronyecs, Jane Regars, advisor Miss Nagy, Barbara Trainor, Betty Ann Brown, Doris Hamilton, Gladys Henry, and Sandina Bombelli; (second row) Catherine Scott, Helen Marinkos, Dorothy Pustay, Dot McNinney, Louise Wainwright, Betty Boyle, Edith Pullen, Virginia Addari, Jackie Dennis, and Eleanor Taylor; (third row) Charles Snow, Robert Brining, Kenneth Reed, Raymond Carugno, George Malmos, Jack Coumbe, and Joseph Paris. (Courtesy of the Florence Historical Society.)

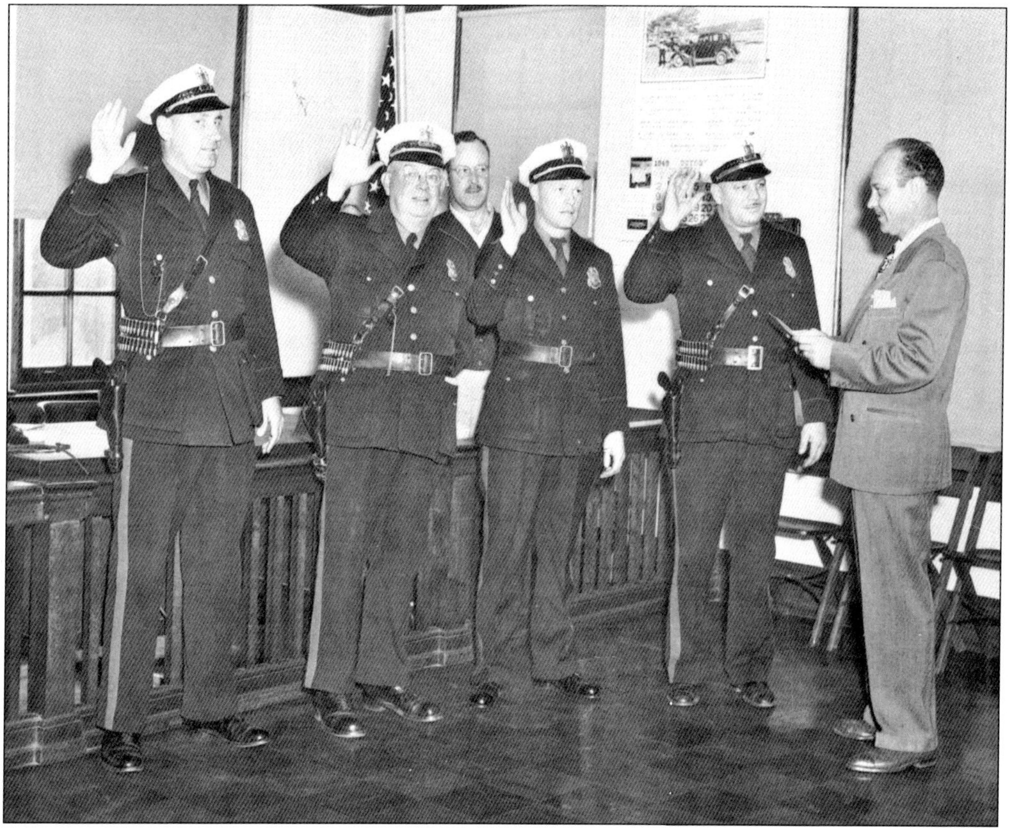

FLORENCE POLICE OFFICERS, 1943. In 1943, the reserve officers were sworn by county sheriff William F. Parker (far right). Being sworn in are, from left to right, David Earley, James Tapper Sr., unidentified, Richard Coates, and Frank "Blimp" Cicero. The location is thought to be the Florence Firehouse No. 1 on West Third Street, which also housed the town jail and police headquarters at this time. (Courtesy of the Florence Historical Society.)

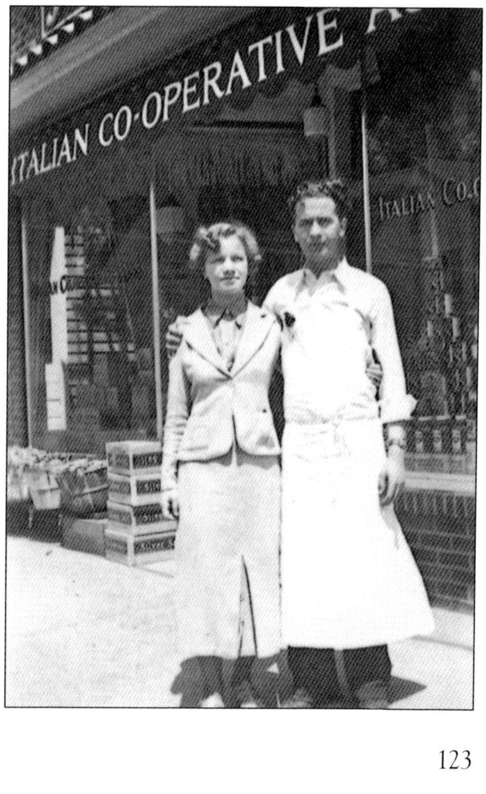

TOTS AND MARIE "GIGI" LEGNAIOLI. Husband and wife Tots and Gigi pose proudly in front of the Italian Co-operative Store downtown, where they were owners/managers in 1938. They opened their own store many years later on West Second Street. (Courtesy of the Florence Historical Society.)

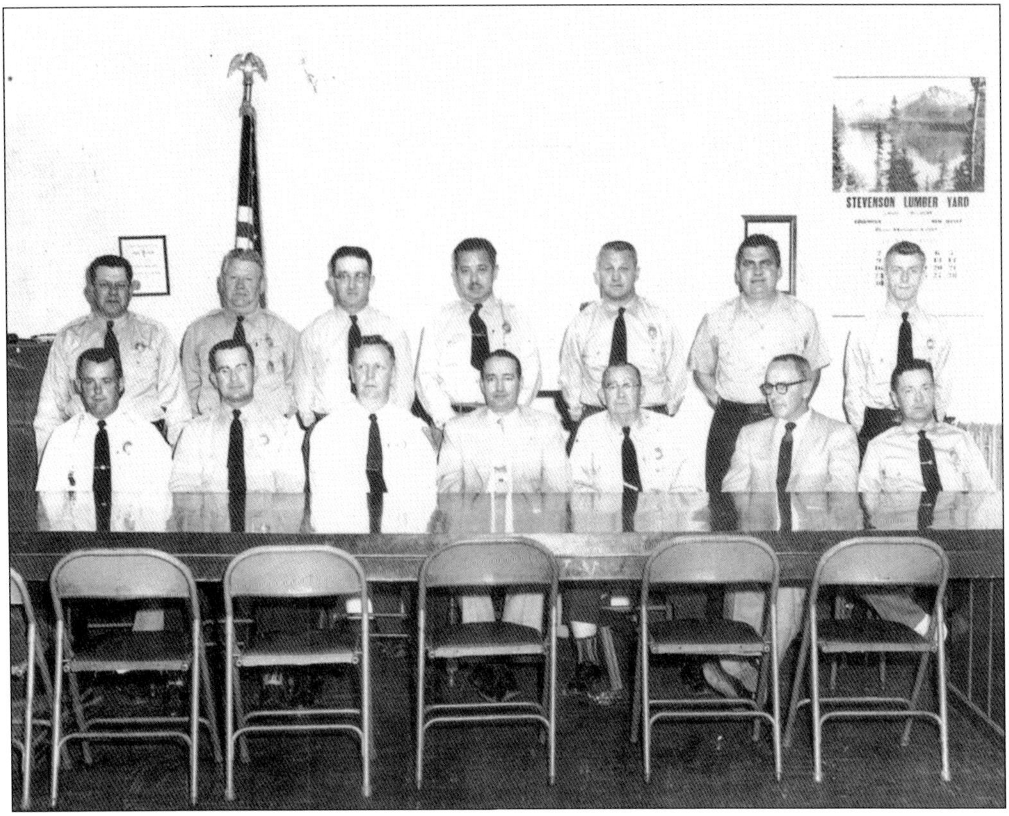

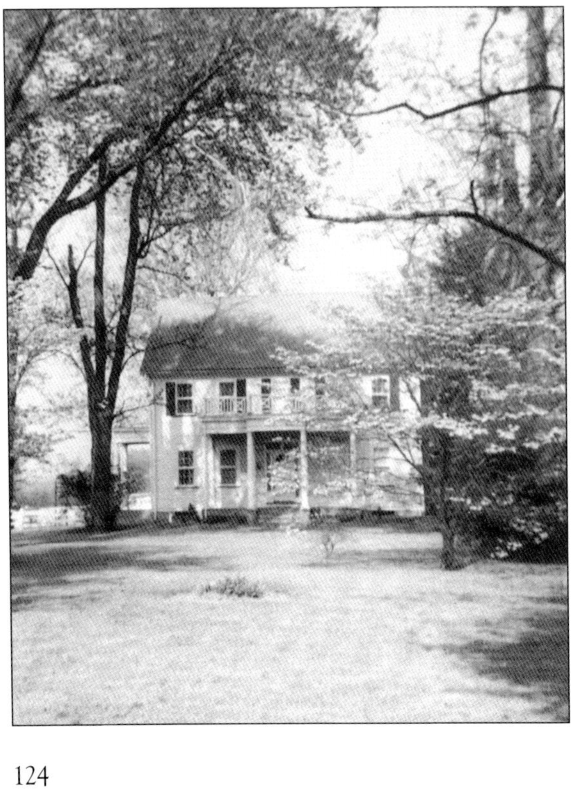

Florence Police Officers, 1958. In 1958, local police officers assembled for a formal portrait at the Third Street firehouse. From left to right are (first row) Harvey Worth, Joseph Czaplicki, Edward Shafle, Mayor Michael Chanti, James Tapper Sr., John McGoldrick, and Richard Coates; (second row) Russell "Icky" Roughton, Fred Miller, Lou Green, Frank "Blimp Cicero, Joe "Schmir" Millerline, Ed Markowitz, and William Doherty. (Courtesy of Mary Tapper.)

The Carty/Stout/Simpkins House. This image was taken in the late 1950s at the house on Cedar Lane, built around 1861. The barn silo, still standing, has the name *Stout* inscribed on it. The home is now vacant and in poor condition. The porch provides an idea of its grandeur. (Courtesy of Hilyard Simpkins.)

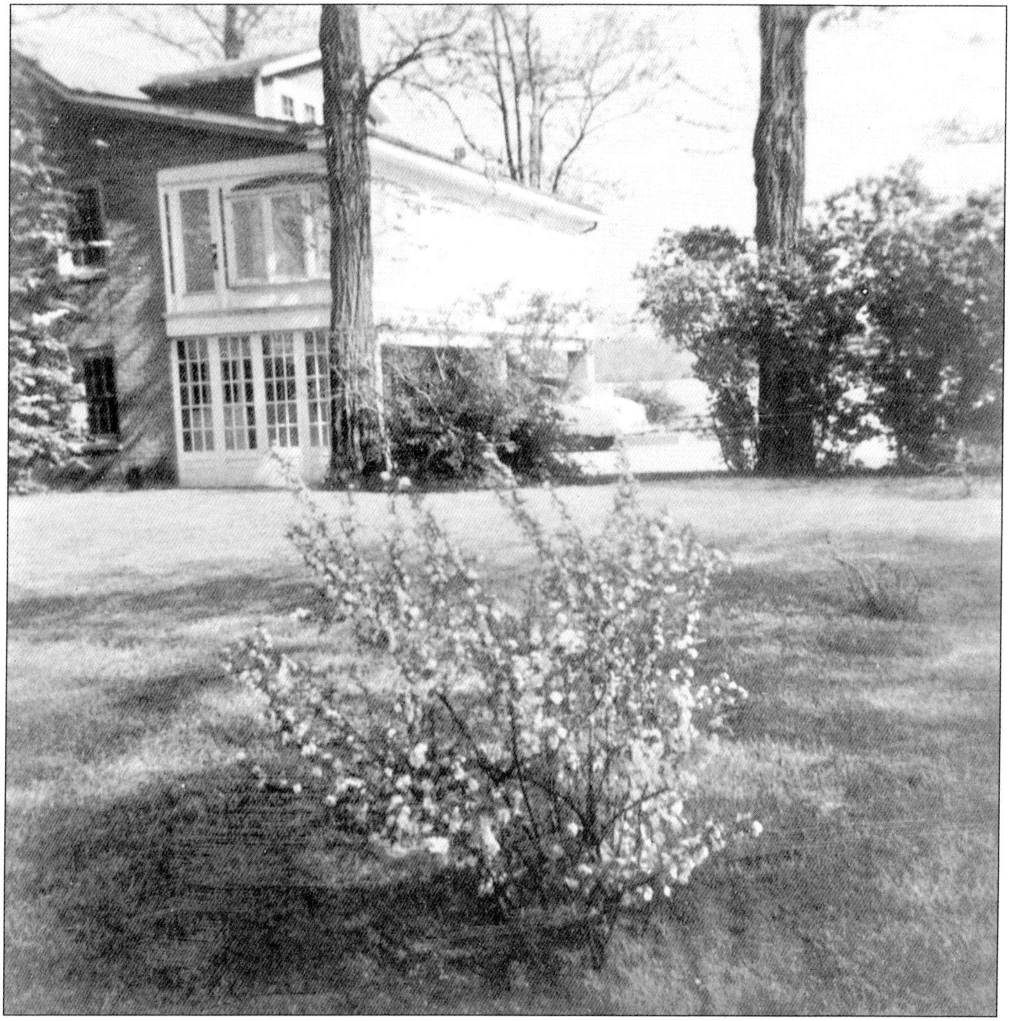

The Carty Carriage House. As part of the Carty/Stout/Simpkins property, this carriage house was to the right of the main house. The second floor is now an apartment, and the downstairs is an artist's gallery and workshop. (Courtesy of Hilyard Simpkins.)

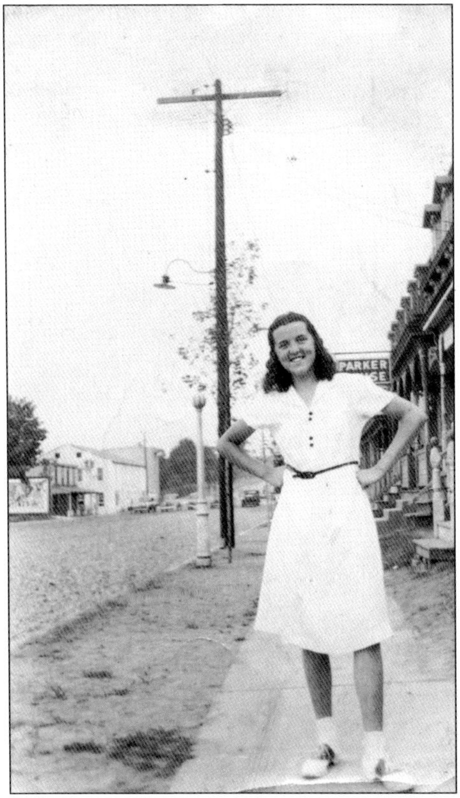

DORIS DURHAM. Doris was about 17 years old in the 1940s, and this picture was taken shortly before she moved out of town. Notice the condition of the street, and the standing gas vent pipe behind her. Streetlights were attached to telephone poles in those days. The Florence Hotel and an older small store are shown on the left behind her. (Courtesy of Jean Petty.)

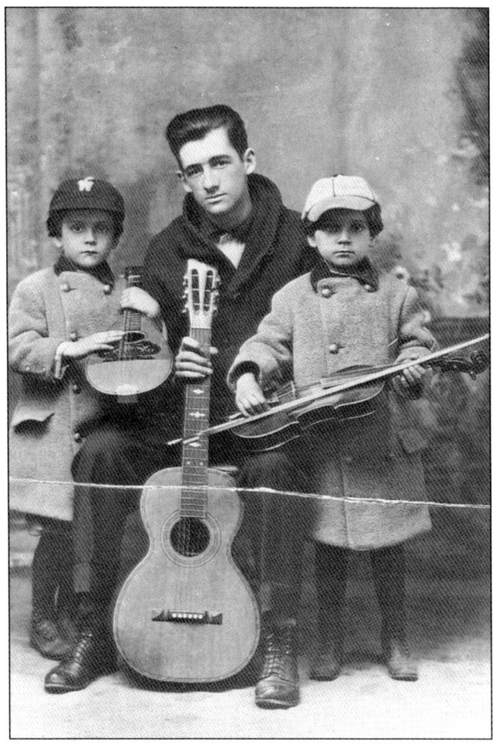

FRANK PEACOCK AND THE BAIRD TWINS. Frank Peacock (center) poses with John (left) and David Baird, though it is unclear if they were musically talented. The Baird boys are twins, and were born about 1907. This picture appears to be from around 1912. (Courtesy of the Florence Historical Society.)

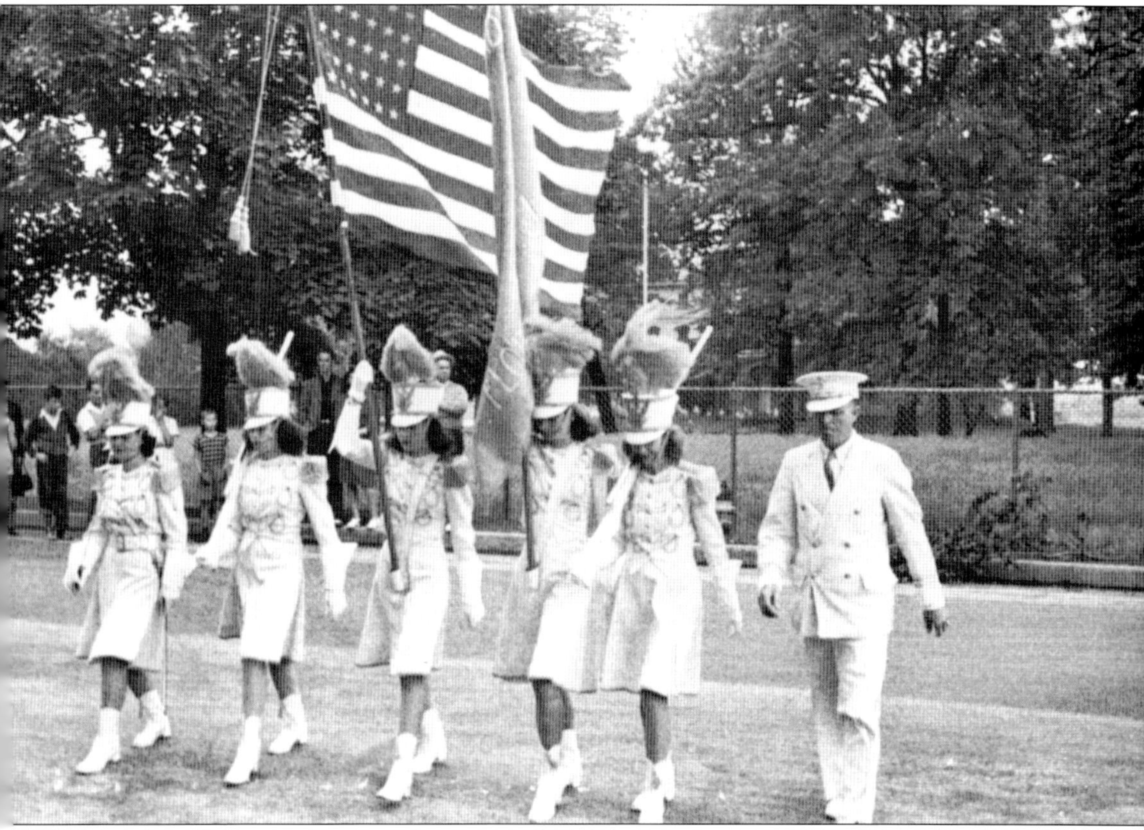

Nichols Drum and Bugle Corps. Harry Nichols, who lived on the Boulevard, organized and managed the Nichols Drum and Bugle Corps. Here, the corps proudly marches in a Florence parade in front of the foundry property on West Front Street, now Wilkie Park. The Jones/R.D. Wood mansion is barely visible behind the fence. As it was demolished after 1949, the picture can be dated to around 1948. (Courtesy of the Florence Historical Society.)

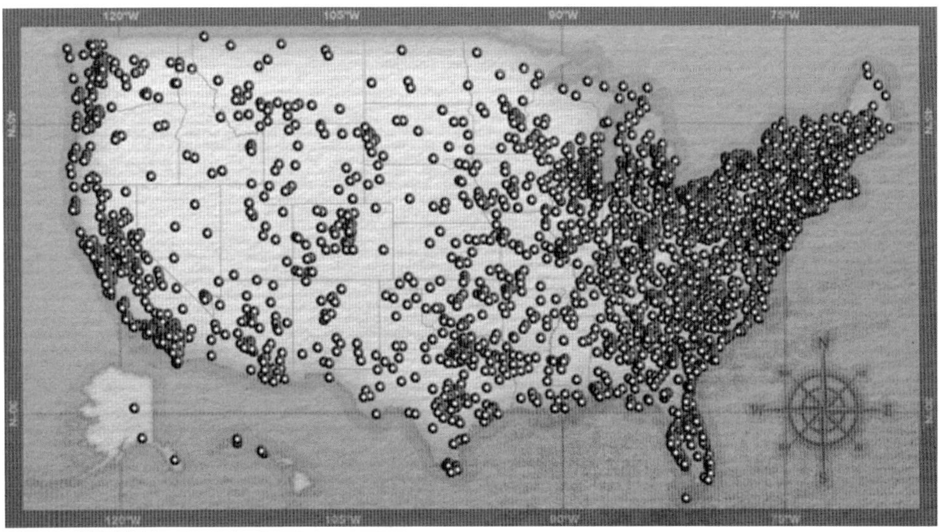